3 9094 00869 8142

G2

WHY I AM

A BAPTIST

By LOUIE D. NEWTON

Good Morning, 1938

WHY I AM A BAPTIST

By

Louie Devotie Newton

THOMAS NELSON & SONS

EDINBURGH   NEW YORK   TORONTO

286
N48

CAMPBELL LIBRARY
SHIMER COLLEGE
MT. CARROLL, ILLINOIS

Copyright, 1957, by Louie Devotie Newton

Library of Congress Catalog Card No.: 57-9779

Second Printing, May, 1959

Manufactured in the United States of America

TO

J. C. N.

WHOSE LOVE AND PRAYERS

HAVE AWAKENED AND SUSTAINED

JOYOUS SERVICE

IN HIS NAME

PREFACE

WHEN THE ORIGINAL INVITATION came to write the Baptist book in the *Why I Am* series, I said No, and for two reasons: first, there were others far better qualified; and, second, I shrank from the inescapable pattern of having to write in a disproportionate use of the personal pronoun. The invitation was renewed, and I set to work to get my friends to say that I should decline. They argued that someone should respond to the publisher's gracious request. I then read Dr. Roy Smith's *Why I Am A Methodist,* and he convinced me that one can use the personal pronoun without being misunderstood. Even so, I trust that the reader will appreciate my feeling that this important undertaking might more wisely have been assigned any one of many Baptists of our generation. I have some satisfaction in the fact that a number of these cherished friends did share in the chapter on "Why They Are Baptists."

May I express the hope that our Baptist people will claim the privilege of reading the other volumes in this series. I have found pleasure and profit in reading *Why I Am A Methodist,* Dr. Roy L. Smith; *Why I Am A Lutheran,* Dr. Victor E. Beck; and *Why I Am A Presbyterian,* Dr. Park Hays Miller.

Also, may I express appreciation to publishers and authors

vii

from whom I have quoted; to Miss Clarice Whitener for her kindness in helping me assemble data for the book and her patience in copying my typing; and to Gorham Munson of Thomas Nelson and Sons for his amazing faith in me and his surpassing patience with me.

LOUIE D. NEWTON

Atlanta, Georgia

CONTENTS

WHY I AM

A BAPTIST

BECAUSE OF A HOME

FOR WEAL OR WOE, the home is the citadel of civilization. Trace the story of man from the Garden of Eden, and his way of life will usually reveal the sort of home his parents provided. Not always, but usually. We see not only the physical resemblance of child and parent, but usually one may observe the intellectual and spiritual bent in the unfolding personality of the child, accounted for in the precept and example of the parents. One reads the meaning of Tennyson's revealing line: "Her eyes are homes of silent prayer," as he feels the hidden power in the child's response to life.

God be thanked, I was born in a home of prayer. My earliest memories portray in vivid overtones my mother's gentle voice, teaching me to say after her:

Now I lay me down to sleep,
    I pray Thee, Lord, my soul to keep.
If I should die, before I wake,
    I pray Thee, Lord, my soul to take.
And this I ask, for Jesus' sake.

Sometimes it was at her knee, she taught me to pray; sometimes it was in bed, when she would come to say good-night,
and whisper a prayer for her boys, calling each by name. One
of my older brothers, talking with a colored boy on the farm,
remarked one day: "The Lord knows my name. Mama has
told Him so many times."

My father was a farmer in Screven County, Georgia. My
paternal grandfather farmed the same land. My father as a
boy accepted Jesus Christ as Saviour and Lord, won to the
Lord by his father, as he delighted to tell his children. One
of the first memories of my father was of his prayers with the
family at the close of the day as we sat about the open fire in
what we called "their room"—the bedroom of my father and
mother. It was in that room we gathered in family worship.
At one side of the fireplace was my father's armchair, and at
the other side, my mother's gooseneck rocker. In between
sat the daughter and five sons. Perhaps I should add that we
were supposed to be seated. One can never predict what five
boys will do. Anyway, we were present, and for a little while
quiet, when the hour arrived for family worship.

My mother usually read the Daily Bible Readings as suggested by the Sunday School Lesson for the week, keeping
always in her Bible the Sunday School Lesson Helps. Also, she
kept in her Bible an outline which would take one through
the entire Bible in a year. Often she would read first the Sunday School Daily Reading, and then turn to the schedule of
chapters for reading the Bible through in a year. Sometimes

the younger ones of us might fall asleep, but she never re-
buked us for that.

When the reading ended, my father would kneel, and lead
in prayer. I could repeat now many of the phrases in my
father's prayers. For example:

"We know that Thou art God—that Thou art good—that Thou
art merciful—that Thy truth endureth forever. Forgive our sins—
the sins of commission, and the sins of omission. We thank Thee
for life, and all that sustains life—for strength of body and mind—
for bread and sunshine and rain—for friends and neighbors—for
the Bible and the church—for freedom of worship—for all good
things. We pray for all mankind. Thy Kingdom come, and Thy
will be done in our lives, here and now, through Jesus Christ our
Lord. Amen."

My father loved music. He played the flute, and often on
long winter evenings, after he had finished reading the daily
paper and any farm journal that had lately arrived, we would
ask him to play the flute. He was never too quick in his response, making sure that the majority really wanted him to
play. If he delayed unduly, my mother would begin humming
some melody that she knew he specially loved. That would
settle the matter. The clear note of the flute would promptly
pick up the tune, and our imaginations would soar to lands
of enchantment.

As Superintendent of the Sunday School in the little country church, my father emphasized singing as one of the major
parts of the program every Sunday afternoon. He usually led
the singing. I can see him now as he stood beside the little
organ, beating out the rhythm of "Blessed Assurance, Jesus
Is Mine." His favorite hymn was "What a Friend We Have
in Jesus." When the time came for suggested "numbers,"
someone would be certain to say, "And now let's sing your
hymn."

Nor was the singing of the grand old hymns of truth and beauty confined to the fireside and meetinghouse. My father delighted to sing or whistle as he worked in the field or about the barn. There were several Negro families on our farm, and having lived there all their lives, the fellowship of the heads of the Negro families was often reflected as these cherished friends would join with my father in some beautiful hymn or folklore tune as they worked together. And after my father had led for a while, then one of the Negro men would come in with a Spiritual, and my father would always take the tenor.

On rainy days, we would often wind up in the barn, shucking corn or picking penders (peanuts). Or maybe it would be mending and greasing harness, repairing farm tools, or other indoor chores. And on such days the singing was extra good. Once when the men folks were repairing the troughs and hayracks in the big horse-shed, we boys slipped in the loft to see if we could spear a rat or two. One of the Negro boys called to us, and said: "Listen what they're singing—'When the Roll Is Called Up Yonder.' Let's get back down there. We ain't in Heaven yet."

My father took little interest in family records, but he did delight to remind his five sons that they were descended from a long line of Anglo-Americans, and he fervently prayed that we would each resolve to bear the name worthily. His concept of life was based on the teachings of the Bible. He would often quote the familiar saying: "You can't break the Ten Commandments, but you can break yourself if you violate the laws of God." Many, many times he would say to us: "Any person who will steal will lie, and a person who will steal and lie will kill you if you get him in a corner." Moving from the prohibitions of the Ten Commandments, he laid great emphasis upon the teachings of Jesus in everyday life.

I have often wished in these after years that I had made a copy of his homilies on salt and light and wind and fire and trees and ants and goats and sheep and mules, specially on mules. He knew the Sermon on the Mount by heart, and when he would begin with the "Blesseds," he would always remind us that we might just as truly say "Happy are the . . ."

My father had deep convictions concerning the social implications of the Gospel. He believed that Christianity is a seven-day-a-week way of life. He regarded the home as the citadel of civilization, and civilization to him was of no consequence if it was not Christian. From the home, all roads seemed to him important—the road to the schoolhouse, the storehouse, the courthouse, and all the houses, with primary emphasis, always, upon the meetinghouse. He served faithfully on the juries, grand and petit, and he would often talk to us about what had happened in court—how men came to grief because they broke the laws of God and man. He served for many years as Justice of the Peace in our Militia District. Many are the times I have listened as some citizen would come to our home, infuriated with a neighbor, and ask my father to issue a warrant. "Let's talk about this before we resort to legal processes," my father would say to the upset man. And in many instances it would wind up by my father getting in the buggy with the man and driving to the home of the alleged criminal where reason prevailed and complete reconciliation was effected.

I remember the occasion when there had been a heavy rain storm, and the cows belonging to one neighbor got into the corn field of another neighbor, where the rail fence had been washed away. They had wrought much damage on the fine corn, just in shoot. My father listened to the plea of the man suffering the damage, and then said:

"Billie, let's go and see Paul. He'll do the right thing. He couldn't help the fact that his cows tore down your corn."

Result of that conference was that before sundown all the neighbors had pitched in and replaced the fence, and the man who owned the cows agreed that he would deliver a two-horse wagon load of corn to his neighbor in the fall.

My father was concerned that each of the five boys would learn to work, and love it. "I can't teach you all that is in the books, but I can teach you what I know in my experience in the university of life," he would say. "You will have to choose your course in life, with God's leading, but whatever that course may be, you will be profited by knowing how to make a living, and that I hope and pray to teach you." And by the time we were half way in our teens, we each knew how to farm, and all that goes with farming in Southeast Georgia. We knew about soils and seasons and seeds and cultivation and harvesting. We knew about horses and mules and cows and hogs and sheep and goats. We knew about every sort of tool from hoes and rakes to plows and reapers. We knew about insects and worms, in the ground and in the air. We knew about drought and flood. We knew about supply and demand. We knew the value of a dollar. We knew the philosophy of work and prudence. We knew how to make a living.

There were six children in the home—one daughter and five sons. Our sister was the oldest child, and I was the fourth, so that she was off to college before I could remember much about her. I can well remember how proud I was of my beautiful sister as she would come home from college. And then the courtship which was soon to take her away from her admiring brothers. She married a young preacher, Rev. J. A. Reiser. I had difficulty with his name, how to pronounce it. They kept telling me to say "Ricer," and I argued that if that was the way to pronounce it, they should change the spelling accordingly, but I lost my debate, as has been my portion in so many instances. I was interested chiefly in the fact that he was taking my sister away, and I told him one day that I didn't like him. He smiled, and said: "You will forgive me. I promise you I will try to be worthy of her love." He did. And it was in their home that I later got to know my sister as one of the really great Christians I shall ever see. Indeed, she proved a second mother as I went to live with them and attend high school. And Joseph Austin Reiser taught me many valuable and lasting lessons, of which I shall later write.

There were five boys in that home, two older and two younger than I. My oldest brother was honored with our father's first name—William. My second brother was named for our paternal grandfather—David. My third brother was named for our maternal grandfather—James Robbins. The youngest brother was named for a great teacher and a great-uncle—Ralph George. Two of these beloved brothers have passed on to the Land and Life beyond—David and Robbie. Willie is a farmer in the beloved old home community in Screven County, and I delight to visit in the home that Willie and Pearl have built into a sanctuary of love and devotion for a half century, blessed by the fellowship of their son, William David. Robbie never fully recovered from the damage of gas in World War I, and when pneumonia struck him, some years following the war, he left his wife and little daughters, entering into the House not made with hands. His portrait as a Captain in World War I holds preferred space on my study desk. David was the victim of an unexpected heart attack, following within a few months the death of his beloved wife, Annie Lee, but death can never erase my memory of his laughing eyes. Ralph is the doctor, and I can well remember how my mother called him "doctor" when he was yet a little boy. Ralph and Irma are happy that their two sons are walking in the steps of their father and their maternal grandfather, seeking to minister to sick people in the name of the Great Physician.

One of my father's favorite books was *Poor Richard's Almanac,* and he delighted to check on our ability to quote accurately the cryptic sayings of Benjamin Franklin. Another source of constant discussion was *Aesop's Fables.* But my father relied chiefly on the Bible for his subjects of serious conversation with his boys. One of my happiest memories is the picture of my father, in his armchair, or somewhere about his work, talking with us about men in the Bible— Enoch, Noah, Abraham, Joseph, Moses.

He loved a good story, and knew, himself, the art of storytelling. I have seen him laugh until tears came in his eyes over some good story. An ardent fisherman, he delighted to describe the ones that got away, and we wondered, sometimes, which ones counted the most—those he landed, or those that broke the line. His idea was that you go fishing for the fun of it, and this philosophy of good humor accounted for his 81 years of joyous living.

My mother contributed the Scotch element in the union which was my home. On her paternal side, reaching back to the McCalls, were several Baptist preachers, and her children rise up and call that heritage blessed. She was one of the most deeply religious persons I have ever known. She gave full acknowledgement and appreciation to good books, but for her there was but one Book. She knew the Bible and she loved it. She could quote chapter after chapter, and for many years it was her rule to read the Bible through annually, from Genesis to Revelation. Her Bible was always bulging with penciled notes and clippings. We knew very well that we were not to allow one of those clippings to fall out as we handled the Book. Periodically, she would transfer these notes and clippings to large pasteboard boxes.

From my earliest recollections, I have associated my mother with the Bible. I can hear her voice now: "Remember, children, this is God's Book. It is the Holy Bible. Its words are truth and life. Never place any other book on top of the Book." And here was something she would say that I could never forget: "Always wash your hands before you put them on God's Book." That sense of reverence for the Bible was the first lesson she taught me in what I would call the field of religion.

Coupled with the Bible was the fact of prayer. I say fact for the reason that my mother would always bow her head in silent prayer before she read the Bible. Once when I listened to an eminent theologian in an address on the Holy Spirit's illuminating function—preparing our minds and hearts for an understanding of the Word of God—I remembered with much satisfaction my mother's example of asking that her eyes be opened that she might read aright and her heart prepared that she might understand what God was saying to her.

My mother not only read the Bible every day, but she would sing the Bible as she went about her household work—in the kitchen, in the garden. She loved the great hymns, but often she would sing not the words in the hymnbook, but use the music for the words of a Psalm or some other familiar passage in the Bible. It is an interesting exercise to note how many passages in the Bible may be sung to the music of the grand old hymns of the church.

This element of praise in my mother's life is one of the major equations in the home where I was blest to be born. How many times I have heard her speak some word of praise as she went about her work! Here was a hen that had just hatched a nestful of beautiful baby chicks. As she lifted them from the nest to the nearby pen where the mother hen was to conduct a kindergarten, my mother would thank the Lord for this new gift to her inventory. Every chicken, every egg, was regarded as a trust from the Lord.

Once when an old sow got into the chicken yard and killed a mother hen, leaving a brood of helpless baby chicks, we wondered what our mother would say. She said two things: "For we know that all things work together for good to those who love God, to those who are the called according to His purpose," and then she said: "Giving thanks always for all things unto God and the Father in the name of our Lord Jesus Christ." That, we thought, was an amazing demonstration of forbearance. Presently, she turned to me and said: "You are to mother these biddies. Get a box and some soft straw and put them in the kitchen by the stove. You will keep them in the box for a week or so, and then you can move them to the woodshed. You will be proud of them, and you will get a blessing from looking after them." I was proud of them, and claimed them as "my" chickens as long as I could identify them.

Along with reverence and praise, my mother kept before us the concept of beauty. Every nook and corner had a flower. Maybe the arrangement wouldn't pass muster today, but she was achieving something in the soul of her children—a sense of beauty. The family exchequer would not allow for store-bought flower pots, but that didn't hinder my mother's purpose. Every sort of box and tin can, even jars and bottles, were brought into service. In the house and on the porches, these boxes and cans and jars and bottles would present gorgeous tapestries of foliage and blossom. And here again would enter the equation of teaching us a sense of responsibility. An assignment I shall never forget, though I did forget it now and then at the time, was watering these plants. "They drink water, just as you drink water," she would say.

One of the grand spectacles in our front yard was a large camellia bush. We called it japonica. This exceptionally large bush, thirty feet high, and I don't know how many feet in circumference, would have literally hundreds of blossoms annually, and from this one bush went armfuls of flowers to sick rooms, the meetinghouse every Lord's Day, and in the parlor and dining room. We delighted to keep a fresh vase of japonicas in "their room." My father and mother rooted many plants from this giant bush for their neighbors. We never knew just how old that bush was.

And in the yards, front and side and back, my mother had every sort of flowering plant in all that region—roses and lilac and gardenia and spirea and crepe myrtle and hydrangea. And please don't forget the "sweet shrubs." One of the remembered stunts of the boys in the family was to pick sweet shrub blossoms and put them in the pockets of our jackets as we started to school or Sunday School, and have the neighbors inquire the "brand" of perfume in the room.

Turning to the kitchen in that home in which I got my training, I must mention the good things my mother and "Aunt Sookie" would prepare. We didn't mind keeping the woodbox well filled, thinking of the hot cakes and delectable pies. My mother believed in plenty of vegetables for growing boys, so that we had to go through with all of that before we could have the deep pan pies of peaches and apples and all the other tasty viands. Clabber was a great dish in our home—clabber with nutmeg sprinkled over it, and a crisp piece of cornbread! Biscuit and homemade "lightbread" were always just right. And never shall I forget those covered dishes—pilau, for example.

Dwelling for a moment in the memories of that home, I

can well understand the emotions of David, when he longed, and said, "O that some one would give me water to drink from the well of Bethlehem, which is by the gate!" (II Samuel 23:15.)

And now, getting on to the assignment, Why I Am a Baptist, let me say quite frankly that my father and mother had much to do in my answer to that question. They were, themselves, convinced Baptists. They didn't argue about it. They didn't assume to decide for their children. They just went on, quietly pursuing their discipleship, always ready to give an answer to every man that might ask a reason of the hope they held, with meekness and fear.

Once when a beloved preacher of another denomination was visiting in our home, I asked him why he was not a Baptist. He handled the situation with gracious consideration of my brash approach, turning an otherwise embarrassing moment into pleasant words of appreciation of my father and mother, declaring: "One can easily understand why their children are Baptists."

Indeed, it was not until the evening in July, 1902, when I surrendered my will to the will of God, praying, "Lord, be merciful to me a sinner," that my father and mother spoke to me about being a Baptist. Until that hour, they had only spoken to me about being a Christian. When they knew that I had accepted Jesus Christ as my personal Saviour, and had declared that I wished to unite with the church, they asked me if I wished to join their church. That seemed a very strange question, but they made themselves quite clear. "You are now a Christian," they began, "but you are not a Baptist until you understand what Baptists believe—until you are fully committed to the doctrines which Baptists hold."

There followed a series of statements I shall never forget—simple, positive declarations of basic doctrines. The long-time pastor of Union Baptist Church was a guest in our home that evening, and as my mother talked with me about Baptist doctrine, my father went to the front porch and invited Pastor Thomas Walker to come to the kitchen. It was a notable session in church history for a ten-year-old boy. Brother Walker went over every step, already covered by my father and mother, helping me to clarify my understanding of personal salvation, and then the Baptist doctrines, one after another.

Supper was late that night, but that didn't matter with my father and mother. They were rejoicing that their son had received eternal life through Jesus Christ, and they were concerned that I should clearly understand what I was proposing to do in asking for membership in a Baptist church. I was convinced then that had I demurred at any of the beliefs of Baptists, they would have advised me against making public my profession of faith in their church that evening. And I know now that they would never have brought the least pressure upon me to join their church against any doubt of their Baptist doctrines. This, I think, is important. I had never questioned the fact that I would sometime be a Baptist. But it would have been unwholesome for me, had they assumed to rush me into church membership without leading me to examine my mind and heart on this matter. Just as I had to act initially in becoming a Christian, so they insisted that I must, insofar as I was capable, determine for myself whether I would be a Baptist or not.

What, you may reasonably ask, could a ten-year-old boy know about such basic doctrines as the priesthood of the believer, the authority of the Scriptures, the equality of believers, etc., etc.? Very well, I testify that I did realize that I must give an account of myself—of my right to believe or not believe—to God. I had come to see that I was a sinner before God. I was of all boys, I felt, most miserable. There was the example of my father and mother in that humble, Christian home. They had something that I did not have, albeit I had been nurtured in the warmth of their love. They had given to me everything they could. I knew that. But they couldn't believe for me! That truth, that fact, that doctrine had burned itself into my understanding. I had heard my mother in prayer on my behalf. I had come, one late afternoon at feeding time, upon my father as he knelt in the barn, praying that his boy might be saved. And I knew that they were asking God to do something for me that they desired above all else, but that God could not settle the transaction with them—that I had to enter the battle between God and Satan—that I held a vote in this election. I knew that. And if I, a ten-year-old boy, could know that much, what, I respectfully ask, could keep me from understanding that I was competent to deal directly with God? And if I could say yes or no to God, must I not also choose between this and that proposal of obedience to His teachings insofar as they related to outward discipleship? Baptism, for example. I had read what Jesus said to John concerning baptism, and what Jesus Himself did, Matthew 3:13-17. Also what Paul said about baptism in Romans and Colossians. I had read about the manner of managing the affairs of the early church, and it seemed quite clear to me that equality of believers was clearly taught. I didn't understand it as fully as I now understand it, but I understod enough to make my decision for that sort of procedure in trying to carry on His work. To that extent I was a convinced Baptist in 1902. And to my father and mother, as faithful Christians and faithful Baptists, I attribute largely my decision to become a Christian and a Baptist. The beloved old pastor had a part in it, as did other good and cherished people in the little church and community, but it was because of that home—that father and mother—that I found my way, early in my life, to the Saviour and to the Baptist faith or denomination, as you may wish to call it.

The Bible, taught daily in the home, and by my mother in the Sunday School, and by the preacher in the pulpit, and by *The Christian Index,* our Baptist paper in Georgia, and by certain books that my mother put in my hands, like *Theodosia Ernest, Grace Abounding, Pilgrim's Progress,* and others —these all had their determining influence. The Holy Spirit, working through my father and mother, and through other persons and instrumentalities, brought me to see clearly that I was lost and undone in my sins for which I was directly accountable unto God, Who loved me, and gave His only begotten Son to die on Calvary, that I should not perish, but have everlasting life.

Yes, I am a Baptist because of a home. That is my first answer, but I wish here to give notice that two other homes entered deeply and finally into my experience as a convinced Baptist, and of these I shall speak later. That first home, far away from the jostling throngs, brought me to the Saviour and to the Baptist faith; the other two helped me beyond all words in the growth in grace and service which God has granted me.

Perhaps I may be permitted here to say that, fifty-five years after that decision to yield my will to God's will, I have never doubted God's promise to save, unto the utmost, even one so unworthy as I. And the decision to become a Baptist in 1902 has been affirmed many times in the intervening years.

Having settled the matter of accepting Christ as my Saviour in that kitchen conference with my father and mother and the beloved pastor, I was supremely happy. When the bell called to supper, I couldn't eat. My mother understood, and nodded her approval when I asked to be excused. While the family and guests ate, I went out in the orchard beyond the syrup house, and knelt by an apple tree to thank God for what He had done for me. Never did the stars shine so brightly. The whole universe seemed aglow.

I ran across the field to the house in which one of the Negro families lived, and whistled for Tom, exactly my age. He came out with a big biscuit and a slice of crisp bacon. He offered me the first bite, but I couldn't eat. I told him what had happened to me. He rolled his big eyes, and in the moonlight I could see deep wonder in his face.

"Tom," I began, "I want you to have what I have. I want you to accept Jesus Christ as your Saviour. He will save you, just as He has saved me. You need Him, Tom. Let's pray."

I put my hand on Tom's shoulder, and asked Jesus to save him. Tom thanked me, and as I started back toward our home, he called to me:

"Thank you for telling me."

A few weeks after that Tom accepted Christ as his Saviour, and I went to Cyprus Pond Baptist Church to see him go down and give the preacher his hand. Later I saw him baptized in the same stream in which I had been baptized.

I ran back across the field to the house, and they were getting ready to go to church. I could scarcely wait for the preacher to give the invitation. How well I remember those words of the invitation hymn:

> "Just as I am, without one plea,
> But that Thy blood was shed for me,
> And that Thou bidd'st me come to Thee,
> O Lamb of God, I come, I come."

And then the people came to welcome me into Christian fellowship. Years afterward, when I was guest in the home of Chief Justice Charles Evans Hughes, I asked him which of all the honors that had come to him did he regard as the greatest. He smiled, and said:

"The day I walked down the aisle in the Baptist Church at Oswego, New York, where my father was pastor, and when he asked the church if they would receive me into fellowship, and they voted affirmatively to accept me into full membership, after baptism, in that church of the Lord Jesus Christ. That, sir, is the greatest honor that ever could come to a boy or a man."

And that was precisely the feeling in my heart that Thursday evening after the third Sunday in July, 1902, when Union Baptist Church voted to receive me as a member. I was not thinking in terms of honor so much as gratitude— gratitude to God for His unspeakable love in Jesus Christ— gratitude to my father and mother and the pastor and all the good people for their witness to His saving grace.

The following day was equally notable for me. We went to the nearby stream for the baptismal service. There were several candidates for baptism, three grown people and three other youngsters my age. My father and some of the other men in the church had gone earlier that morning to trim away the underbrush near the water, providing a wonderful setting. The big trees along the bank, draped in moss, furnished shade for the people as they stood there singing.

The pastor, aided by one of the deacons, walked down into the water until it was waist deep. He turned and faced the audience, and opened the Bible:

"Then cometh Jesus from Galilee to Jordan unto John, to be baptized of him. But John forbad Him, saying, I have need to be baptized of Thee, and comest Thou to me? And Jesus answering said unto him, Suffer it to be so now; for thus it becometh us to fulfill all righteousness. Then he suffered Him. And Jesus, when

He was baptized, went up straightway out of the water; and, lo, the heavens were opened unto Him, and He saw the Spirit of God descending like a dove, and lighting upon Him. And, lo, a voice from heaven, saying, This is My beloved Son, in Whom I am well pleased."   —Matthew 3:13-17.

Another deacon led those of us who were to be baptized into the water, and the pastor began:

"Having accepted the Lord Jesus Christ as your Redeemer, I baptize you, my sister, in the Name of the Father, and of the Son, and of the Holy Ghost," (Matthew 28:19).

And as each believer was quietly lowered into the water, the people on the bank sang:

> "O, happy day, that fixed my choice,
> On Thee, my Saviour, and my God."

In that stream my father and mother had been baptized. Often I have stood on that bank and thanked the Lord for that precious memory. Back at the meetinghouse, we received the hand of church fellowship, and I was a member of a Baptist church.

Had I been asked that Friday afternoon, following my baptism and the hand of fellowship into church membership, what it was that had happened to me, I would have answered in terms of the spiritual experience that I have already likened to light dispelling darkness, joy dispelling sorrow, assurance dispelling doubt, hope dispelling despair. I would have, most likely, quoted the words of the hymn they sang as the people came forward and welcomed me into full fellowship in the little Baptist church:

> "Amazing grace! how sweet the sound,
> That saved a wretch like me!
> I once was lost, but now am found,
> Was blind, but now I see."

I would have answered that afternoon in terms of having become a Christian rather than having become a Baptist. And I am sure that I would have thus reflected what today is my confirmed conviction—becoming a Christian is more important than becoming a Baptist. That point made clear, I move on to say that even that Friday afternoon in July, 1902, I would have been able to say that I was happy in the decision to be a Baptist, though I could not have then supported that decision with the sense of satisfaction that I can today.

In that initial experience of grace—of reconciliation—my primary concern was finding pardon for my sins. I realized that I was lost and undone. I realized that my father and mother had something that I needed—that they wanted me to have it—that they couldn't bestow it—that I must act for myself. I realized that something deep and indescribable was trying to help me in my state of condemnation. I yielded to the drawing Power at work in my heart, and I was saved—delivered—released! That was the great transaction that had consciously gone on in my soul. God, for Christ's sake, through the work of the Holy Spirit, had saved my soul! Amen.

And I was now on my way to find and make my own a reason for the faith that was in me. This leads me to the next chapter—Because of a Book.

TWO

BECAUSE OF A BOOK

STRETCHED OUT on the side porch one noon, taking the after-dinner rest which my father regularly observed, and which he admonished his sons to adopt, I was reading the current issue of *Youth's Companion,* one of the journals my mother subscribed for in exchange for eggs at fifteen cents per dozen.

It was the week after I had professed my faith in the Lord Jesus Christ—the third week in July, 1902. I had already formed a strong admiration for Daniel Webster, having used one of his compositions to win an oratorical contest at a Friday afternoon even in the little rural schoolhouse. Imagine my delight when I came upon a filler in *The Companion* by Webster, an excerpt from his Address at Bunker Hill, June 17, 1843:

"The Bible is a book of faith, and a book of doctrine, and a book of morals, and a book of religion, of especial revelation from God."

I jumped up and ran through the hallway to my mother's room, but was rudely intercepted by one of the older brothers, who held me in a scissors grip, reminding me that: "Papa and Mama are asleep! When will you ever learn any sense?"

"What is it, my child?" came the gentle call of my mother.

I tiptoed into her room, and pointed to the words by Webster. My father was sound asleep in his armchair on the porch just outside the bedroom window.

"Tell me softly what it says," she whispered.

I read the words, slowly. I knew she was listening with the care of a mother when her child is excited, for whatever reason.

"Read it again," she whispered.

Patting my hand, she commented that we would discuss this in the late afternoon when I would be coming in from the field to pick up the eggs and help with other chores about the house. I tiptoed back to my spot on the side porch, and dropped off to sleep.

I dreamed . . . a great curtain, it seemed at first—moving, as if the wind were coming from every direction . . . and now the curtain seemed to form into a great ball—too large to be called a ball—a globe, but so much larger than any globe could ever be . . . and that vast globe suspended in measureless space . . . beautiful, vast space—beautiful tones of inexpressible lustre, though below there appeared darkness, and then a Voice—a Voice as of many waters:

"In the beginning God created the heavens and the earth. The earth was without form and void, and darkness was upon the face of the deep; and the Spirit of God was moving over the face of the waters . . ."

And I awoke. How long had I been asleep? I wondered—
wondered as a child wonders. I was almost afraid to think.
Had they gone back to the field? What time was it? Where
had I been?

The clock in "their room" struck—one! My father yawned.
My oldest brother rang the farm bell. Time to go to work.

It must have been ten to fifteen minutes that I was asleep,
but long enough to dream—to record what God was saying
to a little boy—words right out of His Book—words too great
for any man ever to utter, but words which any man may
understand if he willeth to know of the doctrine, whether it
be of God or of man.

I tucked *The Companion* under the pillow on my side of
the bed which I shared with my brother Bob, and darted
through the house to overtake the crowd on the way to the
field. It was hot weather, and as we passed over a little stream
on the way to the field—the branch, we called it—where we
often waded through the water to cool our feet, I saw a rattle-
snake sunning himself on a low-swinging limb over the dark
water. I called my father's attention to the snake, and he
told David to run to the house and fetch the gun. He motioned to all of us to be still and silent. In the short interim,
I watched that snake—his apparent awakening to a sense of
conflict. I shall never forget that slithering tongue—the deadly
fangs—eyes like lightning!

My brother handed the gun to my father, and he took quick
aim as the monster lifted his head as if to leap into my very
heart. Dragging the long writhing body from the muddied
water, they counted the rattles—ten! Ten years old. Ten years
old? As old as I—here as long as I had been here!

Through the big gate, and on to the field we walked, my
father leading the way. I glanced back at the snake's dead

body, hanging from the gate, and edged nearer my father. He took my hand.

"Why the sweat on the palm of your hand, my boy?" he asked.

I didn't know it was there, and I didn't understand why. And then he began:

"You were frightened by the snake. That is why you have moisture in the palm of your hand. It always happens when you are very nervous. And you needn't be worried about being afraid of snakes. I am afraid of snakes. I reckon everybody is afraid of snakes. Do you know what the Bible says about the snake? What the snake is like? What the snake represents? Whom the snake represents? Perhaps that is the better way to put it."

I could answer that, remembering how many times I had heard my mother read the passage in Genesis three. My father nodded, and then he said:

"If you want to understand God, you must know what He says in His Book. The Bible is the Good News about God—God's love, God's mercy, God's care, God's power, God's patience, God's peace. But more than that, the Bible is God's Book of warning—His warning concerning Satan in all his schemes to deceive man and entice man away from God's love, mercy, care, power, patience and peace. It is His invitation to all men to repent and be saved. You answered that invitation last week. Now, let this experience with the snake this afternoon teach you this lesson. Although saved by the grace of God, Satan is ever lying in some dark place, hoping to snatch you away, to drag you down into some dark water, some dark place, away from God. That is why it is very good to be afraid of snakes, my child. Just remember that, and you can say with the Psalmist:

" 'Yea, though I walk through the valley
of the shadow of death, I will fear no evil;
for Thou art with me;
Thy rod and Thy staff, they comfort me.' "

It was fodder-pulling time, and when we reached the field where the fodder had been pulled that morning and the afternoon before, my father began examining each handful, hanging from the stalk, one end tucked into the vise-like point at which the ear joins the stalk, making sure that it was ready to tie into bundles. The hot, dry day had done its work, and he nodded to the men to begin tying. Fodder, if you are wondering about the word, is the blade of the corn stalk, which if pulled at exactly the right time, and properly cured, becomes a very good feed for horses, mules and cattle. Left on the stalk, the blades dry up. There was a theory, even in those ancient days of farming, that it was better to leave the blades on the stalk—that whatever energy they possessed passed into the maturing grain on the ripening ear. Even so, my father, and most of the farmers of our community, pulled the fodder. My older brothers argued with convincing logic that it was better to pull the fodder, since the net result of the corn was just as good as that where the fodder was left on the stalk. Now, of course, they never think of pulling fodder, since almost all farming is reduced to mechanized devices, and stalk and fodder and ear all go into shock and silo and sack.

Little boys couldn't do much in the process of tying and stacking fodder, except to drag the bundles into piles, where the wagon picked them up for the haul to the stackpoles, usually along the fence row for convenient later hauling to the barn. One of the arts in farm work at that time was stacking fodder and oats and hay—knowing how to place each bundle to make a secure stack, tapered gradually from the ground to the tip of the stackpole to insure drainage of rain to the outer rim of the stack instead of to the center. And every stack must be windproof.

There was an elderly Negro on the farm, Uncle Eli, who knew exactly what to do with every bundle. The younger men delighted to crowd him, hoping to bring him to the top with a mistake; but when they threw up the bundles too fast, he kicked them back to the ground, without a word. And instead of quarrelling with the youngsters, he would hum some hymn.

Maybe he would offer a comment:

"Stid ub try'n ter wurri 'n ole man, yer mighter be larn'n fur yurselves. De pole iz strait. De bundles mus fit. De Lawd watchin' ole Eli."

The sun dropped behind a thunderhead. My father glanced toward the West, and said:

"There's a storm in that cloud. Let's try to get this fodder stacked before it gets here."

And with that announcement, my father took a pole, and two stacks started up at the same moment. We were all working at full strength. All the fodder had now been tied into bundles, and the younger ones of us were getting it to the stackpoles as fast as we could. My oldest brother became the third stacker.

Uncle Eli watched him, offering a word of caution if he placed a bundle falsely. My father was encouraging everyone as the flashes of lightning played across the black, furious cloud.

Uncle Eli started singing:

> "Precious Lord, take my hand,
> Lead me on, help me stand,
> I am tired, I am weak, I am worn ..."

The last bundle was wrapped, cap-like, around the tip of the last pole, as the big drops of rain began to spatter on the hot earth. We ran to the nearest weather house in the field, which was used for various purposes—storing commercial fertilizer in the spring, cotton in the fall, and always a haven of shelter in time of storm. We could see the tall cyprus and pine trees swaying in the gusts that cut sharply through the nearby swamp, and suddenly the whole earth seemed aglow as lightning struck in the open field a few yards from the shelter. We were momentarily blinded, but no one was hurt. Then the torrential rain.

As the thunder lessened into minor tones and the rain slackened to a drizzle, my father said:

"Grier's *Almanac* predicts when it will rain, but we forget what man predicts when God appears in wind and flood."

"Lis'un Lawd, whut de boss is sayin'," said Uncle Eli.

And then my father quoted Cowper's great hymn:

> "God moves in mysterious ways,
>   His wonders to perform;
> He plants His footsteps in the sea,
>   And rides upon the storm.
> Ye fearful saints, fresh courage take;
>   The clouds ye so much dread
> Are big with mercy, and shall break
>   With blessing on thy head."

The rain ended, we started home. A Negro boy, just my age, was first to jump from the weather house into the muddy soil. He yelled:

"Look up there!"

And across the eastern sky was the grandest rainbow I ever saw. The entire group stood in breathless silence and awe for a moment. I managed to get my father's hand. I was still excited—the dream, the snake, the storm. He knew it. And as we walked along the muddy road, he said to me:

"When you grow older, you will understand all this and many other great and wonderful things. God reveals Himself in the Bible, and we see it fulfilled in a thousand ways. I want you to take your own Bible and see for yourself that God is His own interpreter, and He will make it plain—everything, from sin to salvation."

The rain was still dripping from every tree and eave, and my mother called us into the kitchen to see if we were wet and needed dry outfits. The fire in the stove felt good, even on a July evening, and the odor from the sputtering pots presaged a good supper. She directed me to the nearby nests, but suggested that I need not go to the further nests for eggs—that they might wait until morning. I came in with a basketful, and she raised another anthem of praise for God's goodness. Aunt Sookie was humming one of the cherished spirituals as she went about making biscuit for five growing boys.

I remembered what my mother had said about the Webster statement, but she waved me on to the back porch where a row of pans and soap meant washing up for supper. She always had fresh towels on the rollers against the wall, and each boy knew he should have his face and hands clean and his hair combed before he slipped into his appointed place at the table. It was an unusually good supper, with the big covered dish filled with chicken dumplings. A deep pan pie of fresh peaches proved the pièce de résistance of the menu.

"Suppose we have our family worship here at the table tonight," my mother began, "since it will be damp on the porch. And before we read the lesson, I want Louie to get something he read to me at noon today. It is about the Bible. I want each of you to hear it."

I ran to the big room which my father had built for the boys, often referred to as the "yellun shed," and got the copy of *The Companion* which I had tucked under my pillow. Naturally a bit shy to appear "in public" on a theme of such importance, I handed the magazine to my mother. But she gave it back to me, and asked for quiet as I read it. I needed help with one or two of the words, which my father promptly supplied.

"Do you understand what doctrine means? And revelation?" asked my father. "That, you see, is what I was trying to say to you this afternoon. You keep on reading the Bible, praying God to make its meaning clear, and you will find therein a complete rule and guide for your faith and practice."

My mother nodded her assent to the wise words of my father, and then she read the lesson she had selected for the evening worship:

"The heavens declare the glory of God; and the firmament sheweth His handiwork. Day unto day uttereth speech, and night unto night sheweth knowledge. There is no speech nor language where their voice is not heard . . ."

And my father prayed. I never felt before the power of prayer as I felt it that night as we bowed at the supper table. He prayed that we, "each of us," might understand what God says in His Book. I felt he was praying specially for me.

It was my night to dry the dishes—David's night to wash them. As we stood there, side by side, I asked him if he knew what the word "doctrine" meant. He smiled. He had a way of smiling that always seemed particularly expressive to me. He was smiling at me. I was sure of that. Still, he didn't answer my question. Just as he was rinsing the wash cloths, he turned to me and said:

"Ever heard of the dictionary?"

That was just the guidance I needed. I went to the big room, called the "yellun shed," and lighted the lamp. I got the dictionary, and turned to "doctrine." That was the word in the Webster quotation that kept prodding me.

"Doctrine. Teaching, instruction, principle, tenet, dogma." I read all the footnotes in the big book, and found myself somewhat overwhelmed. I needed help. Just then I heard the flute, and blew out the lamp to join the family circle.

Some days later, my mother reminded me that we would be attending church the next Lord's Day at Middle Ground, and I could ask Brother Arnett to explain to me what Webster's statement meant. That sounded good. Everybody knew Brother Arnett, a beloved Baptist preacher in our county. Often he had visited in our home, and I had unhitched his gentle horse and fed him many times. Brother Arnett always thanked me. He had a way of putting his one arm around a boy's shoulder. He had lost one arm and leg in an explosion of an old shell, left in the wake of the War Between the States.

That Sunday morning we got to the meetinghouse early, as was the custom of my father and mother, and my mother went straight to Brother Arnett and told him that I had confessed my faith in the Lord Jesus Christ and had been received into the membership of Union Baptist Church. Tears came in his eyes as he drew me close to his great heart. She left me with him, and after some cordial words of encouragement, he left the door wide open for my question, and I walked right in.

"Brother Arnett," I began, "here is something I read in a magazine, and I want you to tell me what it means."

Putting on his reading glasses, he went slowly through the statement by Daniel Webster, and said:

"Webster was a great man, my boy. I am glad you have

come upon this excerpt from his Bunker Hill Address. Here, you see, are some of the great words of religion—faith, doctrine, morals, revelation. You could, and should, look up these words in the dictionary, and I hope you will. But you will find the best answer to your question in the Bible. Take the word faith, for example. The Bible tells us what faith is and what it does. Let me write down some passages for you to study in the Bible."

And with the nub of his lost arm and hand, he held the Bible, while with his one hand he wrote down passage after passage, mostly from memory. The memo was on the back of an envelope. I kept that envelope for years, and only wish now that I might have preserved it as one of the most precious documents that ever came into my hands. The first passage identified was Hebrews 11:1. When he had finished the memo, he opened his Bible to that passage, and talked to me in terms I could understand about the profound statement concerning faith. And then to John 7:17.

"You asked me to tell you especially what is meant by 'doctrine.' I take these words of Jesus in John 7:17 to mean precisely what they say, that if any man really wants to know whether His teaching is true or false, he may know. And I am glad that you appear eager to learn of Him. That is what we mean by the word 'doctrine'—learning about God the Father, God the Son, God the Holy Ghost. Seek this knowledge, and you will be forever happy and forever blessed. You know Him now as Saviour, but you are just beginning to go to school in the great realm of faith and hope and love. Promise me that you will study these passages, both in the Old and New Testament, and I assure you there will be endless satisfaction in your mind and heart. I wish I might go on talking with you, but it is time for the service. Go, and God be with you."

After that service, we went to the hospitable home of Uncle

Jim McGee for dinner, and Brother Arnett was there. He took particular care to speak again to me, and to encourage me in the purpose to study the Bible as the source Book of my spiritual growth. He turned in his Bible to II Timothy 3:16, and asked me to read it aloud. And then the seventeenth verse, which he employed as a sort of benediction for all that he said concerning the Scriptures. That day I shall never forget.

Indeed, my mother had no intention of allowing me to forget it. She used the memo on the back of that envelope as an outline for what I now think of as my first course in theology. Again and again, she quizzed me on those passages— did I really understand them—did I believe them—had I made them a part of my very being?

The month passed rapidly, and it was the third Saturday and Sunday in August—time for our regular meeting day, and the coming of the beloved pastor for his ministry in our little country church. His name was Thomas Walker, and he lived in Augusta. He would arrive on the Friday afternoon train, returning on the Monday morning train. It was our time to entertain the pastor, and I was specially glad. I asked if I might go to the station to meet him, and the request was quickly granted. My father let me drive on the way to the station. We talked about casual matters for a little of the six-mile journey, and then the main thing—my experience of grace.

"Your Mama and I are very happy that you have accepted Christ," he began, "and I pray that you will ever be faithful to your vows to Him. We are very happy that you have chosen the Baptist doctrines, and I pray that you will continue to test your faith and your practice in the light of God's Book."

The train stopped, and Conductor Barney Cubbedge stepped to the ground, waving his inimitable salute to the three or four people standing near. Captain Cubbedge was the greatest public relations man for the railroad I ever saw. He made one feel that it was an honor to ride with him, and it was.

"I have been honored to have Preacher Walker on my train," he said to my father, "and you are to be honored in having him as your house guest. How I wish I might hear him tomorrow and Sunday in old Union Church. Good-day, gentlemen. All aboard!"

Brother Walker drew me close to his side, and said:

"How's my boy? I've prayed for you every day since I baptized you last month. Tell me, are you happy, deep down in your heart? Glad you took the great step? Thank God."

My father took the lines when we started home. Always, the horses seemed skittish when they had stood hitched at the station. Maybe it was the smell of the strange smoke from the big locomotive. Anyway, they might want to run away, and it was a bit too much for a ten-year-old boy. It was enough to have driven one way, and I settled back to listen to the conversation. Brother Walker turned to me on the back seat, and said:

"I remember that your mother gave you a Bible sometime ago, but I thought you might like to read this little book about the Bible, and I brought it along for you."

He handed me Patterson Smyth's *How We Got Our Bible*. I couldn't tell you what they said on the front seat the rest of the way home. I was eating up that interesting volume. Many times, in these intervening years, I have read that really fine little book, and it has helped me understand as otherwise I probably would not have understood the Bible. I have read many larger volumes about the Bible, but none that helped me quite as much as the gift from my first pastor.

I checked the Webster statement with the pastor during

that weekend, and received real help from him. It was not long until another beloved minister in our section came to preach at Union. His name was Cartin, a university graduate, and a theologian of exceptional ability. He talked with me for an hour, pointing out the meaning of each phrase in Webster's estimate of the Bible, and then he did something I shall never forget. He wrote his name and address on a card—Rev. R. G. Cartin, Guyton, Georgia—and said to me:

"You put this card in your Bible, and when you come upon a passage you don't understand, write to me and tell me what you wish to know, and I will do my very best to help you. It is in this way that you will come to know what you believe and why you believe it. I have been studying the Bible fifty years, and I come upon something new every time I open the Book."

Why I am a Christian? The Bible tells me that God loves me—loves me enough to provide a plan of redemption for me—a plan which cost Him the life of His only begotten Son— a plan which I can understand sufficiently to accept.

That is what the Bible has meant in my life at the point of the greatest decision I ever made—the decision to accept the Great Invitation, as Emil Brunner describes the Divine plan of redemption.

Why I am a Baptist? The Bible, again, tells me that God has created man as a free moral agent, capable of decisions relating to God and His church in the Christian's adjustment to all the processes of discipleship. Acknowledging the very definite influence of the Baptist home into which I was born in turning my feet toward the little Baptist church in that quiet, rural community, I have to say that it was the Bible which these Baptist parents placed in my hands, and which they insisted I must ultimately study for myself, that confirmed my acceptance of the Baptist doctrine and polity.

It is an interesting story as I review the chain of events that followed that Thursday evening after the third Sunday in July, 1902, when I accepted the Great Invitation, and became a Christian.

My sister had married a young Baptist preacher, as I have before reported, and they had accepted a call to a village pastorate at Stellaville, in East Georgia, not far from Augusta. They suggested that I might come and live with them and attend the public school at Stellaville, which offered several advantages over the one-room school I had been attending in our neighborhood. Of this second home, I shall have more to say as the story unfolds.

My brother-in-law, Mr. Reiser, had been reared a Lutheran, but had become unsettled in his convictions regarding the doctrine of the priesthood of the believer as it related the individual to such matters as personal accountability to God, and he had asked for membership in a Baptist church, had been immersed, and had graduated from the Southern Baptist Seminary. Browsing among his books one rainy afternoon, I came upon this title, *Baptist Doctrines,* edited by Charles A. Jenkens, published by Chancy R. Barns, St. Louis, 1884. I was into the Preface, and Jenkins was saying:

"Every religious denomination, perhaps, that wields a very extensive influence among men, has a formulated creed. The Mohammedans have their Koran; the Roman Catholics, their long-established ritual; the Episcopalians, their Book of Common Prayer; the Methodists, their Discipline; the Presbyterians, their Confession of Faith; and the Baptists, the New Testament . . ."

when Mr. Reiser walked in, and asked me what I was reading. Glancing at the title, he admitted that he had not read the entire book, but intended to do so. He turned to the Table of Contents, and commented on the twenty-two prominent

Baptist contributors to the volume. The names meant little to me at that time, but I now remember gratefully almost every name, and the help I gained from the book. Here were some of those stalwarts:

Thomas Armitage, New York City, who had for his text on Baptist Faith and Practice, "We desire to hear from thee what thou thinkest, for as concerning this sect, we know that everywhere it is spoken against," Acts 27:22;

William Cathcart, Philadelphia, who had for his text on Infant Baptism, "Thus have ye made the commandment of God of none effect by your tradition," Matthew 15:6;

William E. Hatcher, Richmond, who had several texts for his article on Why Baptists Do Not Baptize Infants;

Charles H. Spurgeon, London, who had for his text on Baptismal Regeneration, Mark 16:15-16;

Henry S. Burrage, Portland, Maine, who had for his texts on Immersion Essential to Christian Baptism, Matthew 28:19-20, Mark 16:15-16, and Acts 2:38;

Albert H. Newman, Rochester, who had for his texts on Baptist Church Apostolical, John 16:15, Matthew 28:20, and II Corinthians 3:17;

Thomas Henderson Pritchard, Wake Forest College, who had for his text on the Difference Between a Baptist Church and Other Churches, Jude 1:3;

E. G. Taylor, Providence, Rhode Island, who had for his text on Regeneration Essential to Salvation, John 3:3; and,

Richard Fuller, Baltimore, who had for his text on Predestination, Acts 27:22-31.

I read every word in that book of 566 pages, and I asked Mr. Reiser if I might copy some of the passages in a notebook which I purposed to keep. He was pleased that I was treating this question of my Baptist beliefs with such seriousness, and he said he would be glad for me to make the fullest use of his library.

The chapter by Armitage impressed me. For example, after tracing the background of the passage in Acts 27:22, in which Paul was invited to explain "the sect everywhere spoken against," Dr. Armitage went on to say:

"You all know, to begin with, that as a sect (Baptist) we have the unenviable distinction of being 'everywhere spoken against'; for we are not honored in one place, and subjected to obloquy in another—the detraction is pretty evenly spread. Perhaps it does us no injury, as 'a prophet has no honor in his own country,' but that makes it no easier to bear; rather a little harder, because a Baptist prophet has none either there or anywhere else."

The Armitage chapter, I repeat, impressed me—disturbed me. I had never known, until I read that chapter in the Jenkens book, that Baptists were somewhat on the spot. I went on with the Armitage chapter as he outlined "three great foundation principles" which Baptists hold:

"1.   That the book called the Bible is given by the inspiration of God, and is the only rule of the Christian faith and practice. The consequence is, that we have no creeds, nor catechisms, nor decretals, which bind us by their authority . . . Our churches hold that Jesus Christ is the only Law-giver, and the only King in Zion; that His law is laid down in the Scriptures, and is perfect; and, therefore, they refuse to follow all forms of tradition and ecclesiastical ordinations whatever, bowing only to the behests of inspired precept, and the recorded practices of the apostolic churches, as their record is found in the Scriptures.

"2.   Baptists hold that God has given to every person the right to interpret the Scriptures for Himself. As we cannot be Baptists without the Bible, we must know personally for ourselves, what order of obedience it requires at our hands. To give up one of these positions is to give up both. But do not mistake me here, as to what we mean by private judgment, as a divine right. We do not think that men are at liberty to think of the Bible or not, to obey it or not, just as they please. But we think that they are bound to use their judgment, and to govern it, by the facts and truths of the Bible. The liberty that we claim, is not to follow our own fancies, or predelictions, in investigating the Bible, not merely to speculate upon it, and then diverge from its teachings if we choose to do so, because that would be criminal trifling. The right to investigate the truth does not carry with it the right to disobey it, or to doubt it,—that would convert the doctrine into rebellion against its author, which is an evil, and cannot become a right. God allows every man to interpret the Bible for himself, in order that he may discover its facts and truth, and then honestly follow them in obedience. Hence, no church, or class of men in the church, can step in between the personal investigations of the man and the Bible, to interpret it for him by authority.

"3. That a man is responsible to God, and to Him only, for his faith and practice, so far as the infliction of any punishment for disobedience to God is concerned. Right here we deny the right of the civil magistrate, or the State, either to prescribe a form of religion for us, or to punish us for not following any religion they may prescribe. This we call soul liberty, a freedom which we have obtained at a great price; the rack, the dungeon, the 'bloody tenet,' the stake and the gibbet. Baptists have ever resisted the right of the State to establish a church by law, to tolerate the conformists under pains and penalties, or to interfere with the free exercise of a

man's religion, be it what it may. We may regret that all
men are not Christians, and wish that they were, and we may
wish that they held Christian principles as we hold them,
but we have no right to enforce our doctrines by law, and
others have no right to force their doctrines upon us by
human statute. We hold that if a man chooses to be a Mo-
hammedan, a Jew, a Pagan, a Roman Catholic, a Protestant,
or an Infidel, he has a right to be that, so far as the civil law
is concerned. Therefore, all persecution for the maintenance
of this or that religion is radically wrong. The same liberty
which we claim for ourselves, we are bound to claim for others,
for if their rights can be taken away, ours may be also. When
a Baptist shall rob one man of soul-liberty, by statute, penalty
and sword, he will cease to be a Baptist for that reason . . .

"You will readily see that out of these three great principles
spring up (1) *the doctrine of church independency.* Hence,
the Baptist denomination is not a church, but a body of
churches. That is to say, each church or congregation is entirely independent of each other church or congregation, in
all that relates to its government. Every separate Baptist
church chooses its own minister and other officers, receives
and dismisses its own members, makes its own rules and
regulations, and is sovereign in its self-control throughout.
Baptists have no legislative, judicial, nor executive body,
known as a convocation, conference, council or synod. A body
of churches voluntarily organize themselves into an association, but simply for fraternal and missionary purposes. Associations have no power over the churches, each church gov-
erning itself on democratic principles, and being as free
from outside interference as so many private families, in this
or any other city.

" (2) The net result of these principles *a regenerated
church membership.* No person can become a member of a

Baptist church, till he professes to have found the remission
of sins, by personal faith in the merits of our Lord Jesus
Christ. Many fall into the mistake that, in some way or other,
we are sacramentarians; that is, that we associate the moral
renovation of the soul with baptism and the Lord's Supper.
This is a sad mistake. We believe that man cannot be 'born
from above, or made a new creature,' excepting by the sovereign influence of the Holy Spirit on the heart, leading the
sinner to accept the benefits of Christ's atonement, by faith,
to the free justification of his soul. Then, when he is regenerated, or as the word means, generated again, from above,
we accept him as a fit subject for baptism. In that act, he
professes his faith in Christ as his present Saviour. So far
from baptising a man, in order that his soul may be regenerated thereby, we administer it to him because he is
already regenerated by the Spirit of God. We say to him,
'You have no right to baptism till you are born again, till
you have a new heart, and are made a temple of the Holy
Spirit. All the waters on the globe, and all the religious
services that may be used in connection with water, cannot
cleanse your soul of one stain or blot which sin has left.
But now that you are regenerated from above, it is your
duty to be baptized, and your privilege to be baptized, and
by that act to declare that you are already a renewed man.
And, because you are now dead indeed unto sin, and
alive unto righteousness, you must be buried with Christ
in baptism; just as Christ was first buried in the waters of
Jordan, and then in the tomb of Joseph; that, like as He was
raised again by the glory of the Father, even so should ye
walk in newness of life.' This is the doctrine of baptism as
Paul preaches it in the sixth chapter of Romans, and this is
the reason that we immerse men, because when men are

buried, they are covered in the tomb. This is what we understand by burying a believer 'with Christ in baptism.'

"You will see, therefore, that we must (3) *reject infant
baptism.* An infant, we think, cannot be brought to the Lord's
baptism, any more properly than it can be brought to the
Lord's Supper. It cannot discern the import of the Lord's
baptism, any more than it can discern the Lord's body. Therefore, it cannot show forth the significancy of one, any more
than it can the significancy of the other. It is a subject
for neither ordinance. On this point, the *North British Review* exactly expresses our (Baptist) views when it says: 'Scripture knows nothing of the baptism of infants. There is
absolutely not a single trace of it to be found in the New
Testament. The recognized baptism of the ancient church
was that of adults.' But we do not rest there, on this subject.
Professor Lange, of Jena, who is not a Baptist, expresses our
views more fully, when he says: 'Would the Protestant church
fulfill and attain to its final destiny, the baptism of infants
must of necessity be abolished.' Now this learned man thinks
that infant baptism should be abolished, if Protestantism
would reach its 'final destiny.' But he does not give us his
reasons for thinking so. Our own views on the same subject
are these: It seems to us that infant baptism is in conflict with
the great doctrine of the atonement of Christ. We believe that
if an infant dies, it is saved by the virtue of Christ's blood-
shedding, and not by a few drops of water, nor an ocean
full. It looks to us, therefore, to be laying a great stress on
water in salvation, to be christening the child in death, as
well as to foster superstition; as if the death of Jesus were
not enough to save it, whereas in heaven, the ransomed babe
will sing glory, and ascribe salvation 'unto Him who has
washed us in His blood,' and not to him who christened us.

Then we think that infant baptism is a great evil and should be abolished because, if the christened child lives, his christening has introduced him into the visible church, and thereby corrupted the Gospel simplicity of the church relation. The whole of the state churches of Europe are made up of persons who were christened as infants. No wonder that they are corrupt churches. When infant baptism makes all the population members of the church, that act blots out all lines of distinction between a converted church and an unconverted world. But in those churches which are not established by law, but who still think that 'the church is composed of believers and their baptized children,' infant baptism corrupts the church relation. They do not pretend that the christening so renewed the child's moral nature as to make him a saint, but they do claim that it introduced him into the church. Yet, he is not under church obligations and discipline, and he does not share church privileges, such as the Lord's Supper. So that infant baptism, as we (Baptists) see it, corrupts the church by introducing another sort of members into its fellowship, beside those who are converted to Christ. Then we hold that the christening of a child inflicts a serious injury upon him. It leaves the impression upon him, as he grows up, that in some way, he cannot tell how, he is sealed in a a covenant to Christ, as other children are not; whereas, he finds himself just as wicked as other children. And then, if he ever wishes to make a profession of religion himself, it robs him of the right to that religious freedom, by which he can follow his own convictions of personal duty in baptism, without violating the covenant which his parents made for him, by repudiating their act of infant baptism . . ."

Having copied the above section of the chapter by Dr. Armitage, and numerous other passages from this book, I set myself to the task of checking what these men had written

against what the Bible had to say on each particular point
they had discussed. I had entered upon this task with the
clear commitment that I would agree with what any man
taught only on the condition that he must have a "thus saith
the Lord" for his position. I have followed this pattern all
my life.

My brother-in-law was observing my procedure, but he
was not imposing himself upon my thinking. For that, I was
very grateful. I asked him many questions, from time to time,
as we would be working together in the yard or garden, and
he maintained a wholesome attitude of answering my questions, but never seeking to hurry me to conclusions.

It was, of course, still in the days of open fireplaces, with
either wood or coal for fuel, and since there was an abundance
of firewood, my brother-in-law bought pine and oak stock,
20 to 30 feet long, and did his own chopping. I should add
that he actually bought very little wood, since usually some
deacon in his church would keep the inventory at top level.
Anyway, one evening as we sat about the fire, after supper,
my brother-in-law remarked that he would like to find a
man who would come for a day with a cross-cut saw and help
him with some of the big pine and oak stock. I asked him if
he knew where he could get a cross-cut saw—that I would
handle one end of it on any coming Saturday, when I would
not be in school. He looked at my sister, and she nodded approval. The following Saturday morning, we tackled the pile
of logs. That pleased me very much. I felt it would afford me
an opportunity for some man-to-man discussion of why we
were Baptists.

Concerned lest I overtax my strength at the other end of
the saw, Mr. Reiser would insist on occasional recesses, and
we would talk. When I felt that the situation was sufficiently
pliable, I asked:

"Would you mind telling me why you left the Lutheran faith and asked for membership in a Baptist church?"

At just that juncture, my sister appeared with a pitcher of buttermilk and a plate piled high with warm oatmeal cookies. Naturally, that delayed his answer, but also gave my sister an expected inquiry about how we were doing, and what we were talking about. A woman is always needed in every situation. As in so many other instances, my sister provided a timely contribution that morning. It reminded me of a verse I had memorized from the Bible:

"A word fitly spoken is like apples of gold in pictures of silver."
                                              —Proverbs 25:11

She had read my mind all along, and, obviously, had agreed with her husband that I was delving into areas usually reserved for maturer years and wider knowledge than a boy of eleven would likely possess. This is what she said:

"All right now, you boys have a good time with your sawing and your theological discussion, and remember that an open mind and a trusting heart will always take you through."

Refreshed by the buttermilk and cookies, we pulled the saw through another stock of oak, and my brother-in-law motioned me to a seat on the log as he wiped the sweat from his brow. He began:

"It was the Bible."

When he finished a statement of his experience, tracing his struggle with what he had previously believed and what he found in the Scriptures, he concluded:

"In the words of Luther at Worms, I could do none other. Does that answer your question?"

We returned to the saw, and I felt good on the inside. I felt that we had become fellow-students in the great quest for certitude. After that session on the woodpile, I moved

on in my study of the Bible with an assurance that I cherish
beyond all words to describe.

Why am I a Baptist? Because of a home, and because of a
Book.

And now I am ready to move to a third consideration in
explaining why I am a Baptist—because of Books.

THREE

BECAUSE OF BOOKS

M Y BROTHER-IN-LAW accepted a call to the Baptist church at Swainsboro, and after a rewarding summer at home, working on the farm, attending again every Lord's Day afternoon Sunday School in Union Baptist Church, and somewhere to worship in one of the rural churches every Lord's Day morning, I went again that fall to live with my sister and brother-in-law, and to the public school in Swainsboro—a larger school than Stellaville, and more subjects to study.

The superintendent of the Swainsboro public school was Mr. J. R. York, a very fine Baptist layman, who took particular interest in every pupil. A close friend of Mr. Reiser, Mr. York came often by the pastor's home, and I soon got to know him well enough to ask him questions in many

47

realms. Discovering that I was browsing constantly in my brother-in-law's library, Mr. York asked me if I had read certain books—*Pilgrim's Progress,* heading the list. Yes, I had, each of a half-dozen books he mentioned.

"Since you indicate an interest in biography and history, I suggest that you tackle *Plutarch's Lives,* and after that *The Decline and Fall of the Roman Empire,*" said Mr. York, adding that there would be published the following year, 1909, *Harvard Classics,* which he had already ordered, and which he hoped I would set myself to master. And then he said something that meant much to me in those days of reading. He said: "I want you to adopt a rule for your reading, namely, every time you come upon a word that you do not understand, go to that unabridged dictionary there on that stand, and master the word. Don't leave the page until you know what it means—what it comes from—some of its synonyms. You will never know anything worth knowing until you know words, and there is the book that will help you master words. Don't be ashamed to admit that you need to consult the dictionary, and you will be on your way."

Following that conversation, my brother-in-law put in another stimulating word. "I like the books Mr. York suggested and I hope you will regard what he said. I would add to the list, for the present, the Encyclopedia. I have the *Britannica,* and over at the school library I notice they have the *New International.* Stay with a good encyclopedia, and you will be putting money in the bank—the bank of knowledge. And remember this, knowledge is power."

Swainsboro was a town of some 1,500 population at that time, capital of Emanuel County. It was moving along complacently in an agricultural section, with big supply houses, livery stables, a couple of banks, one big general store, numerous groceries, several ginhouses, a cottonseed mill, sawmills, and blacksmith shops. The courthouse was imposing, with a big clock that could be heard a mile as it counted off the hours, day and night. The schoolhouses, white and colored, were imposing to a country boy, and the churches had kept apace with large preaching auditoriums and high steeples. Little attention had been given at that time to educational facilities in the meetinghouses.

I was intrigued by the bell in the steeple of the Baptist meetinghouse. I studied the situation for a few weeks, and finally worked up to the point of asking my brother-in-law if there would be any chance of appointment as bell-ringer. My sister smiled. She understood boys, especially boys that had not been too used to big bells. It was agreed that I might talk it over with the sexton, and if he concurred, it would be all right. When I saw the sexton the following Saturday afternoon, he indicated that the pastor had mentioned the request, and he came up with the proposal that if I would meet him every Sunday morning and help dust the pews and take care of a few other chores, that I might ring the bell for Sunday School, but he would reserve the ringing for worship services, morning and evening, as his responsibility. That was wonderful, and I entered upon my apprenticeship as bell-ringer, which developed into senior relationship—ringing the bell for all services, including mid-week prayermeeting.

I was charmed by the big store, known as Coleman's. I walked many times past the large windows, studying the displays, and finally ventured inside. A kindly disposed gentleman welcomed me, and said he had seen me at church, offering his services for whatever purchase I might have in mind. I thanked him, and darted out. Weeks passed, and I managed at last to inquire of my sister if she thought they might need a boy in the big store on Friday afternoon and Saturday. She was not specially impressed. I hadn't expected that she would be. I later got around to a slanting inquiry of my brother-in-law, as we worked out a grassy corner of the garden. Nor was he too encouraging, though he would be willing to mention the matter to one of his deacons who worked in the big store.

One morning as I rang the bell at the meetinghouse, this deacon tapped me on the shoulder and suggested that he would like to see me when I got through with the bell. He told me that the pastor had mentioned the matter of working at the store on Friday afternoon and Saturday, and they would look for me the next Friday afternoon when I got through at the schoolhouse. My first assignment was pulling nails out of big shipping boxes on the back platform of the warehouse. I moved up next to dusting boxes of shoes as they were unpacked. Then to keeping the glassed-in show cases clean, until, at long last, I was allowed to sell certain items in the department of notions—every item clearly priced. It was a great experience, particularly on Saturday nights, when the doors were closed, and the cleaning-up period began. I felt pretty good as I walked briskly toward the pastorium as the big clock struck eleven, and sometimes twelve. I was paid 50 cents for Friday afternoon, and $1.25 for Saturday. Before I had to give up merchandising, at the end of my stay at school in Swainsboro, I was paid $1.50 for Saturday's work—$2.00 per week. I tithed the income, and started a savings account at the bank.

But of far greater importance, Swainsboro meant an introduction to the larger field of books. I didn't have too much trouble with the class work, and devoted most of my time to general reading. I dipped into *Plutarch,* but found the current a bit swift. I shifted to Gibbon, and went through the *Decline and Fall* with deepening interest and many excursions into the *Britannica.* I felt the winds of the ages blowing through my mind, whipping up my imagination, beckoning me out and up to the level of man's struggle with ideas, even ideals, here and there. I was fascinated.

Every time I think of Swainsboro, maybe passing through by car, or flying over it by plane, I thank the Lord again for my sister and brother-in-law, for Mr. York and my other teachers, for the clock in the courthouse, and, specially, the bell in the Baptist meetinghouse. Nor do I forget the lessons learned in the big store.

Then came the call to my brother-in-law to serve as pastor of the Baptist church at Sylvester, county seat of Worth County, and that fall I entered McPhaul Institute, where I met Mr. William Curry Underwood, who was to have much influence upon my life. And 1909 was to bring me to other horizons—far horizons.

Sylvester, as a community, was much like Swainsboro, about the same size, about the same type of business, agriculture, religion, and all the rest. The pastor's home was next door to the meetinghouse, across the street from the jail. The courthouse had a big clock. The meetinghouse had a bell. Some blocks away was a Negro Baptist meetinghouse with a bell, one of the sweetest-toned bells I ever heard. I kept on listening to the big clock, far into the nights, when the fire was burning low in my room, and when a boy my age should have been asleep, but *Plutarch* had me in the grip of men, some going one way, some another.

The Atlantic Coastline Railway operated fast trains on the line that passed through Sylvester, and soon after arriving in that cherished little city, I made my way to the station one afternoon, and asked the agent if he would let me see the timetables that accounted for those trains—where they were from, and where they were going. Geography came alive for me every time one of those trains thundered through the night. The plaintive whistle seemed to be translating human urge and wistfulness. I would blow out the lamp and stand at the window, watching the great headlight as it played against the night sky, and then the flashes of light here and there along the cars as the train sped across the street down the way from the pastor's home. There—yonder! Whence? Whither? What? Why? Transportation back on the farm ceased with nightfall, but here was another world.

Deacon Westberry bought one of the first automobiles in Sylvester. One day, observing my awe and wonder, he motioned me to come and ride with him!

The Southern Baptist Convention would be meeting in Louisville, Kentucky, in the spring. At home for the Christmas holiday, my mother remarked that she wanted me to go with my sister and Mr. Reiser to the Convention. Surely not, I said. Already they were doing so much for me. I couldn't let them spend that much money. Cotton was selling for six cents a pound. There were younger brothers. She did not argue. She just said that she would find a way for me to go—that she wanted me to go. My father nodded his approval. As he often said: "When Miss Dicie sets her heart on something, she usually finds a way." The thought kept coming back into the fringe of my then crowded mind that next spring I was to go out of Georgia for the first time—that I was to go to the Southern Baptist Convention. Were there Baptists outside Georgia? Were they like the Baptists in Union Church, like the Baptists in Stellaville, Swainsboro, Sylvester? I had compassed the fact, several years before, that there was a Georgia Baptist Convention—had attended a session in Savannah. I had learned a good deal about Georgia Baptist leaders. My middle name was for the first Secretary of Missions in the Georgia Baptist Convention, Dr. J. H. Devotie. Week after week, I studied the names of the preachers and laymen in *The Christian Index*. I had, in that paper, come upon references to Baptists elsewhere, but it was not a clear pattern. Anyway, I might be going to this larger, outside meeting, the next spring. Just why my mother wanted me to go was not quite clear to me, but she did, and that was sufficient to alert my sense of obligation and responsibility.

The church in Sylvester welcomed me, chiefly because I was in the pastor's home. It was in Sylvester that I came upon the first Baptist Young People's Union, known as the BYPU. It was not yet a going organization, but they were exploring its possible usefulness. I worked in the Sunday School, sang in the choir. By that time, my brother-in-law's sermons were beginning to mean more and more to me. I could trace his thoughts—thoughts born mostly from the Bible, but some from books I had been reading. And he was inviting more and more serious conversations, often in the kitchen after supper, as he washed the dishes, and I dried them. He would open up a theme, and then suggest that at some later time we would talk this through. That, I later discovered, was a very good way to deal with a boy—drop an idea into his mind, challenge him with a wall a little taller than he could see over, and come back later to check on the response to the challenge.

Over at the schoolhouse in Sylvester was that man Underwood. He came often to the pastor's home, sometimes for supper, and then to practice with my sister the duet they would sing the following Sunday. He was watching me, but in a friendly way. That I deeply felt. In a little while, I was at home in his presence. He invited conversation, and put himself at my disposal for questions. A graduate of Mercer University, he suggested that he might help me in extra afternoon and evening work to enter Mercer. September, 1910, was set as the goal of preparation. At first he showed me what I would have to do to enter freshman class. Later, he challenged me with the undertaking of entering sophomore class, by the same date, September, 1910. He said:

"You are taking hold of Latin, Mathematics, History and English. If you are willing to work, I believe I can get you ready for sophomore class in the fall of 1910."

I accepted the challenge. He explained that it would mean less general reading than I had been doing, but there would be time later on for that. I must master certain basic courses. He took me one afternoon to the science teacher and asked him if he would give me some extra work in science, explaining what we had set for our goal. The teacher agreed, but I could see that he was in doubt about the wisdom of so much extra work. He put me through the paces, and finally okayed my units in science. I sometimes wonder how I did it—how a boy could have spent an average of 15 hours per day in actual study. Anyway, by the grace of God, and the patience and encouragement of my sister and brother-in-law and Mr. Underwood and my other teachers, I walked into the office of the President of Mercer University one hot afternoon in September, 1910, a week before the opening date, and handed him a note from Mr. Underwood, which read:

"This will introduce Louie Devotie Newton, who is ready to stand examinations for entrance to sophomore class at Mercer University."

Dr. Samuel Young Jameson was President of Mercer University in 1910. He was a big man, physically, intellectually, spiritually. I had seen him a time or two at our District Association, back at home. He had visited my brother-in-law, preaching for him. Dr. Jameson had served several prominent churches in Georgia—West End, Atlanta; First Church, Griffin; and also as Secretary of Missions, before coming to Mercer as President. He was, in every sense of the word, a big man.

Holding Mr. Underwood's note in his hand, shifting his glasses to his lower nose, he pondered. It seemed to me he would never break the spell. But I knew that when he did speak, it would be important for me.

"What does Will Underwood mean, sending you up here to enter sophomore class?"

He wasn't asking me, apparently. He certainly didn't allow for any answer on my part. He went into a soliloquy, it appeared. He kept talking to himself, some of it about Mr. Underwood. He appeared surprised that Mr. Underwood would presume to tell him that I was ready for sophomore work. He kept saying something about Carnegie units for entrance. Mr. Underwood had warned me that this would happen.

Without a word to me, the President arose and walked out of the office, slapping the note between his hands. Presently, he reappeared, accompanied by a gentleman whom he introduced as Professor William E. Godfrey, Department of Physics, and Registrar. Professor Godfrey had small eyes and protruding eyebrows. He fixed those sharp eyes on me for what must have been a full minute. Dr. Jameson then said:

"Son, we have to admire your spunk, and Mr. Underwood's faith, but we question the wisdom of it all. Now, Professor Godfrey will take you to his office for a talk, and I will agree to whatever Professor Godfrey recommends. Good luck, and God bless you."

Over in Professor Godfrey's office, he handed me a catalogue, marked the section on entrance requirements, and turned his attention to other matters. He bade me take a chair by the window for my assignment of examining the catalogue. After ample time for reflection, he turned to me, and said:

"Do you think, after reading the requirements of admission, that you are ready to undertake sophomore work? Tell me, if you will, just what you have done. You see, Mr. Underwood has not given us any detail. He simply says that you are ready to stand examinations for sophomore class. How much Mathematics have you had? How much Latin? How much Science? How much History? How much English? Any French or German?"

I answered his questions to the best of my ability. He excused himself, and went to the President's office. Returning, he said:

"Would you be willing to take examination this afternoon in Mathematics? It just happens that Professor Edenfield is in his office."

Professor Robert W. Edenfield was a tall, handsome man, with a kindly twinkle in his eye. I liked him. He talked with me a few minutes in his office, and motioned to the adjoining class room, where he wrote on the blackboard, in beautiful style, five propositions in geometry and three in trigonometry. Walking over to the chair where I sat, he put his hand on my shoulder, and said:

"Please take your time. It is right important how you come out in this first examination. If there is anything you wish to ask me, I will be in my office."

I sat there, studying the propositions, but thinking also about what he had said about the importance of this hour in my life. I wasn't afraid of the propositions. I only wished that the other examinations would be as easy. What got hold of me was the thought that I was dealing with destiny, at least in that small circle in which I moved. Until now, I had known my teachers—had loved them. Here I was among strangers, and the man had said: "Please take your time. It is right important . . ." I got up and walked over to the window. Across the way was a building with stained-glass

windows. I knew it must be the Chapel. Just beyond that
building, I could see the tip of a steeple. A church, evidently.
Across the campus appeared a Negro man, wearing an apron
and cap like a turban, shuffling along toward the building in
which I stood. He was saying something to himself. As he got
nearer, I discovered that he was singing:

"Take my hand, precious Lord,
Lead me on . . ."

And just in the middle of that line, he looked up—looked
up to the open window, where I stood. What a face! It made
me think of Uncle Eli, back at home, only he was younger
than Uncle Eli. He smiled. I smiled. He began:

"Lawd, bless you, honey child. Is you coming with us? This
is Lee—Lee Battle. I calls all my boys, honey child. I'm here
to help you, and all my chillun'. Lawd, bless you, my child.
Lawd, bless you."

He waved toward the door, and I ran down stairs to meet
him. He threw his arms around me, and kissed me. "You'll
like it here. O yes, yes. Got a room? I'll take care of you. O yes,
yes. Lawd, bless this child."

That, permit me to say, dear friend, was a very great moment in my life. Perhaps you understand. You see, Lee Battle
was summoning the angels to the side of a lonely boy. What
angels? My mother, my sister, my father, my brothers, my
teachers—everybody that believed in me. More than that, he
was reminding me that we are ever in the presence of the
Lord. "For the Lord thy God is a merciful God; He will not
forsake thee . . . Fear not, I will be with thee."

How, I ask you, could President Jameson and Professor
Edenfield have known what was going on? Why were they
standing at the top of stairs as I started back to the class room?

They looked different, especially Dr. Jameson. Holding out his hand as I climbed the stairway, he said:

"You've been crying, son. Don't you understand? Don't you understand that we are interested in you? Maybe we can't say it like Lee Battle, but we want you to know that we are interested in you—that we want to help you."

Professor Edenfield put his arm around me, and walked with me into the class room. He looked at the paper on my chair-arm—saw it was blank—and then he said:

"Is it too much for you, my boy?"

I shook his hand, thanked him, and went to work. When I knocked on his door to hand him my paper, he was not there. I went down stairs to Professor Godfrey's office. He was not there. Across the hall to the President's office, but he was not there. It was late in the afternoon. They had gone home.

What was I to do? It was a week before school would open. I had no arrangement about a place to stay. The big building was empty.

I picked up my small suitcase, carefully packed by my mother, and started out. Lee Battle was watering a flower bed at the side of the building. He motioned me to him. Putting the hose down, he took my bag, and started toward the dormitory. He began:

"President Jameson told me to stay around till you finished, and take you to your room, and bring you on to his apartment for supper. You all right, honey child? Yes, yes, Mercer is so wonderful. You'll like it here. Now, here's my room, where you can always come when you need anything—anything, I tell you, my child—and, let's see, right over here will be good for you tonight. I'll have your bed all ready when you come back. And we'll talk some, too. Here, here's a towel, if you need one. Lawd, bless my new child."

Lee took me to the President's apartments in the Main Building, and there I met a lovely family, and a warm, understanding welcome. Dr. Jameson talked to me for a long time after supper, telling me about the college, the faculty, the students. Yes, he knew my mother and father.

I was trying to get away, feeling that I had broken in on their family plans for the evening, but he reassured me. He walked across the campus with me, describing in detail every building. And at that moment something very important happened. He pointed to a house where a man sat on the porch, and said:

"Let's go by and meet Dr. Forrester. He is Professor of Bible."

As we crossed the road in front of the house, Dr. Eldred John Forrester arose, walked to the edge of the porch, and took my hand. Dr. Jameson told him who I was, and what I was trying to do. Dr. Forrester smiled, waved us to the waiting rocking chairs, and began:

"Mr. President, I feel like I know this boy. Bob Edenfield came by this afternoon and told me about him, and then Professor Godfrey, and to top it all, Lee Battle has given me the whole story, chapter and verse. O yes, I feel like I already know him. By the way, son, I'll give you my examination right here tonight, orally. If you are what I believe you to be, you can prove it right here just as well as you can in the class room. If the President wants to sit in, all right; if he has to go, all right."

Dr. Jameson insisted that he would like to sit in on the examination, and there on the porch that September evening, with a lambent moon silhouetting the tower and steeple of the beautiful old campus, the great theologian examined me for my knowledge of the Bible.

Do you ask me why I am a Baptist? I had to know why that

night, but long before he ever asked me a word about being a Baptist, he had asked me what I knew about God, about Jesus Christ, about the Holy Spirit, about man, about sin, about redemption, about grace, about faith, hope and love.

What time was it? Mrs. Forrester had brought refreshing lemonade. And then she had said quietly that she would go upstairs. Still, on and on, question after question, comment after comment. Lee Battle appeared. Wanted to know what had become of his boy. Dr. Forrester took my hand, spoke heartening words, and reminded me to be in Professor Godfrey's office at 8 o'clock that morning.

I gave my paper in Mathematics to Professor Godfrey, and reported, according to his instructions, to Professor Carl William Steed, Department of English. There, for three hours, I entered another portal—a portal into the life of one of God's good gentlemen. Maybe, some day, I shall be permitted to say to him, along the banks of the River of Life, what he meant to my life. The three hours ended, Professor Steed took my hand, looked with those understanding eyes into mine, and said:

"Shakespeare had to say it for himself, and Browning and Wordsworth and Lanier had to say it for themselves. I have to say it for myself. You have to say it for yourself. And when you finally say it, your life becomes Literature. Jesus put it sublimely: 'And this is life eternal, that they might know Thee, the only true God, and Jesus Christ whom Thou hast sent.' I shall be glad to have you enter Sophomore English. Good-day."

As I started across the campus to the dormitory where Lee Battle had settled me, Professor Godfrey called to me from his window, and said:

"Please come by my office. I have your card ready for matriculation."

Dropping back to 1909, I have to assess the significance of that first visit to the Southern Baptist Convention, in my assignment to say why I am a Baptist. My mother had her horse, Ruby, known as the WMS source of transportation, due to the fact that every time the Woman's Missionary Society met, my mother would drive around the community and pick up the women to go to the meetings, or to one of the homes to sew, or about the neighborhood to visit the sick and shut-ins. And she always had her herd of cattle, based generally on the fact that there would be a sick calf, or an injured calf that she would nurse back to normalcy, and all such patients in the bovine category became her cows. Invariably, they developed into fine specimens. On this particular occasion, she had a heifer that belonged in the fair. She was the finest heifer on the range. A cattle-buyer asked my mother if she would sell the heifer. Yes, she would, provided she brought a certain sum. My mother had already got the price of a round-trip coach ticket to Louisville, Kentucky. Cost of the ticket was $27.17. The cattleman explained that he would have to take the heifer to the scales in Sylvania before determining what she would bring, at three cents per pound on the hoof. The next day he brought the money to my mother—$27.27! Perhaps the reader will understand why I always tip my hat to every red heifer I pass.

My mother briefed me on the men she wanted me to hear at the Convention—Dr. J. B. Gambrell, Dr. E. Y. Mullins, Dr. B. H. Carroll, Dr. George W. Truett, Dr. F. C. McConnell, Dr. B. D. Gray, Dr. R. J. Willingham, Dr. A. T. Robertson, Dr. J. R. Sampey, Dr. L. R. Scarborough, Dr. E. C. Dargan, Dr. I. J. Van Ness, Dr. George McDaniel, Dr. C. W. Daniel and Dr. John E. White. I asked my brother-in-law to tell me about these men. He had attended the Southern Baptist Theological Seminary, after becoming a Baptist, and he was pleased to know that I was interested in men like President Mullins and members of that faculty, along with the others named by my mother. My mother's knowledge of these leaders was based on her constant study of the Baptist journals. She had clippings in her Bible of their pictures and articles they had written from time to time.

I stayed in a boarding house a few doors from the Walnut Street Baptist Church, where the Convention met. I made a deal with the woman who ran the boarding house to give me meals in exchange for washing dishes. It wound up that she would not accept any pay, even for the room. She wanted to know how I learned to wash dishes. I let her guess.

I made friends with the sexton at the Walnut Street meetinghouse the first morning, and he appointed me his official representative to be a sort of trash boy, staying near the front during the sessions to gather up odds and ends of litter about the clerk's desk. He was a deacon in one of the Negro Baptist churches in Louisville, and he said to me:

"Since you want to know these big men, I'll fix it so you can be right in there amongst them all the time."

That was one of the happiest assignments of my life. Mr. Joshua Levering of Baltimore was President of the Convention, a large man of jovial temper, and he called me to his side during the opening session to know what I was doing there. I explained. He chuckled, and said:

"You tell the sexton that you are also my personal page. We'll work this thing together. You keep your eye on me, and I will see that you meet every man on your mother's list. And you also tell your mother I am going to send her a package of the best coffee she ever tasted." He did.

My mother had provided me a tablet—one of those old-time ruled tablets. I started with the first speaker, making quotes and observations. Dr. Lansing Burrows was Recording

Secretary of the Convention, and he suggested that I come
and sit by him, so I would have the table on which to write
in my tablet. He made numerous comments, from time to
time, of Baptist men and matters. These comments centered
in a question, a question I shall never forget. Looking me
straight in the eye, with his arm about me, he drew me close
to his chair, and asked:

"My lad, can you give a reason for the faith you hold?"

He didn't allow for any off-hand answer, but went on admonishing me to be very certain about my belief in Jesus
Christ as Saviour and Lord, about my belief as a Baptist.

"These men you see here—men like President Mullins,
President Carroll, and all real leaders of our Baptist life today
and yesterday—are men of conviction. They are convinced
Christians and convinced Baptists. You tell me that you were
greatly impressed by the address of Dr. Mullins. Very well.
You see, he knows what he knows. He is not a fanatic, but he
is a dogmatist. Do you know what that word means? Then
look it up when you get home. It is a word you need to understand clearly, or you will be misunderstood when you use it.
Here, let me introduce you to Dr. Mullins."

The tall theologian—the tallest theologian I ever saw—held
my hand as Dr. Burrows introduced me, explaining how I got
to the Convention, and what I was doing there, and then Dr.
Mullins said to me:

"Thank God for mothers like yours. Now, I tell you what
I would like to do for you. I have a book, published last year,
The Axioms of Religion, which I would like to give you. In
that book I have tried to say what religion is, and why I am
a Christian and a Baptist."

Dr. Burrows thanked Dr. Mullins for me. I couldn't get
my talking apparatus in action. I had sense enough to know
that I was in the midst of "tall cotton," as we used to say on

the farm, and I was happy to have Dr. Burrows speak for me. After the Bible, this book by Dr. Mullins, and other books from his pen, influenced my life more than any other author. I shall come back to this book presently. Let me finish with the Convention in Louisville in 1909.

I was introduced by either President Levering or Dr. Burrows to each of the men my mother had listed, and I heard each of them say something during the sessions of that Convention. Climax of it all was on Sunday morning, when Dr. George W. Truett preached. I was at the meetinghouse by seven o'clock that morning, helping my deacon friend sweep the floor, tidy-up the platform, etc., etc. I explained that Dr. Truett would preach that morning, and the deacon answered:

"My pastor says Dr. Truett is the greatest preacher in the world. I'm going to check on my pastor's idea of preaching this morning."

Never shall I forget the feeling I experienced when Dr. Truett stood up to preach. Never. I made no notes, but I could tell you now what he said. I heard him many, many times in the after years—in Washington, London, Paris, Stockholm, Toronto, Berlin—but never did he impress me more than that morning in Kentucky in 1909. He was the greatest preacher I shall ever hear.

Among the men I met at my first Southern Baptist Convention, 1909, was Dr. Hight C. Moore, then Editor of *The Biblical Recorder,* North Carolina, later Editor of the Sunday School Board's publications, Nashville, Tennessee. He invited me to go with a group to Mammoth Cave. I can't say now which meant the most to me—seeing Mammoth Cave, or getting to know Dr. Hight C. Moore.

The train had scarcely cleared the station in Louisville until I settled down to read *The Axioms of Religion.* They asked if I wanted any supper. No, thanks. I had other meat.

Dr. Charles W. Daniel, then pastor of the First Baptist Church, Fort Worth, Texas, had received a call to the First Church, Atlanta, and he was on our train, planning to stop off in Atlanta to confer with the pulpit committee. He stopped at my seat in the coach, asked me what I was reading, and said:

"Son, you're mighty young to be tackling a book like that, but I glory in your spunk. If you master that book, you'll know why you are a Christian, and why you are a Baptist. I reckon that book to be the greatest contribution to religious thought in this generation. How did you happen to buy such a book? He gave it to you? How did you come to know Edgar Young Mullins?" The book was published by the Judson Press, Philadelphia, 1908.

By the time the train reached Georgia, I had read the last word of the last chapter, and I was back on pages 73-74.

THE AXIOMS OF RELIGION

1. *The Theological Axiom*: The holy and loving God has a right to be sovereign.
2. *The Religious Axiom*: All souls have an equal right to direct access to God.
3. *The Ecclesiastical Axiom*: All believers have a right to equal privileges in the church.
4. *The Moral Axiom*: To be responsible, man must be free.
5. *The Religio-civic Axiom*: A free church in a free state.
6. *The Social Axiom*: Love your neighbor as yourself.

Mr. Levering had introduced me to Former Governor W. J. Northen of Georgia, himself a former President of the Convention, and just before the train reached Atlanta, Governor

Northen stopped, as he passed through the coach where I sat, and asked me what I was reading. I handed him the book by Dr. Mullins. Glancing at the open pages with the six Axioms, he said:

"The most comprehensive statement I have read in many a day. I intend to buy the book and master it."

Dr. B. D. Gray overheard the Governor's statement, and he said, with a twinkle in his great eyes:

"Son, eat that book like Jeremiah did eat the words of truth, and you will be ready always to give an answer to every man that asketh you a reason of the hope that is in you, to quote the words of Simon Peter."

As I wrote the above paragraph, the postman arrived with the issue of *Time,* November 26, 1956. Turning to the section on Religion, page 55, I noted this quoted statement from Dr. Eugene Carson Blake, President of the National Council of Churches:

"The old question, 'Can I believe?' has given way to the new, 'What shall I believe?' "

Maybe, then, I was not too far out of date in 1909 when I was determined to know what I believed, and to be able to give a reason for my hope and faith and practice. It was the Bible first, and then certain other books that brought me to the point of knowing, to my own satisfaction, why I was a Baptist.

Continuing my study of the Mullins book, I came upon numerous references to other books that I felt I must have. There was a previous book by Dr. Mullins, *Why Is Christianity True?* I borrowed that book from my brother-in-law and went through it. A book which helped me very much was *A Short History of the Baptists,* Henry C. Vedder, 1891, American Baptist Publication Society. Students of that important volume will recall that Dr. Vedder, Professor of Church

History at Rochester Theological Seminary, divided his material into three sections—*The Primitive Church*: (a) The New Testament Church, (b) Marks of Degeneracy and Corruption, (c) The Church in the Wilderness; *The Persecuted Church*: (a) The Church Reappears, (b) The Anabaptists of Switzerland, (c) The German Anabaptists, (d) The Anabaptists of Germany and Holland, (e) The English Baptists, Origin and Doctrines: and *The Evangelizing Church*: (a) English Baptists, the Struggle for Liberty, (b) English Baptists, Freedom and Growth, (c) Baptists in the American Colonies, (d) Baptists in the United States, the Period of Expansion, (e) Baptists in the United States, the Period of Evangelism and Education, (f) Baptists in the United States, Irregular Baptist Bodies, (g) Baptists in Other Countries, (h) Progress of Baptist Principles.

When I had finished the Vedder book, with its rich veins of Baptist history, I could the better comprehend the six Axioms of Dr. Mullins. And because of Vedder's frequent reference to Armitage's *History of Baptists,* 1887, I resolved to get and master that book as soon as I could find the time. It was not until my first year at Mercer, 1910-11, that I got to Armitage, and thereby hangs an interesting chapter in my experience.

A few days after matriculating at Mercer, I saw a very charming woman entering the Library Building, and Charlie Lanier, a senior, with whom I was rooming, suggested that I come along and meet Miss Sallie—Miss Sallie Boone, Librarian. She literally overwhelmed me, and I venture the opinion that every man who attended Mercer University within the 30-odd years of her glorious ministry as Librarian, will agree that she was, indeed, an overwhelming personality. She was vivacious, charming, exuberant, compelling. She knew books, and loved them; she knew students, and loved them. From that day when Miss Sallie overwhelmed me with her cordial, compelling welcome, to the end of my senior year, and then the five years that I taught at Mercer, I went to her daily for help and guidance. There will never be, I fear, another Miss Sallie.

Soon after this first meeting with Miss Sallie, I asked her if she had a copy of Armitage's *History of Baptists*. Holding me by the ear—her favorite method of leading students to the library stacks—she pointed to the volume by the distinguished preacher-scholar, of New York City, and said:

"That, my boy, is a great book. You see, I am a Presbyterian, by birth, I suppose; but if I were to read that book too much, I would, probably, become a Baptist. It is, I repeat, a great book. Now, if you want to read that book, all right; but I warn you, it is slightly above the intellectual level of Nick Carter, though, perhaps, not quite so intriguing. And you promise me, on your life, that you will take care of this book. It is out of print, and we have but the one volume. Do you promise, Louie Newton?"

She was right. One doesn't cruise through Armitage. But I found every page important, confirming Vedder and Mullins. I made copious notes, and returned the book to Miss Sallie, but again and again across my years at Mercer as student and teacher, I went back to Armitage. And Armitage, Vedder and Mullins introduced me, through documentations, to other important books—books that helped me to know that I was a Baptist.

Other books that accounted for my confirmed Baptist beliefs were Cramp's *Baptist History*, Philadelphia, no date; Milton's *Areopagitica*, 1644; Schaff's two volumes, *History of the Christian Church*, New York, 1882-8; Conant's *Baptizein*, 1885; *The Augsburg Confession;* Augustine's *Con-*

fessions; Calvin's *Institutes of the Christian Religion; The Baptist Annual Register,* John Rippon, London, 1790; *Memoir of Luther Rice,* J. B. Taylor, 1841; *The Baptist Encyclopedia,* Cathcart, Philadelphia, 1881; *The Philadelphia Confession of Faith,* 1678; *Principles and Practices of Baptist Churches,* Francis Wayland, 1858; *Memoirs of Jesse Mercer,* Mallary, 1844; *Fifty Years Among Baptists,* David Benedict, 1860; *Life of J. B. Jeter,* William E. Hatcher, 1887; *Life and Letters of John A. Broadus,* A. T. Robertson, 1909; *Memoirs,* Adiel Sherwood; *A History of the Baptist Churches in the United States,* A. H. Newman, Philadelphia, 1898, *A History of Baptists in New England,* Isaac Backus, 1871; *A History of the Baptists,* John T. Christian, 1926, Broadman Press.

To this list I would add many articles in early and later journals, with particular reference to the Letters, Writings and Addresses of Roger Williams, George Washington, Benjamin Franklin, Thomas Jefferson, James Monroe, James Madison, Patrick Henry, Walter Rauschenbusch, John Leland, Rufus W. Weaver, W. J. McGlothlin, W. W. Barnes, Joseph M. Dawson, and other individuals.

Summarizing, briefly, what I have gained from books that confirmed my Baptist faith, I would say that in these books, some of them favorable to Baptists, some of them unfavorable, I came to the conclusion that there are at least six basic distinctives in the Baptist position:

1. The supreme authority of the Bible, and its sufficiency as our rule of faith and practice.
2. The competency of the individual soul in its direct approach to God.
3. The absolute separation of church and state.
4. Baptism by immersion, of believers only.

5. The complete independence of the local church, and its voluntary interdependence in associated fellowship with other Baptist churches.

6. The underlying and all-inclusive principle of voluntariness.

These distinctives include, of course, the priesthood of the believer, and the equality of believers, if someone fears lest I am forgetting or watering down these cherished phrases of Baptist faith and practice.

And now I turn to a fourth Because—Because of a Fellowship.

FOUR

BECAUSE OF A FELLOWSHIP

PAUL VOICED ONE of the deeply revealing experiences of his life when he declared:

"And when they perceived the grace, James and Cephas and John, who were reputed to be pillars, gave to me and Barnabas *the right hand of fellowship.*" —Galatians 2:9

The right hand of fellowship! Why am I a Baptist? Because of a fellowship—a fellowship "of kindred minds, like to that above." No boy, no man, no life, has been more blessed by kindly, generous, gracious fellowship—unmerited, let me quickly add—than this writer. From my earliest recollection, I have felt an arm about me. With Clyde McGee, let me sing:

For sunlit hours and vision clear,
For all remembered faces dear,
For comrades of a single day,
Who sent me stronger on my way,
For friends who shared the year's long road,
And bore with me the common load,
For hours that levied heavy tolls,
But brought me nearer to my goals,
For insights won through toil and tears,
I thank the Keeper of my years.[1]

My parents, my sister, my brothers, my church—these, at
the first. And after this, the second home, with my sister and
brother-in-law, with its widened opportunity and rewarding
fellowships.

And now that third home. There was the home of my birth,
and the home of my sister and brother-in-law—homes of enriching, ennobling, enduring fellowships. For those homes I
ever give thanks unto God. Let no sun rise or set without
thanksgiving for those fountains of faith and hope and love.

The third home! I had dreamed of it, prayed for it. Every
normal young man does. My dreams came true. My prayers
were answered. And in that third home—our home—has been
the crowning fellowship of the earthly pilgrimage.

There was no time, no money, no thought of romance in
my days of preparation for college. O yes, back at home during
the summers, I had my taste of "going with the girls," to be
sure. I would wash the buggy, oil the harness, trim the fet-
locks, groom the mane and tail—all of that to take the pretty
young thing to church somewhere in the community. And,
during my college days, I had a few, very few, dates. I did get
so far, once, as to pinch the pennies from my small earnings
in newspaper work and holiday "clerking" in a Macon store

---

[1] *Quotable Poems,* Willet, Clark & Company, Chicago, 1937, p. 212.

to buy a canary bird, and a fancy cage, for a beautiful young college girl I had met. But that was about it, until one Sunday morning.

Uniting with the Tattnall Square Baptist Church, on the Mercer campus, the first Sunday I entered college, I was teaching in the Sunday School, and singing in the choir. Miss Jessie Rice directed the choir, and on that Sunday morning she made quite a to-do over a young woman, home for the week end from Bessie Tift College. I didn't meet her, but I saw her. She sang in the choir, and I was quite certain that I could hear her voice, though all the way from her at the other end of the choir loft. She was Miss Zollie's niece. I got that much, and I knew Miss Zollie as one of the Sunday School workers—Mrs. Zollie McElroy. That was a good clue.

Presently, the Mercer Glee Club sang at Bessie Tift College, some 30 miles to the north of Macon. After the concert, the young woman to whom I had given the canary introduced me to Miss Zollie's niece—Julia Winn Carstarphen. What a name, I thought, but not very much thought could I give the strange name. I was looking at the girl—*the* girl! I knew it, but did she? That was the 64-dollar question then, and for sometime afterward. Did she know it?

Miss Zollie was my friend, and she invited me to a teacher's meeting at 720 College Street. I had passed that house many a time on my way to *The Telegraph,* the morning newspaper in Macon, where I was already doing some work in odd hours to sustain my little exchequer. Usually it would be about two A.M. when I would be walking past that house—the paper having been put to bed, and me without a quarter for a "hack," and the "belt line" street car far past its last round for the night. It had been only another house, until that evening when Miss Zollie invited me to the teacher's meeting. She introduced me to Mr. Wes, an elderly gentleman, and to

Miss Sallie and Mr. Taylor. I didn't get the significance of
the family group, but I was groping for any key that might
open the door.

The meeting ended, they broke up for refreshments, and
I fell into the custody of Mr. Taylor, a most likeable man.
Yes, he was very much interested in Sunday School work,
taught the Baraca Class at the First Baptist Church. His sister,
Miss Sallie, was a member there, as was Mr. Wes, while Miss
Zollie was a member at Tattnall Square—went out there because her great friend, Dr. Warren, was interested in getting
the church started on the college campus. Okay, so far, but
where did the niece come in?

Now, Miss Zollie was passing the plates, with steaming hot
chocolate and wafers, and she stopped as I took my plate,
and said:

"You understand our family, don't you? Mr. Wes is Julia's
father. He married our sister, Eden, and she passed away
when Julia was a baby. Mr. Wes asked Bob and Sallie and
me to come and live with him and the baby. That's the way
it has been ever since. I lost my husband, and Sallie and Bob
are single. We have such a happy home. Wish Julia could be
here tonight." She didn't wish it half as much as I did.

Then Mr. Wes must be Mr. Carstarphen, I thought to
myself. Just then Mr. Taylor took me over to the armchair
by the fire, where Mr. Wes sat, observing the group.

"This is Mr. Newton, a student at Mercer," he began, and
left me standing there.

"Have a seat," Mr. Wes suggested.

Yes, he lived in Macon, since a young boy. Folks had come
from Scotland via North Carolina. He had been in the whole-
sale grocery business, but now was operating on a smaller
scale. Not too well. Where did I come from? That name suggested English background. Did I know anything about

Scotland? Carstarphen was the American spelling of Korstor-
phin—Edinburgh. Gordon. Drop by sometime, and we would
talk about Scotland. Thanks.

Graduation at Mercer, 1913. An offer to teach at University
of Alabama accepted after trip to Tuscaloosa, by invitation
of President George Denny, with understanding that post
graduate work would be at Harvard. Another year at Bessie
Tift for the resident at 720 College Street would mean that I
would be getting along with my work at Harvard, and maybe
right soon, provided I could get her to see it. I was making
more headway with Mr. Wes and Miss Zollie than with her,
but I was not discouraged. Still, I would be in New England,
and that long, sleek car would be parked in front of 720! He
had met her at Bessie Tift. He lived near where the college
was located. It was just a hop to Macon in that fine car. Woe
is me, I pondered.

Home for the Christmas holidays—holiday, I should say,
since I was working throughout the week in Macon—my
mother remarked that she had to take off a hen that was
hatching a brood of biddies. I walked with her to the nest.
Brown Orpingtons. Just about the prettiest baby chicks I
had ever seen. The scene rang a bell somewhere in my mind.
No, in my heart.

"Mama, what about giving me this hen and baby chicks?"

Glancing at me, the shawl around her head half covering
her face, she studied me for a moment, and said:

"You want them there at the college? No? I see. Very well,
you may have them."

The hen and baby chicks comfortably settled in a large hat
box, I bowed for the prayer at the fireside, and ran to the
buggy where my brother was waiting in the cold to drive me
to the station, six miles away, to catch the night train to
Macon.

"Whadda you think you're going to do with a hen and biddies at college? Something here that I can't figure out," said my brother as he held tight lines on the skittish young mare he was breaking in. I preferred to discuss other subjects—quail, in which he was particularly interested—his work at the college at Statesboro, etc.

Inside the warm coach, the old hen talked baby talk to the biddies, just as Captain Wheeler stopped to take my ticket. He listened. Above the roar of the train, he heard something unusual.

"What have you got in that hat box, son?"

Raising his eyebrows, he started quoting regulations . . .

"But you see, Captain Wheeler, this is for my girl, and I didn't have any way of getting the box checked for express. They don't have an agent on duty at Halcyondale for No. 3. And I just have to take the hen and biddies tonight, so she will have them when she wakes up in the morning. Don't you understand, Captain?"

"Very well. If you weren't Bill Newton's boy . . ."

No. 3 got to Macon at 2:30 A.M. I would ordinarily have walked the two and a half miles to the college, but I decided it might not be good for the baby chicks to stand the long walk on a cold, windy night, so I engaged a "hack" for the journey. I knew the old Negro well—his flea-bitten white horse, and the old "hack," tilted to one side.

"Pretty cold, Uncle Ned."

"Not too cold. Good hog-killing weather. Gid-up! Wish I had stayed on the farm. Beats driving a hoss on cobblestones dis time er day. Gid-up!"

"Say, Uncle Ned, would you mind stopping just a minute right on there at 720, that white two-story house. I will take just a minute."

The old hen seemed to understand that something was about to happen, and she started more of that baby talk.

"Whoa! What's dat I hearh? Chicken? Boy, wha'shu mean?"

I ran to the front door, pulled the screen door open, carefully placing the box against the front door, and closing the screen door back, hoping it would fend off any dog that might be passing.

Mrs. Sellers ran the dining hall, and she was my friend. She motioned me to the table where she and Professor Sellers and other faculty members were eating breakfast.

"Someone wants you at the telephone. Go through that door to my desk in the kitchen."

Ah! Miss Zollie! God bless her!

"You'd better get on over here before she comes down for breakfast. Up late last night. You know, Forsyth. Coming?"

Mr. Wes was sitting in front of a big log fire, the box by his chair. Miss Zollie and Miss Sallie were buzzing around, and Tee had left the kitchen, standing there with her grand old face in rapturous excitement.

"Wait, I'll get her down," said Miss Zollie.

But before Miss Zollie could get into action, Tee was off up stairs, and presently, she was standing in the door to the living room, amazed. What was it all about? Who had a new hat? Most significant, for me, what was I doing there?

Mr. Wes lifted the lid from the box. The old hen talked to the babies. She marvelled for a moment, then ran to her father's side, reached down and stroked the hen's neck.

"Beautiful, isn't she? But what on earth?"

Just then a baby chick stuck his head through the hen's downy feathers, and looked about the strange place. That was it. Tee was down on her knees by the box, lifting the biddies, one after another, into her lap—soft little creatures, with eyes like diamonds. They were picking at the buttons on her sweater, cuddling against her cheek.

Mr. Wes patted me on the hand, asking if I was ready for breakfast. Tee hurried to the kitchen, emitting a blend of coffee and bacon.

Thanks, but I had been to breakfast. Opening the door, she grabbed my hand. One look, and closed the door. It had worked. Without a doubt, it had worked.

Two strides down the sidewalk, she called to me:

"See you tonight? Tee says come to supper. Something good. Okay?"

And there you have it—the first battle won—the first sure promise of that third home. Enough about the battleground and the strategy.

It was Friday morning, April 30, 1915, just at sunrise. We walked together into Mr. Wes's room. He was growing weaker. "Why don't you children go on and marry while I am here," he had suggested some days before. It was to have been in June, but not after he said that. My sister and brother-in-law had come, and Miss Zollie and Miss Sallie and Mr. Bob stood about the room. Mr. Frank and Miss Pearl came from their home across the street. Tee stood near the door, wiping the tears with her apron's tip. My brother-in-law spoke the words, prayed.

While Tee was putting the food on the breakfast table, Mr. Wes said to me:

"She's yours now, and still she's mine. She's all I have ... You'll love, cherish and protect her ... I'll be going soon ... Tee promised her mother she'd take care of her baby ... Be good to Tee ... God be with you ..."

Fellowship! That grand old Scot! I could not know her mother, of course, but there was the portrait, and the stories of her kindliness, her deft touch, her understanding heart.

No wonder they said she was beautiful. Yes, Mr. Wes had often said to me, it was her life, so gentle and good, that took him through. She was such a Christian, such a Christian as no one could withstand. She had led him to Christ—to her church—where he had found sweet and strengthening fellowship. And her sisters had continued that fellowship in the home, and the brother. Fellowship!

Dropping back to the thread of developments, I must deal now with the fellowships of my college days—the faculty, students, visiting speakers—to emphasize why I am a Baptist.

Lee Battle, head janitor, of whom I have already spoken, was not only a great Christian but a strong Baptist. Briefing me, that week before school opened in September, 1910, Lee lost no opportunity to remind me that Mercer was a Baptist school. He went over the faculty, one by one, telling me how long they had been there, what they taught, where they went to church. He then took up the student leaders—football, baseball, basketball leaders—debating societies—fraternities—YMCA—the married students—the preacher boys. Mercer was not co-ed then, of course. And he told me about the other janitors, specially about John, whom I was to know and love, along with Lee.

Realizing that I was very much on the spot in the eyes of the faculty, I pitched in to do my best on that Sophomore schedule of Mathematics, English, History, Latin and Greek. I was advised to postpone the sciences for Junior and Senior years, and also Bible, though Dr. Forrester said he would give me some Bible work at his home. I roomed my first year with Charlie Lanier, from Millen, near my boyhood home. He was a Senior, majoring in Science. He was good to me, very good to me. The first night together, I waited for him to suggest devotions, and he must have read my mind. I walked over to my shelf and took down the Bible my mother had given me. He said:

"You read tonight, and I will read tomorrow night, and we will follow that schedule. When you read, I will lead the prayer, and vice versa."

Fellowship with my roommate! Charlie was an unapologetic Christian, and an unapologetic Baptist. We enjoyed the fellowship of that year, Christians and Baptists.

Professor E. T. Holmes taught Latin. He was a keen man. I was afraid of him for some time. He seemed to look right through me. One day, at close of class, he said:

"Mr. Newton, I would like to see you in my office!"

Man, man. I was literally scared stiff.

"Let's see, now," he began, "your sister married Reiser? Uh-huh. Good student. And he's pastor at Sylvester now? German. Those Germans are smart. And your mother . . . is your mother named Dicie? Uh-huh. I remember meeting her once when I was down there in your community, shooting quail with the Evans boys, Tom and Walker. Your mother told me that you were then at school in Swainsboro, living with your sister—that you were on your way to Mercer—that she wanted you to master Latin. That, of course, aroused my interest in you via your mother, which, I may add, is a mighty good way for a boy to be introduced to his teacher.

"I asked you to stop by my office to express appreciation for a question you asked a few days ago about a passage from Cicero, in which he employed the word *certus*. I hope I am correct in the impression that you felt that Cicero not only knew what he was talking about, but that he deeply believed what he was admonishing young men to believe. Did I interpret your statement correctly? Good. I am deeply concerned that the young men in my classes will go beyond mere words to understand what men like Cicero meant by the use of words. This word *certus* is one of the basic words in the Latin language, and its derivatives in English are equally basic. Take the word *certitude*. Give me a man that knows why he knows, and I will put my money on him every time. I may not always agree with him, but I will have to respect his right to believe, and his right to declare his belief.

"And this principle runs through every fabric of life. A man must be certain about his patriotism, just as he must be certain about his religion. My ancestors, a number of them, were Baptist preachers. As a boy, I was impressed with the fact that they were certain about their faith in God and their doctrines of faith and practice. I was tempted at one stage of my adolescence to resist their certitude. Happily, they would not argue with me. They just let me talk myself out into thin nothingness. I soon saw the fallacy of my vaunted 'broad-mindedness.' I discovered that no one had any respect for my opinion, including myself. I examined the Bible anew, and read some of the books on Baptist doctrine in my father's library. From that time, I was able to give a reason for the faith that is in me. Thanks for stopping by. Cleave to *certus* as a guiding principle of life, and you will be happy. Only this further word, test every idea in the crucible of honest and sincere research. If it stands the test of historic and experiential certainty, adopt it as a working tool in your philosophy of life. For my part, I like to extend the word *certus* to *assurance,* and with Fanny Crosby, sing: 'Blessed assurance . . . Perfect submission.' You see, it comes to this— the only free man is the yielded man. I am not a theologian, just a layman, but I believe that right at this point is found, or missed, the answer to the riddle of the universe. Thanks, and good-bye."

Professor Edenfield, following that entrance examination, had spoken to me several times, encouragingly, but I had

not been in his office since that hot afternoon in September.
Calling the roll one morning in late October, he paused at
my name, and said:

"Will Mr. Newton please come by my office at close of
class."

I didn't know what hypertension was then, but my guess
is that my systolic and diastolic action shot up several points.
What would he say? Pointing to a chair, he began:

"Let me say, first, that your paper on the first quiz is quite
satisfactory, but it is not about your class work thus far that
I wish to speak. I want to talk with you about Mathematics,
as such. Do you know any Greek? Trying. Very good. Now,
please request Professor Murray to give you a conference in
his office, and you ask him to explain to you what the word,
mathematic, an adjective, means. He will put the word on
the board in Greek, and show you what it means. Let me tell
you that it means *to learn.* He will go on and write the word,
mathematics, a noun, and from that Greek word we get the
science of mathematical learning. Then, please ask Professor
Holmes to explain to you the Latin word, *planus.* That is the
word from which we get *plan* and *plane.* And while you are
asking Professor Murray about the Greek word from which
we get *mathematics,* ask him, also, to explain to you the
Greek word from which we get geometry—*to measure.* He
will show you that the word, originally, means *to measure the
earth*—two Greek words put together. Here now is the word,
algebra, which means reduction of parts to a whole—*bone-
setting,* if you please. It is from the Latin, with an earlier
derivation from the Aramaic.

"When you get a clear concept of these words—mathematics,
geometry and algebra—come back to see me. You might very
well explore the word *trigonometry,* but the important ones

are *mathematics* and *geometry,* and don't forget *planus.* Thank you, good-day."

By the end of the first semester, I had talked several times with the five professors under whom I was studying, and in each of these mature men I had found rewarding fellowship. They were men of conviction on every important subject. They were challenging me to do my own thinking, putting themselves at my disposal in friendly, stimulating suggestions of wider reading. Invariably, they would cite the Bible as the final source of truth.

President Jameson conducted the chapel services every morning, and every student was checked on attendance. He knew every student's name, and he swept his keen eye along every pew every morning. There was no escape from his eyes. Absent from chapel meant a check from the President's office on why you were not there. There were 350 students, not counting the Law School with only night classes taught by practising attorneys. President Jameson would have some member of the faculty read the Bible and pray. Then the announcements for the day, and while all of this was going on, he would be looking at the students, seemingly studying each of us, as under a microscope. He would then rise, tall like a pine tree. We knew what his first sentence would be:

"Young gentlemen, quit yourselves like men! Be strong! Be true! Be a man! Be a man of God! . . ."

He never had to warm up his carburetor. He always hit the ball, and started running, not expecting to hold up at first base. He was irresistible. He left us feeling miserable with ourselves. When he would wave those long arms, signalling us to stand for the benediction, he had us hungry of soul for the uplands of God's plans and purposes. I walked out of that chapel many and many a morning with cold sweat on my brow. The man was doing something to me. And the boy beside me felt the same way.

"I can't stand this," remarked a young fellow one morning as we walked together from chapel to Professor Holmes's class. "I've either got to leave here, or go to work. I can't face my father and mother. They're making real sacrifices for me to get a college education, and I've been piddling around all the fall. 'Old Sy' (Dr. Jameson's nickname from his initials, S.Y.) is beating me over the head every morning with a sense of my lack of purpose. I've either got to find myself or quit."

I discovered that President Jameson's office was always open to students, always. And I ventured a gentle knock on that door. He arose, put his arm around my shoulder, and pointed to the chair by his desk. That was my first unhurried talk with him after that evening in his home—my first day at Mercer. He put me at ease with a few general observations— how were the folks at home, did I have a satisfactory room- mate, etc. And then he went straight home to my plans for that day and all the days afterward—what did I expect to do with my life? Why and What and When and Where?

My next discovery regarding the President was to come upon him one midnight as I returned to the campus from work at the newspaper. He was just strolling around. Imagine my amazement, when he recognized me in the darkness, call- ing my name, before I recognized him. He walked with me to the dormitory, slapped me on the back, and bade me good- night. I climbed the stairs to our third-floor room, thanking God for fellowship with a man who was dedicated to the ideal of building Christian manhood. Charlie Lanier was bending over Chemistry. He turned to me as I undressed and got ready to tackle Xenophon, and said:

"Newt, I wouldn't be surprised if some guy comes up one of these days with a formula to split the atom, and when he does, look out! There's something bound up in the atom that God intends for man to use. How to use it without getting his head blown off will be the big question."

Charlie was talking about something I couldn't handle, and I bowed out of the conversation with a report on the late news that had come in from New York and London and Berlin. That, remember, was the fall of 1910. Charlie turned to me and observed:

"Berlin! Watch this prediction, the next big news will come out of Germany. Those boys are smart, and they are working like beavers. Wouldn't be surprised if they have some notions about world conquest. Hohenzollerns!"

I united with Tattnall Square Baptist Church my first Sunday at Mercer. There I found several of the members of the faculty—Professor J. F. Sellers, Professor G. L. Carver, Professor R. W. Edenfield, Professor John G. Harrison. And there were numerous students from the college, a good blending of students and the young people in the community. They were calling a pastor, and Robert Colley Granberry came from Columbus—a young man, graduate of Harvard. He was not yet married, and right soon he was inviting me to come to his study and to his apartment. I could never adequately estimate the value of his fellowship. He did something for me that no one else had done—he helped to map a long-range program of reading, independent of my college work. He felt that, with *Plutarch* behind me, I had done enough reading for the time in the field of biography, and that what I needed was to dig into definite fields of knowledge. He suggested theology as the number one undertaking. He had done his theological work at Newton Centre, following his graduation at Harvard, and he had a well organized small library of theological books. He said to me:

"I want you to start with James Denney, famed theologian

of Scotland. We will move on, after Denney to some of the earlier theologians, but I believe you would do well to begin with this modern scholar. Here, look at this sentence in his foreword to this great volume, *The Death of Christ,* London, 1902, p. viii: 'If evangelists were our theologians or theologians our evangelists, we should at least be nearer the ideal church.' You see, Denney is here making straight for the doctrine of the Atonement—an objective act of God, and, as such, an act which is consistent with God's whole character. I want you to get the primary principles of theology, and it will then be time to deal with the frills and trimmings. This book by Denney will be a start. You will ultimately get to Anselm's *Our Deus Homo,* to Butler's *Analogy,* Watson's *Theological Institutes,* Clarke's *Outline of Christian Theology,* Strong's *Systematic Theology,* Harnack's *History of Dogma,* Abelard, and all the others. I have these books right here, and you are invited to use them, but always, please, in this room. You are not to take them away. I am having a key made to my study, and you may keep the key, thus coming and going, as your time allows, for study here in this room. If I am studying, you will not bother me, reserving your questions until such time as we agree upon. Understand? Accept? Now, in addition to the books mentioned, I would cite one writer—here are his books right here on this shelf—that I specially commend, Edgar Young Mullins. He is President of the Southern Baptist Theological Seminary, Louisville, Kentucky. I regard him as the greatest living theologian."

Noticing a response in my alerted attention, he waited, and I was happy to notify Mr. Granberry that I knew President Mullins—that he had given me a copy of his *Axioms,* and that I had purchased three of his other books. My stock went up with my pastor.

To pursue this story of fellowship with Robert Colley

Granberry would get me out of balance in this chapter. It is enough to say that I did read the volumes he suggested within a period of five years, going over into the time when I was a member of the Mercer faculty, and I count that section of my effort to know the best that had been thought and said, to employ the phrase from Matthew Arnold, as one of the most rewarding in all my life. Mr. Granberry once said to me:

"I realize that you are not a preacher—that you are a layman, preparing yourself to teach History—but that doesn't lessen my intention to see you well grounded in theology. After all, it is the Master Science."

I have already referred to Dr. E. J. Forrester, Professor of Bible, the man who examined me for college entrance on his front porch that hot evening in September, 1910. I put him down in my little book as a man I must know, and the passing days brought about this happy circumstance. He had a fine milch cow, and I had been accustomed to dealing with cows from my earliest boyhood. He explained to me that he had a plan by which some of the married students looked after the cow, did the milking, and he shared the milk with them. He anticipated my offer to help with the cow by saying that I had already more than I could do—that he appreciated my willingness to look after the cow and calf, but wait until later for that. However, he had asked me, long before that, to come whenever I could find an evening, and visit with him.

That was another of the enriching fellowships of my student days. I couldn't take Bible until my Junior year, but he had gone over his Freshman and Sophomore *Outlines* with me, letting me hand in papers on my study, and he assured me that I had the gist of his courses for the first two years. In those conversations in his home, he got down to fundamentals. He knew about my reading in the pastor's study, which he warmly commended, but he wanted to be sure that

I knew what I was getting into. Hour after hour, he briefed me on the doctrines of Christianity and Baptist practises. He was a mature Bible scholar. He had studied under Broadus, Boyce, Manly and Williams. He knew Strong and Clarke and McGiffert and Hodge and all the rest by heart. One night he said to me:

"Paul was a theologian. You master what Paul says in Romans, and you will have little difficulty with theology. All the rest, Corinthians and the other Epistles, fall into line when you understand Romans. The Epistle to the Hebrews can only be understood in the light of the Old Testament and Romans. Paul knew Jesus Christ, and he interprets the Gospels in terms of Who Jesus Christ was, and what Jesus Christ did. Remember that. In my teachings, I have one theme. Here it is: The Divine Plan of Redemption. It is *the righteousness of God for unrighteous man*. I have been working on a book for the past twenty-five years, and it will be published soon. That book is my understanding of the Atonement and all the related doctrines of our most precious faith. When the galley proofs come, I will let you read what I have written."

He did. And that book, and Dr. Forrester's *Outlines of the Bible*, I cherish as one of the greatest blessings ever to come into my life. I took his Junior and Senior courses, and stayed close to him through all the after years. Blessed fellowship.

One other teacher at Mercer helped me in that first year— Professor John Scott Murray. He taught Greek. He was a bachelor, tall and impressive. I never saw him at any time that he was not dressed in perfect taste. He was diffident, modest, shy. But when once he accepted you, he was delightful to know. I was not at my best in Greek. He saw that I had travelled too fast at the first. He invited me to come to his office for some review work. He was the most patient teacher

I ever had. He was determined that I would overcome my handicap, and catch step with the class. After that first year, it was wonderful. There were only four of us in Junior Greek, and he would ask one of the four to read the passages for the day, and then he would close his eyes and interpret what Homer was undertaking to say in the *Iliad* and the *Odyssey*. That, of course, meant an interpretation of History, of Religion, of Art, of everything. He would take us up on flights from the sixth century, B.C., to the Byzantine Period, and the Fall of Constantinople, 1453. And all in and between, from Homer to Triclinius, he would introduce us to Sappho, Aeschylus, Sophocles, Euripides, Antiphanes, Herodotus, Thucydides, Xenophon, Anaxagoras, Socrates, Plato, Polybius, Josephus, Plutarch, Epictetus and Marcus Aurelius.

He started us reading Xenophon—the *Anabasis* and the *Memorabilia*. We wound up reading the *Iliad* and the *Odyssey*. No, that is incorrect; we wound up reading the *New Testament*. I can hear Professor Murray now, as he would say:

"And now gentlemen, listen to Him who spake as never man spake . . ."

Fellowship, let me repeat, is the word that interprets my days as a student at Mercer, 1910-13. Professor G. L. Carver, for example, subjecting us to the ordeal of dissecting dogs and cats and fish and butterflies, then leading us on a field trip to study the upturned face of a violet, the perfect anthem of an evening lark, or the silence of a deep swamp at sunset!

Or Professor William E. Godfrey tracing light rays in the Physics laboratory; or Professor J. F. Sellers assaying austere chemicals in tiny tubes; or Professor John G. Harrison leading us through the forests of philosophy.

Fellowship with keen, dedicated minds, helping us to think God's thoughts after Him! Ask me why I am a Christian?

Why I am a Baptist? I lift my hat to teachers like Steed, Sellers, Murray, Forrester, Holmes, Edenfield, Carver, Godfrey, Harrison.

There were other rewarding fellowships during my student days at Mercer. The debating societies, for one. I joined the Phi Delta Society. We debated with ourselves, and when we thought we were sharp enough, we tackled the gentlemen across the hall—the Ciceronians. Subjects? Politics, Money, Labor, Prohibition, Religion, War, Peace, Poverty, Crime, Race, Evolution, Transportation, Communication, Communism, Humanism—any and every question that anyone proposed. There was real discipline in those debates, and I think of it all now as cherished fellowship.

Religious activities on the campus consisted of the daily chapel, and evening vespers under the auspices of the Young Men's Christian Association. It was a vital, well-balanced diet. We would have the messages by the President every morning, and a quiet praise and prayer service at vespers, conducted by the students. That was long before the day of the Baptist Student Union plan and program. We had real fellowship in those vespers, and I shall ever identify some of my best hours as a student with the 30 minutes we would spend in worship at the YMCA.

I was elected editor of the campus weekly newspaper, *The Orange and Black,* in my Junior year, and that, along with the debating society, the glee club, my church work, and my work at the newspaper kept me on my toes. I had wanted to get into athletics, but I couldn't figure how I could find the time, until one afternoon when Coach Stroud stopped me, and asked why I wasn't in a football outfit. I started arguing about time, but he wouldn't listen. He pointed to the gymnasium, and told me to be on the football field in Tattnall Square Park in 10 minutes. Tutt Dunaway was Captain of the football team, and Homer L. Grice was Assistant Captain. They were 200-pounders, and good enough for anybody's All-America, had we been in position to draw from a large reservoir of players to balance their ability. The following spring I got into baseball and track, but I filled the role of a "scrub" for most of the time. Here again was a rewarding fellowship. In my Senior year, I edited *The Mercerian,* the monthly literary magazine, in which appeared the only alleged poem I ever wrote. Miss Sallie approved it, and Professor Steed managed to smile benevolently.

Having accepted the invitation of President George Denny to join the faculty at the University of Alabama, following graduate work at Harvard, I arrived at graduation in June, 1913, with a feeling of satisfaction and security, until the morning we were to receive our diplomas. We knew that there was a sharp issue pending in the meeting of the trustees, dating back to President Jameson's proposal to move Mercer to Atlanta, but we were not prepared for the announcement in the morning paper that he had resigned and that Dean Sellers had been named Acting President. Lee Battle knocked on my door before breakfast, and told me that Professor Sellers wanted to see me at once in the dining room. Motioning me to a chair by his side at the table, he said:

"You have, perhaps, seen the paper. I am utterly unprepared for this task, but one thing I have decided—you will remain at Mercer instead of going to the University of Alabama. George Denny is one of my closest friends. He talked with me several times before he invited you over for the conference, and I am going to call him and ask him to release you. I will ask you to go with me to the office as soon as you get a bite of breakfast, and we will talk together with President Denny."

Mrs. Sellers came in from the kitchen, and seconded what

her husband had said. I drank a glass of milk and promised Professor Sellers to join him immediately in the President's office. I found Lee Battle, and asked him what I should do. He rubbed his head, closed his eyes as if in prayer, and said:

"De Lawd's doings. Say yes, 'n remember, Lee Battle's wid you."

Hurrying across the campus, I saw Miss Sallie getting out of her car. I told her where I was going, and for what. She put her arm around me, and said:

"You see, my child, if you were a Presbyterian, you wouldn't be in a dilemma. Just look at Romans 8:28, and trust in the Lord. Somehow, by His grace, we'll find the way."

Dr. Forrester and Professor Murray were standing at the top of the stairway as I started toward the President's office. I told them. They said in the same breath: "You stay right here. This is a day when we need to join our arms as the cedars of Lebanon link their limbs against the storm."

Professor Sellers had President Denny on the telephone when I entered the office. He motioned me to the extension in the adjoining office, and said to Dr. Denny:

"Here, George, Newton is on the phone with us. Please tell him what you have just said to me."

President Denny said:

"Mr. Newton, my long-time friend, Jeff Sellers, has explained what has happened there at Mercer, and I told him that I could understand his desire to have you by his side this coming year. If it is your wish, I release you from your contract to come to the University, with the understanding that you may feel free to take this up with me at any future date when you may finish your work with Professor Sellers as Acting President. Let me put it this way, I will keep in touch with both of you. You will hear from me later. Remember, we want you here, when you can come."

President Jameson walked in about that time, and Dean Sellers told him what Dr. Denny had said. Never shall I forget Dr. Jameson's reassuring words as he put his arm around me. I felt that I had done right, though I could not understand it.

I hurried off to town to get my father and mother, who had arrived the night before for my graduation. There at the hotel I found them talking with Dr. Lansing Burrows, the man who had been so gracious to me in 1909 at the Southern Baptist Convention. I summoned a "hack" and we drove to the campus, inviting Dr. Burrows to ride with us. Imagine my feeling when, after the delivery of the diplomas, the President of the Board of Trustees, awarding the honors of the year, said:

"I have asked Dr. Lansing Burrows to deliver the medal for General Excellence, the highest honor any student may receive. This medal is given by the Trustees, upon the recommendation of the faculty."

Dr. Burrows arose, held a tiny box in his hand, and said:

"Will Louie Devotie Newton's mother and father please come forward. I have much pleasure, my friends, in placing this symbol of hard work and lofty purpose on the part of your son, in your hands. God bless you, and your boy."

As soon as my father and mother were on their train, I hurried back to the college, where Dean Sellers and several Trustees were shaping plans for the summer and fall. That conference lasted into the night, and early the next morning there was a meeting of the Faculty. I had slept very little. I had prayed with a deepened sense of my need of Divine guidance. How could I undertake what had been outlined in the conference the afternoon and night before? The words of Romans 8:28 kept coming to my mind and heart. I felt an inward calm. As the meeting of the Faculty got under way, Dean Sellers said:

"Beginning with this hour, and as long as I am charged with this responsibility, with the approval of the committee from the Board of Trustees, with authority to act, Mr. Newton is a member of the faculty, and my assistant."

I sat there trembling. Then, one after another, the men who had meant so much to me in the three years of my undergraduate work, took my hand, welcoming me to the new relationship. When the last of the group had clasped my hand, Dean Sellers asked Dr. Forrester to lead in prayer.

"But," I said to them, "I can't become a teacher on the college level with no graduate work. And if I am to do what Professor Sellers has outlined for the coming weeks, I could not possibly get away for even a summer course. Please consider what you are proposing."

Never was a boy so graciously dealt with. They would accept the responsibility for the situation which I outlined. They had already carefully considered it from every angle. I would stay with Dean Sellers for some necessary adjustments, and then spend the rest of the summer in the University of my choice, taking such courses as were available with definite commitment to my doctorate. After much investigation, it was agreed that it would be to my advantage to do my work in History at Columbia University, and at the end of June I was in New York, mapping my work for the doctorate with the guidance of Professors Dunn, Beard, Robinson, Hazen and Sheppard.

Returning to Mercer in September, I was informed that I would teach Freshman English and Freshman History, and that I would be in charge of Sherwood Hall, the domitory in which I had lived as a student; also, that I would be in charge of campus maintenance, including the janitorial staff, etc. Lee Battle smiled as I met him. "It's all settled, honey child. Me and you is in charge!" he said. He took me to the room on the first floor of the dormitory, next to his room, which he had freshened up, and had moved my few belongings from up stairs. "We'll git a rug for the floor, and run the telephone in here. Everything's okay. Leave it to old Lee. God bless you, little child. Only I have to say 'Fessor from now on, but 'tween us, it's still little child—honey child."

My pastor, Dr. Granberry, saw me as I entered the prayer service that evening in the church on the campus, and he embarrassed me beyond words, as he said:

"We welcome back to Tattnall Square tonight Mr. Newton, to be known from this hour as Professor Newton. Your Sunday School class is expecting you Sunday morning, and Miss Rice will expect you at choir practice tomorrow evening. And, may I add, you will please see me in my study at the close of the service."

Dr. Granberry had wanted me to go to Harvard, his alma mater, but he yielded to Columbia when certain facts were assembled. He wanted me to tell him what had happened at Columbia—the courses agreed upon—the schedule of work there and at Mercer. He seemed pleased with the arrangement. Our fellowship renewed, he sent me on my way that night with assurance in my heart.

It was tough going—teaching an average of 16 hours per week—administering the life in the big dormitory, where many of the students had lived and worked with me as a fellow-student—meeting the delicate problems of first-year students—handling the knotty issues of keeping the buildings cleaned and heated and repaired—to mention only a portion of my duties.

As an interlude, answering why I am a Baptist, let me go

back to my Junior year at Mercer for an event which contributed very definitely to a sense of affirmation that I belonged in the Baptist column. Dr. R. J. Willingham, Secretary of the Foreign Mission Board of the Southern Baptist Convention, spoke one morning at chapel. He told the story of missions, from Abram's response to the call of God to his own experience. At the close of his impassioned appeal, he asked if there was anyone in the student body that morning who would be willing to go wherever God might call. I went to him as soon as the benediction was given, offering myself for whatever service God would indicate. Dr. Willingham talked with me for an hour, drew me to his great heart, and said:

"Do you know why you are a Baptist? You give me every assurance that you are a yielded disciple of the Lord Jesus Christ, but if you are to consider, and to be considered for missionary service, you must know why you are a Baptist. I will keep in close touch with you." He did.

Within a few days, Dr. John R. Mott came to Macon for a series of addresses at the City YMCA. I heard every address, and talked with Dr. Mott more than once. I told him about my talk with Dr. Willingham. Dr. Mott emphasized the importance of working with my own denomination, but urged me to make every possible contact with the missionary movement. I went that year, 1912, to Black Mountain, N. C., when they were pouring the foundation for Robert E. Lee Hall. Dr. Robert Speer, great Presbyterian missionary statesman, was the principal speaker. I talked with him and Dr. Mott at Black Mountain. They agreed that I would be wise to explore all possibilities to go, if I did go, as an appointee of my Baptist board of missions. Dr. Speer, who was in the after years my guest on two occasions at Druid Hills Baptist

Church, said to me, in the presence of Dr. Mott, at Black Mountain, 1912:

"You are a Baptist, a convinced Baptist, and you will not be happy in missionary service outside the Baptist pattern."

Dr. Willingham came to Macon during the winter of 1913, and spoke again at chapel. Holding my hand, he said:

"I am convinced that you are in the will of God. You offered to go to China, but God appears to be pointing to Mercer." That settled another question in my mind.

My experiences at Columbia University were varied, but altogether rewarding. I had a letter of introduction to Mr. Frank Cobb, Editor of *The New York World,* from my cherished friend, Mr. George H. Long, Managing Editor of *The Macon Telegraph,* which got me an appointment for part-time work on *The World,* first covering Brooklyn Bridge, afterward special assignments for interviews. I have often gone back to those hectic nights around Brooklyn Bridge as very good preparation for the ministry—studying human beings on Broom Street, for example. It was a situation where you telephoned the bare facts of a murder to the City Desk, or a child run over by a lumbering truck. All the desk wanted was the name, address and hour of the killing. When some desperate victim of alcohol or repressed self-judgment leaped from the Bridge, it was just another incident.

One of the first assignments I had was to interview Dr. Walter Rauschenbusch. I had soaked up his *Christianity and the Social Crisis,* 1907, and *Christianizing the Social Order,* Macmillan, 1912, so that I had a springboard for my approach. Dr. Rauschenbusch was an overwhelming person. I felt absolutely awed by the man's personality—his sense of mission. I asked him about Hell's Kitchen, dating back to the Second German Baptist Church. That sparked him off for a review of his father's great life. August Rauschenbusch, a graduate

of the University of Berlin, came to America in 1858, to teach
at Rochester Theological Seminary. He had met and talked
many times with Johann Oncken, leader of German Baptists,
before coming to America, and had left the Lutheran ministry to become a Baptist.

That led to a totally unexpected vein of conversation in
the interview, and without any suggestion on my part, Walter
Rauschenbusch was telling me why he was a Baptist. Reaching into a drawer of his desk, he handed me a brochure, *Why
I Am a Baptist,* published first in *The Rochester Baptist
Monthly,* 1905. "There," he said, "you will find my reasons
for following in the steps of my father as a convinced Baptist."
I forego the temptation to report further on that, and subsequent conferences with Dr. Rauschenbusch, because I am
sure that the reader would like some direct quotes from Dr.
Rauschenbusch's brochure:

"My First Reason: Religion has taken a great variety of
forms in the various Christian bodies. Take a solemn mass
in a Roman Catholic cathedral, with the dim religious light,
the swelling music, the candles, the trooping of the priests
and acolytes, the wafting of the incense, the tinkle of the
bell, the prostration of the people as the wafer is miraculously
transformed into the very body of the Lord. Take on the
other hand a little experience meeting in a country church
where one simple soul after the other arises to tell in rude
words of its dealings with God. How far apart they are! And
yet it is only fair to believe that all Christian bodies aim
at the same thing: to bring the human soul into saving contact with God through Christ and to secure for it the knowledge and power of a holy life. Let us rejoice that we are all
one in that fundamental aim.

"But on the other hand it is only true to assert that some
religious bodies seek to attain that aim by means that hinder

the soul from finding God more than they help it. Judaism, too, sought God with its elaborate temple worship, its bloody sacrifices, its detailed forms. But Christ taught us to approach God by a simpler and more spiritual way. The all-important question of just where to worship and how to worship was relegated to the background as obsolete and outgrown for those who had learned to worship God in spirit and in truth. All religious bodies carry with them a good many clinging remnants of their childhood stage, beliefs and customs that were superstitious in their origin and never belonged to genuine Christianity. And some religious bodies have squarely refused ever to strip these things off; they cherish remnants of heathenism as their most precious and fundamental possessions. Thus it becomes a matter of importance for an intelligent Christian to inquire where he can find Christianity in its least adulterated form. Where is the fundamental aim of bringing the human soul into saving fellowship with God attained most clearly? Where is worship most spiritual? Where is attention least diverted from what is essential in the religious and ethical life?

"The Christian faith as Baptists hold it sets *spiritual experience* boldly to the front as the one great thing in religion. It aims at experimental religion. We are an evangelistic body. We summon all men to conscious repentance from sin, to conscious prayer and forgiveness. We ask a man: 'Have you put your faith in Christ? Have you submitted your will to His will? Have you received the inward assurance that your sins are forgiven and that you are at peace with God? Have you had experience of God? If anyone desires to enter our churches we ask for evidence of such experience and we ask for nothing else. We do not ask him to recite a creed or catechism. The more simple and heartfelt the testimony is, the better we like it. If it is glib and wordy, we distrust it. Ex-

CAMPBELL LIBRARY
SHIMER COLLEGE
MT. CARROLL, ILLINOIS

perience is our sole requisite for receiving baptism; it is fundamental in our church life.

"We apply the same test to our ministry. The first thing we ask a candidate is about his conversion and Christian experience. The next thing we ask him is if he is conscious of being personally called to the work of the ministry; that also probes for experience with God. Finally we ask him for his views of doctrine, but there, too, we discourage any mere recitation of what is orthodox, and are best pleased if all his intellectual beliefs are plainly born of inward conviction and experience.

"Thus our church membership and our ministry are both based on religious experience. So is the ordinary course of our church life. Take our churches right through and nothing so draws and wins them in preaching as the note of personal experience of God; nothing so touches and melts them in the social meetings as the heart-note of experience. When we insist so strongly on true baptism, it is not an insistence on external forms, but a protest against any external form that has no experience back of it. Baptism of believers is an outward act *plus* an inward experience. Infant baptism, we believe, is an outward act minus any inward experience, and we will have none of it . . .

"I like to think also that a church body which demands religious experience and that alone is deeply democratic. It takes a trained mind to understand the fine distinctions of the creeds. It takes a good deal of historical information merely to understand the ritual and symbols of some of the old churches. If anybody knows just what each garment means which a Catholic priest wears before the altar, and how this garb originated and what changes it has passed through, he knows enough history to write a book. On the other hand, experience of God is open to the simplest mind, just as love is. A little child can love before it can think. A poor German or Italian mother cannot follow the new learning which her children get in this country, but she can outclass anybody in loving them. The intellect is aristocratic; human love and religious faith are both democratic.

"When we Baptists insist on personal experience as the only essential thing in religion, we are hewing our way back to original Christianity. The gorgeous ritual that drapes the limbs of the ancient churches was wrought out piece by piece in later generations, and modern historical scholarship is constantly making it clearer that the shimmering silk of which those garments are made and the golden threads with which they are embroidered, were taken from the heathenism of the ancient world. The insistence on correct thinking, an exact orthodoxy of definition, was likewise a product of Greek intellectualism after Christianity had amalgamated with the Greek civilization of the heathen world. These things were not a part of Christianity as the apostles knew it. Much less were they part of the Christianity of Jesus Himself. Original Christianity was exceedingly simple; it was just a new life with God and a new life with men. Faith in Christ was a spiritual experience. Those who believed in Him, felt a new spirit, the Holy Spirit, living in their hearts, inspiring their prayers and testimonies, melting away their selfishness, emboldening them to heroism. Paul called that new life 'faith.' That word with him does not merely mean an intellectual belief. It is a kind of algebraic symbol, expressing the inner religious experience and life in Christ.

"I am a Baptist, then, because in our church life we have a minimum of emphasis on ritual and creed, and a maximum of emphasis on spiritual experience, and the more I study the history of religion, the more I see how great and fruitful such a position is.

"When I claim such a purely spiritual religion for Baptists, I am well aware that not all Baptists possess it. Many do not even realize that that is the essence of our Baptist faith. We have some who insist on immersion in a purely legal and ritualistic spirit. We have others who would be only too glad if we had an ironclad Baptist creed with a thousand points that they might insist on it. I know, too, that 'experience' with very many is a very shallow emotion, copied often from others, and passing away again without changing life and conduct at all, unless it be to add religious conceit to all other faults. This is the smallness and pettiness that is inseparable from human life. But our Baptist faith, like our American political constitution, is founded on great principles, and even if some misuse it or misunderstand it, or are inwardly traitors to it, its greatness lifts others up to it. Baptists uphold Baptist principles; and Baptist principles in turn lift up Baptists . . .

"*My Second Reason:* To my mind the essential matter is not that a church body is very ancient, or that it has a continuous history, but that it embodies the Christian spirit in the method of its organization, and by its very constitution offers the largest possible opportunity to its members to live a truly Christian life together. The fundamental question is not even whether a certain church order is Biblical, but whether it is Christian. The Bible merely helps us to see if it is Christian.

"Now I think our Baptist church organization, though it is faulty in many ways and though it creaks and groans as it works along, just as all other human organizations do, is built on very noble Christian lines and therefore it is dear to me, for the following reasons:

　　1.　It tries to create an organization of really Christian people.

2. Our churches are Christian democracies.
3. Our Baptist churches recognize no priestly class.
4. We have no hierarchy within our ministry.
5. Our churches have home-rule.
6. Our Baptist churches decline all alliances with the State.

"My Third Reason: The first reason which I gave for embracing my Baptist inheritance with heartiness and intelligence, was that personal religious experience is cultivated among Baptists. The second was that our church organization is approximately Christian in its essence. My third reason deals with the conception of worship . . .

"To anyone who knows the dense pall of superstition that has hung over mankind, it is a wonderful relief to pass from this smoke of incense and burnt-offering to the outdoor air and sunlight in which Jesus walked with his Father. The crew of supernatural despots who want sacrifices and who love to see men cringe and implore, has vanished away, and the Best Being in the universe bows down with fatherly love. Holy places, holy times, holy formulas, holy experts are all left behind, and the only thing God asks for is love for Himself and love for our fellowmen. The old cowering fear of the slave is gone, and instead we see the free love and obedience of the son and child of God. Jesus did not pray because He had to or because He wanted to get something from God, but because He loved to pray and speak to His Father. To become a disciple of Jesus means to learn to think of God and live with Him as Jesus did, and to let all life be transformed by that new knowledge and faith . . .

"The Reformation was a rising of the religious and democratic and national spirit against this dead inheritance of the past. Among other things the Reformation simplified worship and swept out a great mass of superstitious ceremonial. In some countries the break from Catholic forms of worship was far more thorough than in others. The Calvinistic churches in Switzerland, France, Holland, Scotland and parts of Germany were very thorough; the Lutheran churches in Germany and Scandinavia not quite so thorough; and the Church of England least of all. The Baptists, and all those bodies with whom we are historically connected, marched in the vanguard of Protestantism. That is one reason I am a Baptist, because by being a Baptist I am a radical Protestant. I can help to cleanse Christianity of the mass of heathen influence which leaked in during the early centuries and was afterward so religiously preserved and cherished. I can help to bring humanity to that simple, ethical, spiritual worship which Jesus taught and which has been so sadly overlaid by the gilded and jeweled worship of a paganized church.

"Baptists are, in fact, more Protestant than the great Reformers on some points. The Reformers all retained infant baptism. But infant baptism was part and parcel of that very paganizing tendency which I have tried to describe. It grew out of a double root: the belief that original sin damns even infants to hell; and the belief that baptism regenerates. If baptism saves and if children need salvation, of course human love wanted the children to be baptized in order to save them from the risk of hell. There was widespread doubt about infant baptism at the beginning of the Reformation, but to reject it would have meant churches of baptized believers and would have unchurched the great mass of men. The reformers recoiled from so sweeping a change, largely for political reasons, and infant baptism was maintained, defended and extolled. It was an alien element in Protestantism, and has been most subtly influential in opening the door to other alien elements in worship, organization and doctrine. It is now slowly dying out. Modern Protestant Christians no

longer believe that unbaptized infants go to hell through their
original sin, nor do they believe that baptism regenerates.
And if a baby does not need baptism and if baptism does not
do it any good, why should the baby be baptized? Other senti-
mental reasons are now used to prop the custom, but the
number of infant baptisms is constantly decreasing. People
are sensibly concluding to give their children a chance to be
baptized when it will mean something to them. Of course
Baptists have largely helped to bring this result about. They
made a cleaner sweep of the old pagan leaven at the outset,
and the slow development of the purified Christian spirit in
modern Protestantism is swinging their way . . .

"*My Fourth Reason:* Because Baptists have always insisted
that they recognize the Bible alone as their sufficient authority
for faith and practice . . .

"This is the last reason which I shall give for being a
Baptist. Baptists have not bound the religious intellect by
the adoption of a creed, and they have undertaken to learn
what the Bible can tell them and to guide their life thereby.
This is to me satisfactory adjustment between the two great
principles of Freedom and Authority; between the initiative
of the individual and the authority of the church; between
faithfulness to the past and obedience to the call of the future.
I do not mean that Baptists have been faultless in their application of these principles; they have sinned and bungled
more often than not. But the principle is right and has a
saving power of guidance in it."

There were other rewarding fellowships during my student
days at Columbia, including Dr. Harry Emerson Fosdick, Dr.
Curtis Lee Laws, Dr. William Heard Kilpatrick, Dr. Hugh
Black, Dr. J. H. Jowett and others too numerous to name.
I found particular fellowship as a Baptist when I interviewed
Mr. John D. Rockefeller, Sr. He sent me away confirmed in

my faith. "Yes," he said, "I am a Baptist, and mighty proud of it."

I am a Baptist, then, because of a Fellowship—a fellowship which began in my place of birth, widening and deepening through my experience at Columbia University and my experience as a teacher at Mercer University, suddenly terminated with the declaration of war by the United States, April 2, 1917. That significant day thrust me into a conflict, which leads me to the next chapter.

FIVE

BECAUSE OF A CONFLICT

If any of you lacks wisdom, let him ask God who gives to all men generously and without reproaching, and it will be given him. But let him ask in faith, with no doubting, for he who doubts is like a wave of the sea that is driven and tossed by the wind.   —James 1:5-6

WOODROW WILSON CAME TO MACON in 1912 in his campaign for the presidency of the United States. We had already organized a Woodrow Wilson Club at Mercer, with Clem Powers, my classmate and boyhood neighbor, as president and I was secretary. We went to Mr. Charles McKinney, chairman of the Macon Wilson Committee, and besought him to let us have Mr. Wilson for a rally in the Mercer Chapel, inviting the girls from nearby Wesleyan College. Mr. McKinney demurred, but we hastened to overwhelm him with the argument that Woodrow Wilson had been president of Princeton, and that he would appreciate having the college students lined up, going on to remind

Mr. McKinney that if he didn't let us have Mr. Wilson for the college rally, the Republican students would be certain to arrange a rally when Mr. Taft came to Georgia, and what if Teddy should organize a college chapter of Bull Moosers? That turned the tide, and Mr. McKinney gave us the green light.

Mr. Wilson stood there that afternoon in the jammed chapel, and said:

"Young people, I congratulate you on the prospect of living in a world at peace."

That night, after hearing Mr. Wilson in the big downtown rally, a group of us were walking back to the campus, analyzing what he had said, but harking back, ever and anon, to his statement in the chapel, that we had good prospect of living in a world at peace. We agreed that he knew what he was talking about—that he had taught Political Science at Princeton—that he had been Governor of New Jersey—that he was an acknowledged scholar. Few of us were old enough to vote, but Woodrow Wilson was our man. He was predicting the sort of world we wanted to live in—a world at peace. It is only fair to Mr. Wilson to say that he had warned us against the lurking danger, always, of complacency, when every prospect pleases. Anyway, we felt very hopeful about our world.

I could remember, as a small boy, when they talked about a war—about the Rough Riders, and blowing up a ship, and an old woman trying to sweep back the sea. That was in 1898, and I was six years old. I knew it was something terrible. That was about all I could comprehend about war in 1898. Then came 1904, and the Russo-Japanese War, but it seemed very far away to a twelve-year-old boy, dwelling in the quiet of a Christian home and a peaceful land. I remembered Port Arthur and Mukden, but not very clearly. I was thinking peace, not war, and Woodrow Wilson was confirming my wishful thinking.

On the evening of June 28, 1914, I walked into the newsroom of the New York *World* with my story on an interview that afternoon, and everybody seemed crazy. I started to ask what it was, when, with scornful mien one of the men at the copy desk shoved me an AP dispatch, telling about the murder of Archduke Francis Ferdinand and his wife in Sarajevo, capital city of Bosnia, by Gavrilo Princip, one of a group of young Bosnian Slavs who had planned the assassination. The Managing Editor motioned me into his office, and said: "I am sorry, young man, but this probably means a world war, and if my fears come true, you will probably, spend your earthly days in a world struggle, unprecedented!"

I stood around several minutes, listening to the older men talk, and walked toward the door with the copy in my pocket. The City Editor waved to me, wanting to know what had become of my assignment. It was like that the rest of the summer. I listened to my teachers at Columbia, both in class and in private conversations after class, waiting wistfully for some hopeful prediction from these scholars of History. None ever fell from their lips.

On July 23, 1914, the Austrian government delivered its ultimatum to Serbia. Five days later, exactly one month after the pistol shot in Sarajevo, Austria-Hungary declared war. On July 31 Germany delivered its ultimatum to Russia, and on August 3 Germany declared war on France. Then followed the tragic story of Belgium, and on August 4 Great Britain was at war with Germany.

I had discovered Dr. J. H. Jowett a few Sundays after I went to New York City, back in 1913, and the Sunday following the assassination in Sarajevo, Dr. Jowett called the congregation of the Fifth Avenue Presbyterian Church to prayer.

It was always a time of heart-searching when that man led me in prayer, but on that Lord's Day he helped me as rarely I have been helped. He led me to pray that I might have an understanding heart, and that I might find and follow the will of God. After the hour of worship, I asked Dr. Jowett's secretary if I might talk with him at an hour convenient to his schedule. Returning from the pastor's study, I was invited into Dr. Jowett's presence. He received me graciously, motioning to a chair. Yes, I was a graduate student at Columbia, doing some work on *The World*. He was kind enough to say that he had read my story, interviewing Rudyard Kipling. He wanted to know about my courses of study at Columbia, nodding approval, and, commenting that my teachers were among his favorite authors in the field of History. Then, turning in his restful chair, Dr. Jowett said:

"Young friend, we are entering upon a time of great turmoil. I beg you to lash yourself trustfully to the Holy Spirit's leading. Read your Bible. Pray. Meditate. In such mood, God will speak to your soul. His blessings be with you."

Back at Mercer for my role as a young teacher that fall, I announced to the class in Junior History that I would be glad to meet with any young men who might wish to devote one evening each week to an informal forum on world conditions. This led to the organization of what we called the History Club. Other members of the faculty cooperated, and we had to shift our meetings to the chapel. By commencement the following spring, we had a number of people from the community in our weekly meetings. Guest speakers from neighboring states widened the appeal of the History Club until, in the winters of 1915 and 1916, the chapel was filled every Thursday evening. I was kept on my toes as I tried to guide these discussions on world affairs in the years from 1914 to 1917, and all the while I was remembering what Dr. Jowett had said, and what such writers as Dr. Harry Emerson Fosdick, Dr. Hugh Black, Dr. Charles E. Jefferson and others were saying. I gleaned the daily papers for any word that President Wilson had spoken. It was in that period that I started reading *The Congressional Record.* There I found the speeches of men like Lodge, Borah, Glass, and other able members of the Senate. I had read the famed speeches of William Jennings Bryan, and now that he was constantly in the news as Secretary of State, I followed his career with renewed zest. The sinking of the *Lusitania,* May, 1915, had highlighted American concern in the frightening war, and I wondered.

Dr. W. L. Pickard, pastor of the historic First Baptist Church, Savannah, Georgia, had been elected President of Mercer University in 1914, and now and then at the Chapel Hour, he would set aside routine affairs and preach. *He was a preacher.* On the morning following the sinking of the *Lusitania,* President Pickard preached on the text: "To Whom Shall We Go?" It was the sermon I needed. I had not listened to Dr. Jowett for some time, and I needed to hear a man preach who not only felt certitude in his own heart, but could impart it to another.

That evening, I went to Dr. Forrester's home for one of those unhurried seasons of fellowship with a man in whom I had come to deeply trust. We reviewed the sermon of the morning, and then Dr. Forrester said:

"You see, this whole thing means crisis—crisis for nations—crisis for systems of philosophy, science, economics, culture, religion. It means, ultimately, crisis for the individual. One must know what he believes, and on the basis of his belief, his doctrine, his philosophy of life, must take his stand. It does not greatly matter what happens to me, but it does greatly matter where destiny finds me. Now, right at this point, let me ask two questions: First, are you as sure about Jesus Christ as your personal Saviour and Lord as you were back there in those calm, complacent days? Second, are you as sure about your basic doctrines as a Baptist as you were back there when there was no challenge of what men believed about the individual's relation to God and to society? Tell me what you feel in your heart tonight on these two points, and we will proceed with the tangled web in which our troubled world finds itself tonight."

I needed that goad—that spur. I had been driving hard, as had everyone about me. I had been ordained a deacon in the Tattnall Square Baptist Church, on the Mercer campus, and had just been named Superintendent of the Sunday School. We had been married, April 30, 1915. My work in the college and in the church, plus my continuing studies toward my doctorate at Columbia, plus the war psychology that enveloped every waking moment, all of this had meant that I had allowed too little time for that examination of one's soul, urged by Socrates and Plato, and named as the number one requisite for triumphant living by our blessed Lord.

Conflict! "Arms on armour clashing bray'd horrible discord, and the madding wheels of brazen chariots rag'd—dire was the noise of conflict." I was thinking for the moment of Milton's militant lines in *Paradise Lost*. But it was more than noise—this conflict into which I had been thrust, back there in the second decade of my Century. And as I prowled through the recesses of memory, groping for something that would help me state the case—properly evaluate the situation—I thought of this sentence in a speech that William Henry Seward made, March 11, 1850: "It is an irrepressible conflict between opposing and enduring forces." That helped. Still, I reminded myself, I must understand the forces, opposing and enduring, of 1917, even as Seward seemed to have understood the forces of 1850. In that period of inner conflict, I went back to Dr. Mullins' *Axioms of Religion,* the book that had helped me so much in 1909, and ever afterward. And then to Habakkuk's "The just shall live by faith," to Paul's interpretation of this great doctrine, and, finally, to Martin Luther's words at the Diet of Worms.

I was back on the track. Perhaps I had not been off the track—just out on a siding. Whatever else might happen, I was now aware of conflict on a world scale, and of assurance that God is, and His mercy is everlasting, and that His truth endureth forever. I was reassured that the basic Baptist doctrines of the priesthood of the believer, the equality of believers, the necessity that man be free if he is to be responsible—all that Dr. Mullins had said—all that Luther had said —all that Paul had said—all that Jesus had said—had to be true, and was true. I knew then, as I could not have known apart from crisis, why I was a Christian—why I was a Baptist. I turned to Wordsworth's *Happy Warrior,* and read:

> And through the heat of conflict keeps the law
> In calmness made, and sees what he foresaw.

In that period of conflict, there was much to learn. I kept going back to a phrase in Woodrow Wilson's first inaugural address: "Here muster not the forces of party, but the forces of humanity." I went back and read Jefferson's first and Lincoln's second inaugural address. The President called Congress in extra session in April, 1913, addressing the two bodies in person, thus breaking a precedent of more than a hundred years. During his first term as President, Mr. Wilson put through tremendous legislative reforms, including the reduction in tariff, anti-trust laws, the Federal Reserve banking system, the income tax laws, a farm loan act, new labor laws, and so on through the amazing list of achievements of a man committed to the welfare of humanity—a great Christian layman!

Not content with his domestic legislation, President Wilson moved for a new foreign policy. His first concern was Latin America, and well may we be grateful for his address at Mobile, Alabama, October, 1913, when he said, addressing his remarks to Latin America: "The United States will never again seek one additional foot of territory by conquest." He went on to declare that he would have no part of "dollar diplomacy," and moved swiftly to correct the terms of the Hay-Pauncefote Treaty of 1901, the Panama deal of 1903, the terms of loans to China, and other foreign policy actions that had engendered Latin American fear of "American Imperialism." All of this was happening against the back drop of a world conflagration, centered in Europe. Henry Ford had launched his "peace ship," and other sincere efforts were appearing here and there by which our participation in war might be averted. It was a time of conflict.

Meanwhile, President Wilson was leaving no stone unturned to throw the weight of American policy and conviction into clear relief regarding the tragedy of war as a means to international settlement. He offered the good offices of the United States in the role of mediation between the warring nations. Mr. Edward M. House conducted continuous conversations with representatives of the warring powers. Came finally the President's speech to the Senate, January 22, 1917, when he talked of a "peace without victory," laying down some of the principles later set forth in his Fourteen Points. Germany replied by announcing, on January 31, her campaign of unrestricted submarine warfare, going on to send the telegram, intercepted by England, to Mexico, promising Mexico Texas, New Mexico and Arizona, if Mexico would join a concerted attack upon the United States. President

Wilson answered Germany's threats by dismissing the German ambassador on February 3, and on April 2, 1917, the President addressed both houses of Congress, asking for a formal declaration of war. Four days later, April 6, Congress, by an overwhelming vote, declared war on Germany.

"An age on ages telling." All day, April 6, 1917, I kept hearing that phrase. But whether or not to dare complete the thought—"to be living is sublime"—was something else. I couldn't do much with breakfast that morning, except the steaming coffee. Off to my eight o'clock class, I walked through Tattnall Square Park, glancing at the storied towers, thinking, praying. There was no radio, of course, which meant that we were dependent upon the wire stories for hourly developments in Washington, London, Berlin, Paris, Moscow. The young men in my first class that morning were serious—serious as I had never before known those young men. "Professor," one of them said as I walked into the classroom, "what can you say to us this morning?" I answered: "Let us pray." The roll call that morning was on the Book of Remembrance at the Throne of God. When the bell rang, the class was still bowed in prayer. The next class was a period of prayer. The bell for chapel assembled the third prayermeeting of the morning. President Pickard announced that there would be no further classes that day, urging every member of the faculty and every member of the student body to spend the day in prayer and meditation. He did call a meeting of the faculty at 3:30 that afternoon. Another prayermeeting. At the close of the season of prayer, I arose and asked the President and Faculty to accept my resignation—that I had been that noon to Camp Wheeler, a few miles from Macon, to offer my services to my country. I had cleared the decision, in prayer, with Mrs. Newton. That was my last meeting with the faculty—my last day as a teacher at Mercer.

President Wilson had said in his address to the Congress
that this was a war to end war—to make Democracy safe. I
didn't know about that, but I did know that I must do whatever I might as a witness to what I believed. I had talked
with General Walter Harris, and Colonel Thomas—both
Macon men. They sent me to General Leroy Lyon, Commanding Officer, with a brief note of introduction. General
Lyon was a Regular Army man. He looked at me—looked
through me! "You are a teacher. You have been working
with young men in a particular field, that of education. I
suggest that you go to the Army YMCA headquarters building, just down the way from this office. I will telephone
them. We need someone to take charge of the educational
work of this Camp, under the National War Work Council."
That was it. I started to explain that I would need training
before undertaking the task. The answer was: "We are at
war! The General says for you to do this job!" As I had
entered the General's office, I remembered reading a sign:
"It Can Be Done . . . It Must Be Done!" Exclamation points
began to take on new meaning.

By noon, April 7, 1917, I was in uniform and at my desk.
A man entered my cubby hole, and said: "I am Arthur J.
Moore. I arrived an hour ago, and the Boss told me to come
over here and talk with you about a job we are to do. He said
you would have charge of the educational work, and I would
have charge of the religious work of the National War Work
Council for Camp Wheeler, serving the 31st Division. What
do you know?"

If those days and nights of 1917-18 at Camp Wheeler had
meant nothing else in my life than getting to know Arthur
J. Moore, today the Senior Bishop of Methodism in the
United States, I would reckon those days of inestimable meaning and blessing. What a man! What a friend!

As my duties at Camp Wheeler unfolded and widened, I found myself in charge of a faculty of several excellent gentlemen from American colleges, seeking to help 30,000 young Americans understand their situation and panoply themselves for the hour of destiny. There was, for example, the task of providing a library—a collection of books that young men facing death would find interesting and rewarding. There was the task of providing entertainment—entertainment that would bring some suggestion of release from the taut nerves of young men who had expected to live in a world of peace. On the point of recreation, I joined head and hand with the man in charge of athletics, and after a boxing match on the temporary platform out on the parade field, I would have ready some singer, or group of singers. Letting off steam during a boxing match, we found that the soldiers were ready for something that would speak to their hearts of home, of loved ones left behind, of dreams and hopes, despite the dark horizon of guns—of death!

I could speak of many singers who came to bless the lonely hearts of the 31st Division, but I guess top place would have to go to Louise Homer. Never shall I forget the night she stood there on a boxing platform and sang *Home, Sweet Home*. We had just got a train load of men from Camp Pike, and an old boy from the Ozark country stood there crying like a three-year-old that had stubbed his toe. A colonel was brushing hot tears from his eyes as the private wept, and the colonel slapped the private's shoulder and said: "Cheer up, son, I've been away from home twenty-five years." The boy from the hills glanced at the colonel, and said: "You don't look like that big a fool." Madame Schumann Heink was another favorite with the men at Camp Wheeler. She had a son fighting on both sides of the lines in Europe. As I drove her back to the hotel in Macon one evening, she said: "I wonder how much more my poor old heart can stand."

Arthur Moore brought some of the leading preachers of the United States to Camp Wheeler, and, always, he would tell them: "Don't stand up there unless you have a sure and certain word from God for these men. This is no time for frills." The officers and enlisted men preferred Arthur Moore to any of the guest preachers he ever brought. He talked straight to their hearts about God the Father, God the Son, God the Holy Spirit. He called sin by its real names, and summoned their burdened hearts to the Throne of Grace.

The winter of 1917-18 saw the havoc of the worst epidemic of flu at Camp Wheeler in any American military camp. I used to remember how many died, but I was glad when I could forget the figure. Arthur Moore spent all of his time during the epidemic at the Base Hospital, and I was there much of the time. I stood one early morning hour, holding the fevered hand of a boy from Wisconsin. "I am dying," he said. "Tell me what to say to God. Don't tell me wrong." Before the first streak of dawn, 14 other men in that one ward had answered the final bugle call.

The war ended, President Wilson moved on toward the League of Nations. It broke his heart. After the months of invalidism, he looked up as the faithful doctor told him that the chariot was bending low, and whispered: "I am ready."

Conflict! It was, indeed, a time of conflict. Everyone had rejoiced with the cease-fire on November 11, 1918, but deep in our hearts we felt that it was only an armistice. Walking across Camp Wheeler late that evening, Major Henry said to me: "When will we know peace?" I answered "When men everywhere invite the rule of God's will in their hearts."

A major event within that period of conflict was the birth of our first daughter, Elizabeth Eden, March 15, 1918. I had

forewarned all and sundry that when I got the call that Mrs.
Newton had gone to the hospital, I would be off and on my
way. There was a narrow strip on the back side of the second
story of the hospital, and seeing that something had to be
done to get me out of the way, a nurse led me through a back
door on to that strip, and left me with the moon and stars.
All night I did sentry duty on that narrow strip—back and
forth—back and forth. Now and then I would peep through
the blinds to get any possible nod from the friendly nurse,
but it was always a shake of the head instead of a nod. That
night goes into my book as one of the vigils of faith and hope
and love. With the first radiant glow of the rising sun against
the smoky horizon, I heard a tap on the window, and saw a
smiling face, like that of an angel, holding a bundle of answered prayer in her arms.

Macon had very strict laws at that time with reference to
cars parked all night on the street. After a little visit with
Mrs. Newton, and one more look at the baby, I darted out of
the hospital to hurry back to Camp Wheeler. A hospital
orderly was arguing with two big policemen as they milled
about my car. It seems that they had put two tickets on it
during the night, and were now waiting for the wrecker to
arrive to haul it in for impoundment. "No, boss, dat man is
a soldier, and he been waitin' all night for a new baby. You
mustn't do dat to him," my friend was saying to the police.
I walked out just at that moment, adjusting my disheveled
hair, and buttoning up my uniform. They looked at me,
smiled, and waved me on my way. The guard at the Robert
E. Lee Gate to the camp, waved frantically as I slid up to his
post.

"What on earth," he yelled. I broke the news to him.

"Man, wait a minute. Read this telegram," he said. It was
from Michigan, announcing the birth of their first baby. He

grabbed my hand, almost breaking every bone in it, and
waved me on—two happy papas! General Anderson had arrived to form a new division—the 31st having joined the over-
seas forces—and as I circled the headquarters for a parking
spot, General Anderson was entering his private mess hall
for breakfast. He motioned me to join him.

"I can see it has arrived. Tell me, girl or boy?" he asked.

"O, a little girl! Nothing so sweet as a little baby—a little
baby girl . . ." And his great eyes filled with mist, as his strong
hand gripped mine. "We lost our little baby girl. Pardon me,
please." When I got back to the hospital, there was a beautiful baby arrangement—from "General and Mrs. Anderson."
I stood there looking at mother and baby . . . and from
George MacDonald's *Song at the Back of the North Wind*
came the memory of these lines:

> Where did you come from baby dear?
> Out of the everywhere into the here.
> Where did you get your eyes so blue?
> Out of the skies as you came through.

And we held one another's hand as we thanked God for
His precious gift—fulfillment in a time of conflict!

Asked to continue at Camp Wheeler through the tedious
weeks of salvaging the buildings and equipment of the National War Work Council, I had a good deal of time to myself, waiting for bidders to make up their minds on plumbing,
electrical supplies, lumber, etc. A letter from the President
of Mercer University reminded me that my place on the faculty was reserved for whatever date I would name. I thanked
him, and declined the generous invitation. As I folded that
letter there in the quiet of my little office on the abandoned
military post, something welled up within me. No more
work on my doctorate at Columbia? No more challenging

hours before a class of young men on the second floor of the Chapel Building? But even as the feeling came, it seemed to go. And I sat there, wondering. I recalled the prayer of Dr. Jowett about being in the will of God. I recalled the words of my pastor, Dr. Granberry, about life's choices. And the words of Dr. Forrester about certitude.

The envelope still in my hand, I saw a car threading the winding road across the parade grounds. The roll of dust seemed to symbolize the blurred horizon somewhere in my mind. The vice-president of the largest bank in Middle Georgia got out of the car and walked toward my office. He came immediately to the point. His directors had authorized him to offer me a place on the bank's staff as public relations officer, with the rank of vice-president. I smiled as he talked. No, I could never be a banker. It was good to contemplate security, pleasant associations, a sense of sharing in the building of a greater economy; but I could not see it as my life's investment.

The telephone rang that evening. Would I come by the next morning on my way to Camp Wheeler? It was an offer to sell automobiles—twenty counties—a very fine car! Thanks, but I could never fit into that pattern. Yes, I did know people throughout Middle Georgia, and it would, undoubtedly, be a profitable career; but. No. I couldn't quite say why—why I didn't take the offer at the bank—why I didn't accept the offer to sell a very fine car. Thanks, just the same.

Arriving at the lonely little office at Camp Wheeler, I telephoned Mrs. Newton to know if the man had called the house that was supposed to be waiting at my office to buy the last lot of odds and ends. No, but there was a long distance call from New York City. Would I like to go to Australia? What? Yes, for an indefinite assignment, and later, perhaps, to India. No. And as I explained why—the mother

and little baby—the invalid father-in-law—the voice came
back with something about the opportunity of a lifetime. No.
Very well, and good luck.

The man came and bought the last lot of stuff. I pinned his
check to the final report, picked up the few little things that
had collected on and in my desk during the hectic days of
war, and as I reached for my Bible, it opened to these words,
Proverbs 3:5-6, which Mrs. Newton had marked one night
as I was leaving her to take the train to New York:

> Trust in the Lord with all thine heart;
>   And lean not unto thine own understanding.
> In all thy ways acknowledge Him,
>   And He shall direct thy paths.

The big truck pulled away, and I dropped my face into
my hands on the dusty little desk, and prayed.

The Mercer people asked me to do some temporary work
on the alumni list, trying to find out how many alumni had
been engaged in the war, how many had been killed, what
the alumni might do in the days ahead. It was a rewarding
bit of service for my alma mater, but what about the future?
Conflict!

The telephone rang. Would I come to Atlanta immediately? Southern Baptists had just voted, May, 1919, to launch
a great missionary, educational and benevolent effort to raise
$75,000,000 for the postwar program of advance. Dr. J. B.
Gambrell, President of the Convention, was talking from his
room in the Piedmont Hotel in Atlanta. Yes, I would come.
What did it mean? I didn't know, but I did know that I was
on the right road. On to Nashville that night, with Dr. Gambrell and Dr. Lee Scarborough, President of the Southwestern
Seminary, where preliminary plans were adopted, and I was
up to my chin in a task that would mean work, day and night,

for the rest of 1919. Grabbing a train now and then for Macon, I would have a few hours with the little family, then off to Texas or Virginia or Nashville, with Atlanta as a sort of home base for the months of arduous, fascinating work. "Millions for the Master" was the theme of the campaign. Dr. Scarborough was the director of the mighty effort, and to his side he summoned hundreds and hundreds of pastors and laymen, affording a young man the rarest opportunity imaginable for fellowship in the Lord's work.

In addition to constant fellowship with Baptist preachers and laymen, I had interviews with editors, bankers, lawyers, educators, governors, seeking statements from leaders of capital and labor, from farmers and manufacturers, from moulders of the South in the unfolding opportunities to build a sound and enduring civilization. I wrote copy for daily newspapers, weekly newspapers, Baptist newspapers, and it had to be trigger copy, sure-fire reader appeal. I received much good training under Mr. Frank Burkhalter in the Nashville office. And all in between I was used as a substitute speaker at rallies for the fellows that had got sore throats, stiff joints, unexpected weddings, and the inevitable funeral calls. How I missed ulcers is still an interesting reflection. Maybe it was that cast-iron digestive system that turnip greens and cornbread and sugar cane syrup and raw peanuts developed, plus plenty of hard work in the good fresh air and sunshine of Screven County.

Again and again, during the last half of 1919, as I met new people, many of them non-Baptists, I was asked, Why are you a Baptist? What is it you Baptists are doing that you couldn't do just as well in one big church, representing all the denominations? What is the difference between a Baptist and a Roman Catholic, or Methodist, or Presbyterian, or Episcopalian, or Lutheran, or Disciple of Christ, or Congre-

gationalist, or Nazerene, or Mormon, or Quaker, or Christian
Scientist? These people were thinking of the Inter-church
Movement.

I had got to know Dr. J. B. Gambrell well enough to talk
quite freely with him, and one night as we ate together on a
train out of St. Louis, I said:

"Dr. Gambrell, would you tell me why you are a Baptist?"

He held his buttered slice of bread half way from his plate
to his mouth, tilted his kindly face a bit, and said:

"I can't be other than a Baptist until the good Lord sees
fit to revise the New Testament. If that sounds over-simpli-
fied, and too cocksure, then re-examine it for yourself, and
tell me where you would have difficulty in being a Baptist.
Ever read the New Testament with this question in mind,
What is a New Testament church? Or what it says about soul
liberty? Or what it says about the competence of the individual to deal directly with God, through Jesus Christ our great
High Priest forever? Or what it says about the ordinances of
baptism and the Lord's Supper? Take all the creeds of all
the other churches and study them carefully and without bias,
and then read again what the New Testament says regarding
every doctrine and practice, and see where you will wind up.
I have many friends in other denominations, and I have
sought earnestly to compare my beliefs with theirs, trying
to make sure that I had a reason for the faith that is in me as
a Baptist. I hope that every Baptist does as much to insure
that he knows why he is a Baptist. Understand this, I am not
as good a Baptist as I should be, but I am a convinced Baptist.
And if you or anyone else can point me to a denomination
that is nearer to the doctrines and polity of the New Testament church than Baptists, I'll start that moment to the nearest such church and ask for instruction and acceptance."

Dr. Lee Scarborough sat across the table from us in the

diner, and when Dr. Gambrell had finished answering my question, Dr. Scarborough said:

"I'm glad you asked Uncle Gideon why he was a Baptist. You see, down there in Texas, we lean right heavily on this grand old leader. I came up under him and Dr. B. H. Carroll, and when I finished at Yale, I wanted to be quite sure that I was right in my Baptist beliefs. I came home and asked Dr. Carroll exactly the same question you asked Dr. Gambrell tonight. He talked with me an entire evening, and sent me to Dr. Gambrell's office the next morning. They both insisted that I must not be satisfied about my Baptist beliefs merely because of their convictions—that I must establish my beliefs on what the Bible says. I wish every young Baptist in the world would do just what they asked me to do—test your faith in the light of what the Bible says. That is why I am a Baptist."

There was an important meeting in Nashville in October, 1919. Dr. Scarborough summoned a group of "key pastors," as he called them, to map the final strategy to raise $75,000,000 before the end of the year. It was the first close-range touch I had been privileged to have with some of those men—Dr. George W. McDaniel, Virginia; Dr. Fred Brown, Tennessee; Dr. M. E. Dodd, Louisiana; Dr. George W. Truett, Texas; Dr. F. C. McConnell, Georgia; Dr. Charles W. Daniel, Georgia; Dr. S. J. Porter, Oklahoma; Dr. Claude Duke, Florida; Dr. Clyde Turner, North Carolina; Dr. B. D. Gray, Home Mission Board; Dr. I. J. Van Ness, Sunday School Board; Drs. J. F. Love and T. B. Ray of the Foreign Mission Board; Drs. E. Y. Mullins and W. J. McGlothlin of the Southern Seminary; Dr. B. H. Dement of the Baptist Bible Institute; Dr. William Lunsford of the Relief and Annuity Board; and others. Mr. Burkhalter thought it would be a fine thing if I would secure from each of these leaders a brief statement about the purposes of the campaign—what it would mean in the furtherance of the Kingdom of God. The first man I tackled was Dr. W. J. McGlothlin, Professor of Church History in the Southern Seminary, Louisville, Kentucky. He lifted his great eyes, as if peering into the unborn centuries, and said:

"Because Baptists believe in freedom, that is why we must do this thing. The world writhes in bondage—the bondage of false concepts of freedom. Baptists believe in the liberty wherewith Christ makes men free. That is why we must do this thing."

Why am I a Baptist? I knew why that day in Nashville as I had never known before. A man who knew what he was talking about was confirming what I had come to deeply believe. He was underscoring every word, every thought, every conviction in my heart.

The Baptist 75 Million Campaign ended in victory—$92,000,000 pledged over a period of five years. It was not all paid, but 60-odd million was paid within the period of five years, and many paid their pledges in subsequent years. I saw a statement in the fall of 1956 that a Baptist somewhere paid a 50-dollar pledge made in 1919. That campaign meant more for Baptists than anything that had happened to them since the Southern Baptist Convention was organized in Augusta, Georgia, on May 8, 1845. Colleges, seminaries, orphanages, hospitals, mission boards—all were undergirded for a new and greater day of ministry, for Christ's sake.

A man came into my life in connection with the 75 Million Campaign of whom I must here say a word. Dr. Arch C. Cree was the Executive Secretary-Treasurer of the Georgia Baptist Convention at that time, and I got to know him quite well during the last six months of 1919. He was a Scot. He was a hard worker—a man of tireless energy and compelling zeal.

As we neared the end of December, Dr. Cree, seeing that the campaign was a success, proposed to his board that Georgia Baptists buy *The Christian Index*, the Baptist weekly newspaper in Georgia. It was privately owned at the time, edited by Dr. B. J. W. Graham. The Convention approved the recommendation, and the paper was purchased. Dr. Cree called me in his office and asked me if I would accept the editorship, provided the committee recommended me to the board. "I realize that you are only 27 years old," he said, "but with your experience as editor of the campus papers at Mercer, as editor of *The Stars and Stripes* at Camp Wheeler, and your newspaper work in Macon and New York, I believe you have enough know-how, and we will all pitch in and help you with the very essential responsibilities incident to the editorship – meeting and knowing and understanding Georgia Baptists and the far-reaching program of our denomination."

The board of directors, charged with the responsibility of securing an editor and launching the paper's role under Convention ownership, was composed of Drs. F. C. McConnell, Charles W. Daniel, Henry Alford Porter, W. H. Major and Arch C. Cree. Dr. McConnell called me to know if I would meet with the directors at the Winecoff Hotel, December 12, 1919. They invited me to the editorship. I told them that I would not accept the editorship, but I would serve as managing editor for three months, during which time I would have some opportunity of discovering what was involved, and whether I might feel that it was what the Lord wanted me to do, provided Mrs. Newton concurred in that decision. I would be going to Macon for the weekend, and they would have my final answer on Monday. They agreed. I then inquired what they thought the paper should be and do. They weren't too clear in their answers. "We want it to serve the Kingdom of God, if you understand what I am saying," said

Dr. McConnell. Yes, I thought I did understand, and I was very pleased that they didn't have all the answers. I knew very well that I could not be editor of the paper if there was any circumvention of my freedom as editor. They agreed.

I submitted the proposition to Mrs. Newton, and, as in every such instance, she said very quietly and helpfully: "You do what you feel the Lord wants you to do, and I will be at your side."

At lunch with the directors the following Monday, the decision was reached, and I was on my way to 41 Ellis Street for a conference with Dr. Graham. He introduced me to the staff of the paper, and to the men in the printing plant. He explained that his firm would be glad to go on printing the paper as long as the directors wished—that he would help me with the first issue—and then he was going fishing. I glanced at the calendar in Dr. Graham's office, and, lo, 1920 began on Thursday, and Thursday was publication day! "You'll have to have all your copy ready for the linotype operators by December 21, since they will all be off three days for Christmas," he remarked. The copy was ready, and I read the galley proofs on the one day I had with the family that Christmas. My first issue of *The Christian Index* bore the dateline, January 1, 1920. It was far from satisfactory, but it was a beginning. Letters of approval and disapproval were fairly balanced. I knew I had a job to do, and deep down in my heart I was happy.

There was a little nook in the building at 41 Ellis Street, known as the Book Department. The young woman in charge was Miss Erva Blackstock. I talked with her about the possibilities of her department. Couldn't we expand it gradually? Couldn't we promote the sale of Bibles and religious books through the paper? She was enthusiastic. I met a young woman in the circulation department who impressed me as a person of deep conviction. Her name was Miss Leta Hill. She came to me the second week in January, and said: "I love the work here, but I want to be a missionary. I believe God is calling me." Correspondence with Dr. J. F. Love of the Foreign Mission Board led to her appointment, and she went to Japan. And there was Miss Susie Browning, who became a nurse. Within a month, we had moved the little inventory of Bibles and the circulation department to the Flatiron Building, where the Convention headquarters was located. I struggled to get favorable space for the Book Department, but we had to take a rather secluded and limited corner. But that didn't discourage Miss Blackstock and me in our dream of a Baptist Book Store one of these days.

I buckled down to the task of building reader interest into the paper, from cover to cover, every week. It was not easy. There was the limiting factor of money. Dr. Cree, with his Scotch background, would applaud my suggestions, but cautioned me to watch the weekly cost sheets. Dr. Porter helped me with the editorials, and Dr. McConnell wrote the page on the Sunday School lessons. The first cable I ever sent was to Dr. J. F. Love, then in Belgium, studying the havoc of war. I asked him for manuscript on what he found up and down the battlefields. On January 8, my second issue, I carried his first article. I started that week a box, announcing the leading articles for the following week. I inaugurated an Open Forum, publishing some of the critical letters. That was one smart thing I did, if I may be permitted to say so. Baptists do well when allowed to talk out in meeting. Some of my fiercest critics became my staunchest supporters. When they discovered that I respected their opinions, they joined up. I took a long chance in the second issue, January 8, by publishing an article by Ian McLaren, "Shall the Old Minister Be Shot?" He was writing about Dr. Osler's facetious remark that it might be advisable to chloroform all men who reached the age of sixty. That article really pulled a reaction. I was remembering what newspaper men like George H. Long and Frank Cobb had told me about reader-interest.

I devoted the back page to "The Changing Order," and by the issue of January 29, 1920, I had quotes on that page from General John J. Pershing, Dr. Henry Van Dyke, Governor Charles E. Hughes, and Mr. Herbert Hoover. I had dealt with my first front-page personality study in that issue, selecting Dr. A. T. Spalding, Chaplain of the Georgia Baptist Orphan's Home, who had been a subscriber to *The Christian Index* since 1847, a span of 73 years. He had written me: "In these 73 years I have never missed an issue of *The Index,* and it grows dearer to me with every passing issue." I received over 100 letters of appreciation of that first personality feature. That prompted the decision to run one such feature each month.

Within the first quarter of 1920, I had established a Book Review page, with four prominent pastors editing the page one week each month. That page was to become one of the stronger points in my decade of editing the paper. I was working on a page for Agriculture, Business, and other features. Mr. Richard H. Edmonds, Editor of *The Manufacturer's Record,* Baltimore, contributed the first article for the page on Business, and Mr. F. J. Paxton, Atlanta merchant prince, accepted the editorship of the page. Dr. A. M. Soule, head of the state's Agricultural and Mechanical College, contributed the first article for the page on Agriculture, and Dr. Phil Campbell of the A. and M. faculty, accepted the editorship of that page. I had secured commitments from a dozen prominent Americans for leading articles, paying them for their manuscripts, and it looked as if we might be on our way.

Dr. McConnell called me to meet with the directors on

the first Tuesday in April, 1920, in the same room at the Winecoff Hotel in which, three months before, I had been invited to make the experiment with the paper. The lunch consumed, Dr. McConnell said: "We have had a meeting earlier this morning, and we wish now to invite you again to become the editor of *The Christian Index*." I was ready. I had talked the thing over from week to week with Mrs. Newton, when I would run down to Macon for a change of clothes, and we were convinced that this was the Lord's will. I had talked with my mother and father, and they encouraged me. I had talked with my friends at Mercer, including Lee Battle and Miss Sallie Boone. I had talked with friends like Dr. J. C. Wilkinson, Dr. Walter Pope Binns, Dr. R. C. Granberry, and others, and I felt assured and reassured. Conflict was yielding to assurance.

Having been separated from the little family since April, 1917, except for snatched visits here and there, I was glad enough to contemplate establishing residence in Atlanta, though I shared Mrs. Newton's love for Macon. We bought a house at 286 Moreland Avenue, without being allowed to look inside. Houses were that much in demand in Atlanta following the war. It turned out to be a happy dwelling place. Mrs. Newton and the baby, her father and Tee, along with the dog, were soon in charge at 286, and the first thing we did was to join Druid Hills Baptist Church, a couple of blocks away. The church had been constituted in 1914, and had called Dr. F. C. McConnell, widely known Baptist preacher and denominational leader, at the time serving the First Baptist Church, Waco, Texas, and before Waco he had been pastor of the First Baptist Church, Lynchburg, Virginia, and the Calvary Baptist Church, Kansas City, Missouri. A native Georgian, Dr. McConnell was a graduate of Mercer University and the Southern Baptist Theological Seminary, and had also served as Secretary of the Home Mission Board. Coming to the little band of Baptists at Druid Hills, January 1, 1915, Dr. McConnell was happy in the realization that he was in the crowning chapter of his illustrious ministry. At the time we joined the church, they were worshipping in a boarded shanty, through which the cold wind seemed to blow in gales from six directions—the four sides, through the floor which had been built of green lumber, and the roof. We got both cold air and rain through the roof. There was a central stove, which was kept red hot, and the situation made for close communion. I had been attending Druid Hills whenever I could during the months before Mrs. Newton came to Atlanta, and there was no question about our new church home. Mrs. Newton agreed that it was the church for us.

It was a happy coincidence that Dr. McConnell was chairman of the board of directors of the paper of which I was editor. I was invited to membership on the board of deacons and the building committee. After a few weeks, I made my first motion in the board of deacons, that the church put *The Christian Index* in its budget, and to my great satisfaction, the motion prevailed and the church voted unanimously to send the paper to every home. That was the first church in Georgia to take such action—a plan which now accounts for a subscription list of approximately 100,000 in the rural and urban churches of Georgia. My second motion was to recommend to the church that we adopt the plan of rotation for terms of service on the part of deacons, with the lapse of one year before a deacon could return to active service on the board. This recommendation was unanimously adopted by the church.

The building committee had a big job—procuring additional land, and bringing to the small, but growing congregation, comprehensive plans for an adequate house of worship and study. Dr. McConnell was a great preacher, and he made it quite clear to the building committee that it was his responsibility to build a church while we built a meetinghouse —that he would try to have a church ready to occupy the building when it was ready. That impressed me. Moreover, Dr. McConnell was impressing me as the greatest doctrinal preacher I had ever heard. When asked to teach the Men's Bible Class, I said I would need first to talk with the pastor. He gave me an evening. He began with his boyhood experience at Hiawassee, in the high Georgia mountains. He told of several revered prophets of God who had taught him, particularly Uncle Elijah Kimsey and Uncle John Corn. Evidently, they were men of great spiritual perception, though strangers to the cloistered walls of college or seminary. They knew the Book. They preached the Word. And they perceived that young McConnell, though strongly set to become a merchant, was endowed of God—that he would some day answer the call to proclaim the Good News—that he would become a herald—that he would trumpet forth the Gospel. And they were right. After he had married and was operating a mercantile establishment, Fernando Coello McConnell answered the call and was ordained to the ministry. He took his family with him to college and seminary, preaching somewhere every Sunday, happy in the assurance that he was serving the Lord.

Somewhere during the evening, I interrupted to ask, Why are you a Baptist? That seemed to please him, and for an hour he gave me his answer. It was an interesting course in theology and Baptist polity. That he was a convinced Baptist, he left no ground for speculation. His creed was the New Testament, without subtraction or appendage. From that memorable evening, I lashed myself to this great man of God, receiving from him strength and encouragement and inspiration. I go back again and again to his sermons, from 1920 to his death, January 12, 1929, with thanksgiving. He was sitting in his study in his home on Friday morning, January 11, having just written his text for the following Lord's Day across the card: "For God so loved..." when the short pencil dropped from his fingers, and his body crumpled to the floor. Summoned to his side, we managed to get him into the car, and I drove as hurriedly as possible to the Georgia Baptist Hospital. The light flashed red as we neared the intersection where the Druid Hills meetinghouse, just opened the July before, stands. He seemed to gather strength and some use of his voice, as he said, pointing to the place of worship: "God's house, God's people, God's program. For God so loved the world...that He gave..." These were his last coherent words. His body lay in state from 10 o'clock on Sunday morning until three that afternoon, and then the funeral. The people stood in the cold, damp wind in the churchyard, heads bowed, hearts saddened. A great man had gone from us, but his spirit went marching on. On his tomb in Westview Cemetery is the symbol of the open Bible, and the words chiseled into the marble: "For God so loved the world..."

Teaching that Men's Bible Class was a rewarding responsibility. Lawyers, doctors, merchants, architects, engineers, teachers, bankers, salesmen, mechanics—men with a sense of responsibility—men with faith in God and man—eager, purposeful, sincere men. One dared not face that class of 200 men without careful preparation. It meant mastery of the Scripture for the hour. It meant readiness to give a reason for the faith you had and sought to impart. A judge said to me one morning at the close of the class: "Keep telling us the truth about God and about man. We need it." Conflict was steadily yielding to assurance.

My work as editor of *The Christian Index* grew with every passing day. Before the end of 1920, I had lined up a steady reservoir of manuscript from men like F. W. Boreham, Australia; J. H. Rushbrooke, England; O. C. S. Wallace, F. W. Patterson and Charles George Smith, Canada; and from the United States, such well-known men as E. Y. Mullins, George W. Truett, A. T. Robertson, S. J. Porter, Richard H. Edmonds, John Freeman, Rufus W. Weaver, John R. Mott, Robert Speer, George W. McDaniel, W. J. McGlothlin, and Curtis Lee Laws. The centennial of the paper loomed as one of my largest tasks that first year, and the research in putting together that 100-page issue was another of the profitable experiences of my decade as editor. The very next year was the centennial of the Georgia Baptist Convention, and I got my second degree in examining what the founding fathers were thinking and doing.

Mrs. Newton's father had rallied from the illness that had brought him so low at the time we married, and to our great joy he lived to see our first baby born, and to be with us for some time after we moved to Atlanta. How he did love that baby! But the sands were running fast, and he began talking about the Home over there. One evening as he sat in his rocking chair before the open fire, he spoke softly to me, motioned toward the Bible nearby, and managed to say: "Read to me once more . . . about my shepherd . . . about the house not made with hands . . . call them quick . . . I'm going Home . . . my dear, dear ones . . . J e s u s . . ."

And the grand old Scot was gone. I think the little girl never quite got the sense of shock. She came again and again to that chair for his words of affection—for the stick candy he always kept in his pocket—for his intriguing stories about Scotland where little lambs played in the heather. And when she would come to the empty chair, Tee would say: "He's wid Jesus. You know, don'shu?" And she would nod her little head. One comment by Mrs. Newton helped me through those days. She would say, so understandingly: "There is no death for those who trust in Jesus."

Another event of major importance was the birth of our second daughter, Sarah Catherine, February 25, 1921. The first daughter had been named for her maternal grandmothers. The second daughter was named for two of her aunts—Mrs. Newton's Aunt Sarah and my sister. We were now doubly happy, doubly grateful—two lovely little daughters. They have been our joy through all these years, and we give thanks unto God upon every remembrance of them. I have before spoken of Tee—Mrs. Newton's "Black Mammy." Her name was Celia Anne, but Mrs. Newton couldn't say Celia when she was a tiny little girl, so she solved it by saying Tee. Mrs. Newton's mother knew that she couldn't live, and she called Celia to her bed and said: "Take care of my baby." She did. Only the good Lord knows how much we loved Tee. She not only was a mother to Mrs. Newton, but she often said: "If I knew how to raise you, I knows how to raise your own baby, and dat I fully 'spect to do, the Lawd helpin' me." Tee lived to see our first little girl off to school, off to Sunday School, off to picnics. She lived in the home with us, and was a very real part of the family. And then one night, as she sat by her little bed, singing:

> "Swing low, sweet chariot,
> Comin' fur tur carry me Home..."

she felt a "ketch" in her chest. Eden was fast asleep. She smiled as Mrs. Newton rubbed her arms and neck. The doctor came quickly, giving all possible stimulants. He looked at me and shook his head. She knew without his saying so. A few whispered words of affection and assurance, and the

Chariot swung low . . . We took the body back to Macon, where she had said she wanted to be buried. I shall ever think of Tee as one of the Lord's noblest handmaidens—a great Christian, a convinced Baptist.

The Baptist World Alliance was to have held its third Congress in Berlin in 1916, having accepted the invitation of the Baptists of Germany in Philadelphia in 1911, but the Kaiser had vetoed all such plans in the bloody teens of the new century. However, through the courageous leadership of James Henry Rushbrooke, British Baptist statesman and Baptist Commissioner for Europe, the Alliance was summoned into session in Stockholm in 1923. Dr. Robert Stuart MacArthur of New York's Calvary Baptist Church had been elected president of the Alliance in 1911, but he had died, and it was Rushbrooke's conviction and enthusiasm that made possible the call for the meeting in Sweden. I had read in *The Christian Index,* as a boy, about the first World Congress of Baptists in London, in 1905. And as an undergraduate at Mercer, I read again in *The Index* about the second Congress in Philadelphia, in 1911. President Jameson had attended the London Congress, and again in 1911 at Philadelphia. He took several chapel hours to tell us about the meeting in 1911—about the Russians and the Chinese and the Baptists from all the other lands. It was just at that time that I had volunteered to go as a missionary, and my heart was warm and responsive to the voices of catholicity that seemed to be sounding everywhere.

The telephone rang, and Dr. E. Y. Mullins was inviting me to share his stateroom on the Canadian Pacific *SS Drottingholm,* New York to Gotenberg. Could it be possible? Was this tremendous theologian asking me to make the journey with him? I said I would give him my answer that afternoon. I drove the little Model-T home at top speed to see what

Mrs. Newton thought. Certainly, I would accept, she said. And I did.

Why, I have often asked myself, did Dr. Mullins invite me to share that beautiful stateroom with him? He was the guest of the steamship line. We sat at the Captain's table. Dr. Mullins might have had any one of a hundred prominent American Baptists as his guest. Why did he invite a young, unknown chap? True, I had met him in 1909, when he gave me *Axioms of Religion*. True, I had been writing him back and forth as editor, securing from him numerous manuscripts for the paper. True, I had been with him several times in the fall of 1919, during the 75 Million Campaign. But it did seem very strange that he would invite me to make that trip with him to Sweden.

The first night out of New York, Dr. Mullins suggested that I get out my portable typewriter for some work. He would dictate the first draft of his address at Stockholm. The stateroom was spacious, allowing him room to take several steps back and forth, as he dictated directly to the typewriter. After three hours, he smiled, suggested that we dress and go on deck for a walk. I carefully assembled the many pages of copy, clipped them together, and placed them on his bed. He reached over, tore them into shreds, and threw the wad into the waste basket. There was a twinkle in his eye as he said: "Didn't I say the first draft?" We walked for an hour. It was a wonderful night—quiet sea, rising moon, stiff breeze. After we went to bed, following one of the most beautiful moments of devotion I shall ever know, I thought about it all. I remembered how he stood on the aft deck, pointing with his long arm and sensitive finger to the opal-like path of the ship, quoting Swinburne's exquisite line: "Where the wind's feet shine along the sea," and then how understandingly he had read the words of the Psalmist:

> If I take the wings of the morning,
>   And dwell in the uttermost parts of the sea;
> Even there shall Thy hand lead me,
>   And Thy right hand shall hold me.

Shuffle board, checkers and walking. That was the morning
schedule, and after lunch, a nap and reading. Dr. Mullins
had brought along a dozen books, and he suggested that I
begin with P. T. Forsyth's *Justification of God,* a book I very
much needed to read at that very time when the backwash
of the war was beating fiercely against the ramparts of Christian thought and action. Dr. Mullins would read awhile, and
then he would suggest that we review for one another what
we had read the hour before. I felt that he was trying to help
me through the deep forest of Forsyth's theology. He did.
And then he would interpret for me what he was reading—
Strong, Denney, Broadus, Connor. He would then swing his
long legs off the side of the bed, and begin:

"That makes me think of a funny thing that happened
when I was a boy, working as a telegrapher. An old man came
running in one night, said he had to send a message to his
brother up near Amarillo to bring him some medicine, that
his cattle were all sick, and when I asked him for the address,
he said he had plum forgot."

Dr. Mullins loved a good story, and he reminded me again
and again that a sense of humour is as essential as physical
exercise. "Come, let's go for a swim," he would say. It was a
rare mixture of theology, poetry, history, humour, walking,
swimming, eating, sleeping. The second night, after a delightful conversation with the ship's Captain, Dr. Mullins
turned quickly to me, and said: "I am afraid we are taking
too much of the Captain's time. Let's get to our work." Another three hours of dictation, and again the whole sheaf of

manuscript in the waste basket! Striding around and around
the deck at midnight, he stopped quickly, put his hand on my
shoulder, and said: "You see the idea I am working on for
the Stockholm address. Tell me, what do you think? After
a night or two more, we'll keep a carbon copy, and you make
your criticisms and I will make mine, and then we'll begin
the job of polishing. I must spend tomorrow morning in the
ship's library with the Encyclopedia. I am not too sure of one
or two allusions. You will please take the literary allusions,
and I will run down the historical and scientific references.
Only we must not neglect our checkers and shuffleboard.
Agreed?"

It went on like that throughout the nine-day journey.
When the final draft of the address was made, it reminded
me of a great marble column—beautiful, strong, enduring.
The experience taught me the value of hard work, honest
thinking, fearless leadership. The meeting in Stockholm
would be the first world gathering of any major religious
group following the war. Dr. Mullins' address was the peak
spot on the week-long program. He had been invited to speak
on "Religious Liberty—Chief Contribution of Baptists." He
knew very well that there would likely be Baptists there
from Germany. He knew that he would be speaking in a
country with a state church. He knew that the postwar situation was tense with unresolved questions of liberty—the liberty of the individual to think and speak and write. With all
of this in his mind, Dr. Mullins was determined that his address would stand the acid test of any school of thought—
political, cultural, religious.

When the hour arrived for his address, the AP man from
London whispered: "Do you recommend any space for this
guy?"

I had been doing practically all the stories for the AP,

since this friend knew very little about religious matters, and had stuck by me from the first day, promising the best pudding in London when the meeting was ended. I suggested that he listen to the address for five minutes, and decide himself whether it merited any space on the wire story for the day. Dr. Mullins had spoken only a few sentences when my friend punched me, and said: "Most extra-ordinary. This chap knows what he is talking about. I tell you, most extraordinary. What do you say we make this the lead?"

As a matter of fact, the Mullins address was the story of the day for AP, and the Stockholm papers carried it in full. It set the tone of the Third World Congress of Baptists. Dr. Mullins was elected President. I had run off one thousand copies of *The Christian Index* for the week of August 2, 1923, with Dr. Mullins' picture on the front cover, announcing his election on that day (August 2) as the new President of the Alliance. I had left special instructions that should I cable to shift that front cover to stand-by copy, they would be certain to follow instructions. I had the package of papers in the stateroom, and Dr. Mullins asked me several times what was in that package. I dared not let him know. I took the package to the meeting that morning, and had several friends ready to distribute the papers as the people left the meeting. It was something of a scoop to have the new President's picture on the front page of a paper, published four thousand miles away, within a few minutes after his election. I shall never forget the glint in his eye as he walked in our room at the hotel. "I see, I see. You really put a fast one by me, my boy," he said. Dr. George W. Truett knocked on the door, coming across the hall to congratulate Dr. Mullins. He had missed getting a copy of the paper at the convention hall. He looked at it for a moment, and said: "Ed, did you know this boy had these papers right there in the stateroom as we came across?" Dr. Truett laughed heartily, declaring that it was the quickest service he ever expected to see in a Baptist newspaper.

I cannot dwell on the Stockholm meeting, further than to say that two Southern Baptists really dominated the Congress —Dr. Mullins and Dr. Truett. Dr. Truett's sermon was based on Romans 1:16, and was one of the most powerful messages ever to fall from his lips. Hour after hour, during that week in Stockholm, I listened to those two great leaders as they talked about Baptists and the Kingdom of God. If there had ever been any doubt in my mind about why I was a Baptist, it would have been completely settled after that notable week. After the stay in Sweden, I travelled with some friends down into Germany and France, and rejoined Dr. Mullins in London for important conferences with Dr. John Clifford, then very frail, and other Baptist leaders. I made a kodak picture of Dr. Clifford and Dr. J. B. Gambrell, which hangs in my study, and which many Baptists from many lands have admired. The Eastman people did a grand job of enlarging it. Dr. Clifford, it will be remembered, was the Baptist preacher who challenged the British tax for the support of the established church, forcing the government to come each year and levy on a piece of furniture in his house and sell it at the front door. There was always a deacon present to bid it in, pick it up and return it to its place in the pastor's home. His contention that he would not voluntarily pay the tax was the straw that broke the camel's back.

There was a stack of mail at the Baptist Church House in London, including several issues of *The Christian Index* that had come from the press since I had sailed in early July. President Harding had died suddenly in San Francisco, August 2, 1923, and on the front cover for August 9, they had used the pen and ink profile of the President which I had

used for the cover when I interviewed Mr. Harding at his golf
headquarters in Augusta some months before. Another friend,
Robert Loveman, whose poems had appeared in the paper,
had died, and they had a photograph of the famed Georgia
poet, and a poem for the occasion by Uncle Frank L. Stanton,
regular contributor to *The Index*. Uncle Frank had opened
the tribute with these lines:

> A song, and then—the Silence
> Where many singers throng,
> And music gone from earth to God—
> The melody of song;
> For the notes that are the sweetest
> He leaves not with us long.

It was amazing to see how well the paper had fared in the
absence of the editor! One friend had written: "I suggest
that the directors arrange for the editor to spend more time
outside the country." Joking aside, it was a wholesome experience to be convinced that the editor was not indispensable. It revealed the wonderful *esprit de corps* of the faithful
staff and directors. Dr. Rushbrooke and Dr. Mullins had been
urging me to go on with them to the Middle East and Pales-
tine in particular, and this evidence of the paper to prosper
under my absence was the determining factor in that decision.

The 20's were interesting years for Baptists. The Baptist
75 Million Campaign had given confidence and vision to
Southern Baptists, and under the leadership of men like
Mullins, Scarborough, Gambrell, McDaniel, Truett, Mc-
Glothlin, Brown, Dodd, and Crouch, the foundation was
laid for the present sustained advance of missionary, benevolent and educational ministries of our people. Dr. Austin
Crouch had emphasized the importance of coordinating the
appeals for money and the channels through which the local
churches would direct their gifts to the agencies and institu-

tions, state and south-wide. He knew his history, and he knew
Baptists. He cited the purpose of the founding fathers of the
Southern Baptist Convention:

The messengers from missionary societies, churches and other
religious bodies of the Baptist denomination in various parts of
the United States, met in Augusta, Georgia, May 8, 1845, for the
purpose of carrying into effect the benevolent intention of our
constituents by organizing a plan for eliciting, combining, and
directing the energies of the denomination for the propagation
of the Gospel . . .

—Preamble to the Constitution
of the Southern Baptist Convention

Upon this principle, declared by the founding fathers, Dr.
Crouch developed what he wisely called the Cooperative Program. The Convention considered the proposal for more than
a year, and, in 1929, adopted the Cooperative Program. He
also proposed the enlarging of the Convention's executive
committee and its responsibilities. Dr. Crouch later proposed
a Business and Financial Plan for the Convention, which was
adopted in 1938. These are but a few of the major contributions of this cherished Baptist statesman. He served with
great distinction and inspiring faithfulness as Executive Secretary of the Executive Committee of the Convention until
1946, when, at the Miami Convention, he was presented a
scroll, expressing the deep affection and admiration of Southern Baptists. Dr. Crouch has been one of the men in our
Baptist saga whose witness has strengthened my convictions
as a Christian and a Baptist. He knows why he is a Baptist,
and on every basic doctrine of our denomination, he has
spoken and written with compelling understanding.

Events in the 20's brought me face to face with at least
four important decisions. Dr. A. W. Van Hoose was the successful President of Shorter College, and his enthusiasm for

that historic Baptist college for women was irresistible. I first met him back in the teens when the Mercer Glee Club performed annually at Shorter. He took several of us one cold wintry afternoon in an old Buick touring car up the wet, clay trail to the top of a commanding hill overlooking the City of Rome, Georgia, and pointed out the stakes where the new buildings would be built as the college moved from downtown to its new home. He thrilled me as he stood there in the gusts of wind, waving his arms, describing the new campus. A decade later, he called me and asked me to meet him at Durand's for lunch. "I want you to succeed me as President of Shorter," he said. "I am not well, and will not live very long. I want you to come and get the swing of the job while I am there to help you." I couldn't see it, but he held me to the promise that I would think about it—pray about it. "Go home tonight and talk with your wife, and then bring her with you for a visit to the campus. This is more important than you now realize. This, I hope, is your life's work. You will hear from Mr. Cooper."

Within a few days I got a call from Mr. Paul Cooper, President of the Board of Trustees, asking me to visit the College. I had engagements. Then Mr. Cooper came to my office. "We want you to come, and we want you to come before Dr. Van Hoose dies," he said. And then the telegram—Dr. Van Hoose had answered the call—"for whom the bell tolls!" Weeks passed, and I made the trip to Rome. Mrs. Newton could not leave the little girls, but she was thinking and praying. Mrs. Cooper regretted that Mrs. Newton could not come, for, she said, "I had wanted to show her where I propose to build the President's house. That will be my contribution, and I want the house to be like your wife would like it. You have two little girls. They can grow up in the Shorter tradition. But I can go over that with her."

Mr. Cooper drove me, in his attractive buggy, to the college, where we studied the charter, the financial statement, the architect's plans for the future buildings. Mr. Cooper kept emphasizing the fact that they were asking me to invest my life in the college. The long conference ended, he drew from his pocket a check in seven digits, and said: "When you accept the Presidency, I will sign that check." We drove back to the beautiful home atop another hill, had lunch, and then the train for Atlanta. When I walked in my office in the Flatiron Building, there was a long distance call from Miss Martha Berry. "I hope you will come to Shorter," she said. "We will be working toward the same great goal—opening gates of opportunity for tomorrow's men and women." Berry Schools—Martha Berry! Think of such a neighbor and such a task!

We prayed. And then the answer: "Thanks, but we feel that we are in the Lord's will." It was not easy to write that letter of declination.

Then the letter from Dr. Curtis Lee Laws, asking me to come to New York for a conference. I couldn't go then, but I would be passing through New York on my way to Toronto a little later. That would be agreeable. When I got to New York, some weeks later, Dr. Laws had his desk covered with papers, some of them quite frayed and faded. They represented periods in the long history of the oldest Baptist newspaper in America, *The Watchman-Examiner,* established 1819. Wouldn't I like to be editor of the oldest Baptist paper in America? I was ready for that one—wasn't I already editor of the second oldest Baptist paper in America, 1821, and the oldest Baptist paper in the South? Yes, but there were other considerations, he argued. For example, I would live in New York City—in touch with everything! "Listen, friend," I said, "I lived here long enough, during my student days at Columbia University, to know that I wouldn't subject my little family to the provincialism of this community for all the secondary advantages which you are pointing out. Remember what Will Rogers said about 'little old New York City'? No, thanks a million, but I prefer to serve Baptists where Baptists are. This long-range proposition of trying to serve them from the banks of the Hudson wouldn't appeal too much to me." But it was not an easy decision, at that.

Back in Atlanta, Dr. I. J. Van Ness, Secretary of the Sunday School Board of the Southern Baptist Convention, was asking me to become Book Editor of the Board, a new department. This third invitation to leave my work with *The Christian Index*—to leave my native Georgia—to leave the civic responsibilities I had added, as Editor of *The City Builder,* monthly organ of the Atlanta Chamber of Commerce—to leave Druid Hills Baptist Church as deacon and Sunday School worker— all of it was adding up in my mind as a sort of nagging question: Was I, after all, in the will of the Lord? It didn't bother me too much, but I decided to sift the sheaf, hoping to separate the chaff from whatever grain there might be. I wrote Dr. Mullins, telling him that I had just gone through the ordeal of turning down three invitations to other fields of the Lord's work and would he please tell me how to interpret these offers. He wired me to meet him for breakfast in the Terminal Station on Thursday morning. We sat there and talked, but I couldn't get him around to the point of my concern. Finally, they called his train, and as we walked to the gate, he touched me on the arm, and said: "Had it occurred to you that the Lord was merely confirming your mind and heart that you were in His will?" Like a bell at dawn, I had the answer. Assurance!

In the spring of 1928, when everything was pointing toward Toronto and the Fourth World Congress of Baptists, Dr.

Mullins sent a batch of manuscript for the paper, with this disturbing postscript: "I must ask you to acknowledge this as my '30'. I am not feeling too well, and when I complete my Presidential Address for Toronto, I shall rest for a while." I read those words again and again. Somehow, I seemed to see between the lines that he was saying more than appeared at first. He was to give some lectures at Meredith College, just before the Alliance in Toronto, and it was there that the stroke occurred.

I stopped by Raleigh to see him as our little family motored to Canada. I knew when I saw him that it was indeed "Sunset, and evening star." He said good-bye with his eyes—wonderful eyes. Mrs. Mullins handed me the manuscript of his address, asking that I deliver it to Dr. Truett in Toronto. I walked out under the majestic trees and wept. What would the Baptist World Alliance be without Mullins? He had been at London when it was organized in 1905, at Philadelphia in 1911, at Stockholm in 1923. He had done so much of the basic thinking for this new-world fellowship of Baptists. What would it be without Clifford and Maclaren and Strong and Bystrom and Shakespeare and MacArthur and Mullins? A line from Dryden's *Absalom and Achitophel* came to mind: "His tribe were God Almighty's gentlemen." I walked on toward the car, and these lines from Coleridge's *The Good Great Man* seemed written for the hour:

> Greatness and goodness are not means, but ends!
> Hath he not always treasures, always friends,
> The good great man? Three treasures—love and light,
> And calm thoughts, regular as infants' breath;
> And three firm friends, more sure than day and night—
> Himself, his Maker, and the angel Death.

In the absence of President Mullins, Dr. Truett presided at most of the sessions in Toronto, 1928. He read the Presidential Address to the hushed audience of Baptists from many lands. We knew that a mighty man had fallen. Dr. John MacNeill was elected President, and the invitation to meet in Berlin in 1933 was accepted. Dr. J. H. Rushbrooke had succeeded the late Dr. J. H. Shakespeare as General Secretary of the Baptist World Alliance, and, at Toronto, he clarified some of the misconceived purposes of the Alliance, making it clear that it was a "fellowship," rather than an administrative or legislative body. Dr. Rushbrooke was now the acknowledged Voice of Baptists throughout the world, and we left Toronto in 1928 with new vision and purpose. Dr. Rushbrooke insisted that I make a trip with him to the Orient, but I could not consider being away that long for more than one reason. My duties with the paper were becoming heavier and heavier, and my beloved pastor, Dr. F. C. McConnell, was growing weaker and weaker. As chairman of the board of deacons, he was relying more and more upon me to help where I could. There would be another day for the Orient and Australasia, maybe, but not then.

Returning to Atlanta for the first Sunday in July, 1928, we entered the new meetinghouse at Druid Hills, Dr. McConnell preaching at the morning hour, and Dr. Truett in the afternoon and evening. Dr. McConnell baptized our daughters that evening. We had much time to talk with them on the long motor trip through Canada, and they made it quite clear to their mother and me that they had accepted Jesus Christ as their Saviour, and that they wanted to become Baptists. Dr. McConnell's strength waned through the autumn of 1928, and on January 12, 1929, he joined "the blood-washed throng about the throne of God." I have already described that great event in the life of our church and in my own life.

There had been a period of conflict, yielding to assurance,

but little did I dream of what was ahead for me—what that ultimate sense of assurance would mean. I go back to it now and then, and, always, I recall how, during the freighted days of autumn and winter, 1928, I found myself singing, praying:

> Take my will and make it Thine
> It shall be no longer mine;
> Take my heart, it is Thine own,
> It shall be Thy royal throne.

The lines are by Frances Ridley Havergal, 1836-79.

SIX

BECAUSE OF AN ASSURANCE

"Let every man be fully assured
in his own mind." Romans 14:5

DR. MOSES G. CAMPBELL was our senior deacon in
Druid Hills Baptist Church when our pastor, Dr. F. C.
McConnell died, January 12, 1929. He was not only a good
doctor, but a good student of the Scriptures. On the way from
the church to the cemetery on the Sunday afternoon when
we buried our pastor, I was assigned to the same car as Dr.
Campbell. None of us felt like talking, but somewhere along
that sad procession, Dr. Campbell whispered to me: "When
you get back home, read Romans 14:5 and then Hebrews
4:16. That is all I will say now, but remember, I shall be
praying for you."

What did he mean? Back at our little bungalow on Bonaventure, I opened the Bible to the passages, in the order
prescribed. It was time for supper, and I left the Bible

opened at the passage in Hebrews. It seemed queer not to be going to the meetinghouse on the Lord's Day evening, but it had been announced that there would be no evening worship—that the people remain in their homes, thanking God for our beloved pastor—praying His guidance in the days ahead. The dishes washed, and the breakfast table set, the little girls and I listened to their mother as she told a beautiful Bible story, and then the prayer. The fire softened into a wondrous glow as the clock ticked on into the night. Mrs. Newton came softly from the room where the children slept, and read the passages I had underscored before supper. The telephone rang, and it was Mrs. George Garner, President of the Woman's Missionary Society. She talked at length to Mrs. Newton. No comment when she returned to her chair. She had turned out the reading lamp, and we sat for a long time, looking at the fading embers—"faces in the fire"—until she recalled the line from Tennyson: "The shadows flicker to and fro."

Suddenly it dawned on me that the paper must go to press by noon Monday, and the wire tributes to Dr. McConnell, requested on Saturday, would be coming in by seven o'clock. I dropped off to sleep, tossing about in my mind a suitable lead for the feature story on the death of Dr. McConnell, beginning on page three. Should it be: "Moses my servant is dead; now therefore arise, go over this Jordan . . .?" Or perhaps: "A good minister of Jesus Christ. . . ."

Before eight o'clock Monday morning, I heard footsteps in the outer office, and turning from my typewriter, I saw a dozen or more deacons, led by the vice-chairman, Judge Thomas. "Don't leave your work," said Judge Thomas, "we've come by to tell you that some of the deacons got together last night to talk about the meeting you have called for tonight to face the task of setting up a committee to call

a successor to Dr. McConnell, and we simply wanted to drop
by this morning and tell you that we are praying. Let's have
a word of prayer now. Brother Ches, will you lead us?"
Brother Ches was Mr. W. Ches Smith, Sr., the deacon who
seemed always to have an open wire to the Throne of Grace.
The prayer ended, they were gone as suddenly as they had
appeared. I got up and closed the door to my office, and
wondered. Why had they got together the night before without letting me, as chairman, know about it? Why had they
come by my office before eight o'clock in the morning? Why
had Dr. Campbell suggested that I read those passages? Why
had Mrs. Garner talked so long to Mrs. Newton? But here
were more telegrams about Dr. McConnell, and the lino-
types were waiting for copy. The paper must go to press at
noon. I was in my overalls at the plant by ten o'clock that
morning, and the paper was in the forms when the whistle
blew for twelve o'clock.

I had promised Mrs. McConnell that I would come to her
home in the early afternoon for the inevitable conference on
the many responsibilities that must be faced for the week,
both from her personal standpoint and that of the church.
"You will please do whatever you feel best about the affairs
at the church," she began, "remembering this, I shall be praying for you and the other leaders, but I can't do more than
that. You know how my husband relied upon you, and I
have the feeling that he is still relying upon you and all the
other dear friends to carry on the work which he so much
loved."

When the deacons met that evening, in called session, a
motion was made that the chairman recommend a pulpit
committee to the church, with the chairman of the deacons
as the chairman of the pulpit committee. As soon as that
motion was passed, I was asked to leave the room. I went down

in the basement where carpenters were installing blackboards and served an apprenticeship with them for a couple of hours. Returning to the place where the deacons had met, I found the room dark. Walking the several blocks to our little home on Bonaventure, I thought of something Dr. McConnell had often said in sermons and conversations: "Be not anxious about tomorrow. Ask God to lead you and strengthen you, step by step. He knows the way—He holds the key."

"What are you thinking about so seriously?" asked Mrs. Newton as I settled down in front of the open fire. "About someone to fill the pulpit next Sunday," I answered. We agreed that it would be most desirable if Dr. B. D. Gray would come and preach on the first Sunday after Dr. McConnell's death, remembering that Dr. Gray had led in the constituting of the church in July, 1914, and had piloted the little band through the months until Dr. McConnell arrived, January 1, 1915. I called Dr. Gray, and he was glad to render this significant service. Bishop Warren A. Candler preached at both services on the last Sunday in January. Bishop Candler and Dr. McConnell were great friends, and his sermons, like the sermons of Dr. Gray, helped us in an hour of deep and poignant grief. Other preachers, on succeeding Sundays, were Dr. Arch C. Cree, Dr. Fred Brown, Dr. J. C. Wilkinson, and Dr. C. C. Davison. That had got us to the second Sunday in March, and several of the deacons came to my office and said that they would like to take over the duty of filling the pulpit that Sunday. I was quick to swallow hook, sinker and line. They smiled, and said: "Louie Newton will preach next Sunday!"

I cannot go into all the detail of events that led up to the proposal—of two proposals of the committee, asking me to consider a call to the church, and my prompt declination in each instance. There had been many conversations in which the dearest friends I had in the church had insisted that I allow them to present my name, but I couldn't see it. How could a layman, without any formal theological training, follow a preacher like F. C. McConnell? "But that, you see, is not the primary concern in our hearts," Dr. Campbell would say. "It is the fact that we feel that you are God's man for this place. We have tried to consider the men you have proposed, but we don't get any bobble of the cork. There doesn't seem to be anything on the other end of the line, to use a good old South Carolina fisherman's expression."

Brother Ches came to my office and closed the door. He had telephoned that he wanted to talk to me without interruption. I had wanted to talk to him, but I had hesitated to take any initiative in the delicate situation. I dared not allow the slightest human persuasion to enter the picture, and to ask Brother Ches to advise me might, I reasoned, suggest that I was trying to decide it rather than the Lord. He began by saying: "Let us kneel, please." It would be well nigh sacrilegious to attempt any report of that hour. I shan't run the risk. The prayer ended, he held my hand for a minute, or more, hot tears streaming down his noble face. He arose, and walked away, closing the door behind him. I had not noticed the envelope he had placed on my desk until he had gone. I opened it: "We hope that you will preach for us next Sunday. We shall be praying for you. Miss Ada and Brother Ches."

I took the telephone and called Mr. Z. A. Snipes, Secretary of the Pulpit Committee, and told him that I would try to do what they were asking me to do. I shall never forget what that dear friend said.

Sunday, March 10, came. I had not slept, and Mrs. Newton had not slept. We had waited before the Lord. What I said that morning and evening has always puzzled me. I had tried to prepare, but I felt my utter unpreparedness. I wondered if that would not be the Lord's way of settling the whole matter—that the people would be convinced that they were mistaken. I somehow felt relieved when the last person left the meetinghouse that evening. Maybe it was all over, I said. The janitor was waiting for me at the back door. He held my hand, and said: "I prayed, and God answered my prayer." I walked around to the Highland side of the building, and there stood a group of men. "Pretty chilly for you boys to be standing out here," I ventured to say. "Not tonight," answered Mr. Orlando Shepard. Judge Thomas called to me as I walked away: "Who do you have for next Sunday?" I told them that President Aquila Chamlee of Tift College would be the preacher. Dr. Chamlee had baptized Mrs. Newton when she was a student at the College, and she had wanted him to come and preach.

Dr. E. M. Poteat was pastor of the Second Baptist Church in Atlanta, and it had been announced that he would speak to the pastors that Monday morning on "A Divine Call to the Ministry." I was at the office by daylight, rounding up the last copy for the plant, and I slipped in to the preachers' meeting just in time to hear Dr. Poteat, and slipped away with his closing sentence. After supper that evening, I excused myself from the little family to run over to the church to check a water valve that had been acting up. I saw a light in the church office, and several cars parked in the yard. I went quietly down to check the valve, and out through the back door. I checked the cars, and found that they represented the Pulpit Committee. Although chairman, I had not known of several recent meetings until some word would drop in a conversation, here and there, as we pitched horseshoes. I have to say something about the horse-shoes.

A few Saturdays after we moved to Atlanta, when genuine

homesickness for Macon had got a real grip on our hearts, Mrs. Newton suggested to Tee that we fix a basket and have a picnic somewhere. We had heard about the zoo in Grant Park, so that was the place to go—the little girls could see the animals, and there would, surely, be some spot to spread the picnic supper. It was a beautiful park, but not quite like Macon. Tee spread the checkered cloth on the grass, and began setting out the food. We noticed a little group of people, not far away, and a man called: "Why not pick up the rations and come on over here with poor folks?"

That man turned out to be John M. Rudesal. The women folks added their invitation, and we moved over with them. The children were easier than the grown-ups. They were soon calling one another's names, quite happy. All right. John's wife was Pauline, and their children were Miriam and Little John. Estelle's husband was Steadman Burgess, and their children were Steadman, Jr., and Beverly. Sadie's husband was Carlisle McCoy, and their children were Louise, Ralph and Henley. "We've been seeing you over at the church," said John, "and we thought we might as well claim kin. We're just a bunch of every-day Baptists, grew up over here in Capitol Avenue Baptist Church, played all over this park when we were chillun', and we come back over here right often so our little ones will see where we came from. When we get through eating, we'll pitch some horseshoes, and let the women talk to their hearts' content, that is if you're enough of a countryman to know what horseshoe pitching is." That was the way the Newtons got to know the McCoys, Rudesals and Burgesses. That was a Saturday afternoon in 1920. The four families ate supper together every Saturday night from that time on until the children married off, and now the old folks continue the delightful tradition, welcoming in any and all the children and grandchildren as often as they are in reach. Never was Christian fellowship sweeter or more rewarding.

On Saturday afternoon, March 16, 1929, John and Carlisle and Steadman wanted to know if I would be at church next morning. No, I was going by train that night to Thomasville to conduct the funeral of my dear friend, Dr. W. M. Harris, for years pastor at Thomasville, and after retirement, living in Little Rock with one of the children. Dr. Harris had served as one of my Book Editors, and he had asked that I conduct his funeral, although I was a layman. When I explained that I would not be at church the following morning, I saw them glance at one another. They weren't accustomed to excluding me from their counsels, but I knew I was outside the ropes in that instance. We went on and enjoyed our game, and when I suggested that we would have to be getting home so I could pick up my bag and catch the train, they said they would be by presently and take me to the station.

Mrs. Newton was carrying on a running conversation with the little girls as she put them to bed, and I fancied that she was intending that I hear all she was saying: "Daddy needn't worry about tomorrow. We'll entertain Dr. Chamlee, and we'll be thinking about Daddy, won't we? And now for our verses tonight, I want you to say this after me:

> Trust in the Lord with all thine heart;
> And lean not unto thine own understanding.
> In all thy ways acknowledge Him,
> And He shall direct thy paths.

Hugs and kisses from the little girls, and at the door, she whispered: "Remember, my love, His grace is sufficient."

There had been unusually heavy rains, and when the Central of Georgia's overnight express got to Montezuma, it stood there for sometime. I pushed up the shade. The moon was full. What could be delaying us? The porter explained that the Flint River between Montezuma and Oglethorpe had covered the tracks for a mile! I slipped into my trousers, followed the porter to the door, and there was the water on the edge of Montezuma. Just then the whistle's answer to the signal to proceed under caution. "Slip off your shoes, boss," said the porter. "If we do have to swim, let's be ready." The water sloshed against the steps. We swung out, looking toward the locomotive, and it was pushing the swirling current into white caps, glistening in the moonlight, like tigers' teeth! "We're half way," whispered the porter, "which means we over the deepest water! Lawd, help us, please!"

On the bulletin board in Albany in the early dawn, I read these words: "No Trains South Today." I conferred with the railroad agent. No, not a chance for the Coastline's train to Thomasville, bridge under water, unsafe! What about a car? No, the river had backed out for three miles on the highway to Thomasville—the highway was under guard by the State's Militia! No, the only private plane in Albany had gone to drop bread and medicine to people at Newton and other communities! Why was it so necessary for me to get to Thomasville? Dr. Harris' funeral. Ah! Dr. Harris had buried his mother!

I telephoned my friend, Dr. Cecil Cooke, pastor of the First Baptist Church in Albany. In ten minutes he was at the station. Yes, he had read that I was to conduct the funeral. Let's go and talk with the Chief of Police. In the Chief's office we met the Sergeant in charge of the guard on the Albany end of the flooded highway. He, too, knew Dr. Harris, had been baptized by Dr. Harris. What did the Sergeant think about my chance of getting through, if someone would let me have a car? Dr. Cooke offered his Chevrolet, but thought it impossible to drive through that water. The Sergeant motioned me outside.

"Preacher, if you promise me to do what I tell you, I'll call the Captain at the other end of the guarded stretch, and ask him to let you try it," he said. We got two bath towels, wrapped them around the carburetor and generator, and I listened as the Sergeant drove me to the water's edge. "Listen, we've driven stakes every 100 yards, showing where the pavement is. At every bridge, we have four stakes—one at each corner of the bridge. The water is running swift at places, specially where there are bridges. Promise me, preacher, if you see it is getting away from you, jump! I'll stay by the telephone until the Captain reports. God be with you."

I came at last in sight of the soldiers, and they were waving like children. That grand little old Chevy didn't miss a lick, though the water had covered my feet at times. How that little engine kept going, how I managed to hold those wheels on that pavement, only the grace of God can explain. I reached Thomasville ten minutes to eleven, and though my feet were soaking wet, I joined the procession as the congregation stood, and the organ moved into Chopin's funeral march.

Dr. T. F. "Snap" Callaway had succeeded Dr. Harris as pastor of the great church in Thomasville, and I sat with "Snap" and Ruth at lunch, following the funeral. It was long distance, she said, calling me from Atlanta. "Listen, Louie," said Judge Thomas, "I'm calling you before you get the telegram. We've called you again today, and I just wanted to say that we hope you will see it as we see it—that you will feel it as we feel it. That's why I called you. Dr. Chamlee preached a great sermon, and we asked him to let us have a church conference. He handled it just right. He feels like we do. That's all. Just listen to the Lord. That's all. Goodbye."

I dismissed their question about the call, and we were in the midst of pleasant conversation. The door bell. Yes, he would sign for it. "Snap" handed me the telegram, and I put it in my pocket. "Listen, buddy, we were all amazed when you got out of that car, wondering how in this world you could have managed that water, and now you answer long distance as if it was nothing, and when I hand you a telegram, you calmly poke it in your pocket. Am I dreaming? What is all this crazy acting?" said "Snap." Again, the doorbell. Thirty-seven telegrams. "Snap" started tearing them open, handing them to Mrs. Callaway. "Let me see the one you put in your pocket," he demanded. I handed it to him. Tears came in Mrs. Callaway's eyes. "Let us pray," said Dr. Callaway.

When I got to the water on my return trip that afternoon, the Captain smiled, and said: "You'll have it a little better going back. It has fallen several inches since you came through this morning. Only let me caution you that you will be hitting it up stream. Watch those swirls at the bridges." I had my faithful camera in the little bag, and I got several shots that afternoon—Negroes, for example, killing fish as they fluttered across the pavement on the highway. Morgan Blake, Sports Editor of *The Atlanta Journal,* reproduced the pictures in the Monday afternoon edition. Letters poured in, doubting even the camera's candid report. I preached on Sunday night for Dr. Cecil Cooke in Albany, thanked him for the use of his wonderful little car, and got the sleeper for Atlanta. The same porter, and we agreed that we would not go to bed until we "swam" the river between Oglethorpe and Montezuma. It wasn't quite so high Sunday night, though still covering the tracks.

Mrs. Newton met me at the train Monday morning. That was unusual. Why had she got up so early? There was no conversation. None needed, perhaps. As she turned into the drive at 619, I said: "What do you think?" Turning off the switch, she kissed me, and said: "Just what you think."

We agree that I should go and talk with my father and mother, and on Monday night I got the train for Halcyondale, Screven County. After breakfast—the sort of breakfast every mother knows how to prepare for her returning son— we sat about the open fire in "their room." Yes, they had heard about the call. My father spoke first: "When your mother read the story in yesterday's *Morning News,* we didn't know what to say. We just prayed that the Lord would make clear His will." There was a long silence—our eyes focused on the fire. My mother opened the Bible, and read:

I will instruct thee and teach thee in the way that thou shalt go.
                                                            —Psalm 32:8

There was another pause, and then my father bowed his head. My mother put her hand on my hand. We were all bowed in prayer, though no human voice was heard. I have often gone back to that Tuesday morning hour as one of the times of assurance in my heart.

Mrs. A. B. Brown had been my secretary since 1923, having resigned a very desirable position, paying more money, because, as she said, she wanted to devote her life to definite Christian service. Miss Mattie Straughan had gone to Greensboro, N. C., to open a book store. I relied a great deal upon Mrs. Brown's judgment—her intuitive understanding of men and matters in the work of God's Kingdom. I had never asked her what she thought about the call until that Wednesday morning when I returned from Screven County. She was handling the telegrams and letters, piling up as a result of the stories in the Monday papers. Maybe, she suggested, I should read some of those messages. No, I would do that later. Then she said: "I have always thought that there would be something else for you, but I had not tried to figure it out. This, of course, is between you and the Lord, and He will make it clear." And with that, she handed me a message that Dr. T. F. Callaway had sent for the paper: "It is a good thing I am not the Lord. He would stay on with *The Index* if I were."

I talked that week with many friends—Dr. Cree, Dr. Wilkinson, Dr. Major, Dr. Mell, Dr. Chamlee, Dr. Christie, Dr. Poteat, and to as many laymen—Clark Howell, Jim Nevin, John Paschall, Luther Brittain, Judge Jenkins, Judge Sibley—to members of our Baptist headquarters staff—to friends on the street. But there was no help to be had from men, even one's closest friends. It had to be between the Lord and me. Mrs. Newton had known it, and she knew before I did what it was.

Why am I a Baptist? How much easier it would have been if I might have gone to some earthly priest or bishop for the decision. Easier, perhaps, but not surer. It had to be settled through my Great High Priest. I had to yield in His presence, for His sake. Dr. B. D. Ragsdale, long a cherished leader in Georgia Baptist affairs, was to preach for us the following Sunday, and he went to our home for lunch. Neither of us mentioned the call. He directed his attention to the little girls until they were ready to leave the table, then he said:

"I accepted your invitation to preach to the people today, chiefly because I wanted to see the situation—to feel the atmosphere of the congregation—and most importantly, to be with you two people in what must be the most trying ordeal of your Christian experience. I have got the atmosphere of the congregation. It is reassuring. But I am not quite sure about you, my dear friends. I have been trying to discover what is in your hearts. Would you mind telling me?"

Mrs. Newton looked up. "Ah, I see. I understand," he said. "God bless you, my dear children in the Lord." Dr. Ragsdale bowed his head, and prayed. How I do wish we might have a copy of that prayer!

We talked and prayed a long time about it all on Thursday night of that week, and on the back of one of the many telegrams, we agreed on these words:

Mr. Z. A. Snipes, Secretary
Pulpit Committee, Druid Hills Baptist Church,
Atlanta, Georgia
Dear Mr. Snipes:
Fully convinced that it is the will of God for me to accept the invitation of Druid Hills Baptist Church to become its pastor, I am herewith asking you, as Secretary of the Committee, to convey to the Committee, and through the Committee to the Church, my acceptance, effective April 1, 1929.
Cordially yours,
March 28, 1929   LOUIE D. NEWTON

Mr. Snipes read the message to the church on Sunday morning, April 1, and I preached at both hours. Three people came forward on profession of faith, fourteen by letter. I baptized thirteen that night.

One passage of Scripture lived in my heart that day, John 7:17. Dr. Truett had telephoned early in the morning to thank me for the message that I would accept the call, and he concluded his reassuring comment with the words of Jesus:

If any man will do His will, he shall know of the doctrine, whether it be of God, or whether I speak Myself.

Assurance! Blessed Assurance! I knew that day what Fanny Crosby meant when she wrote the beautiful hymn. I understood, as never before, why Blessed Assurance means Perfect Submission. Why am I a Baptist? Because I have walked the way of soul liberty, with its searching implications—its terrific responsibilities.

I made it clear to the church that I would like to be ordained by my home church in Screven County where I made public my profession of faith in the Lord Jesus Christ, and where I became a Baptist. The people graciously agreed. The ordination was arranged for Saturday, April 20, in dear old Union Baptist Church, where my father and mother had served so long and joyously, and where my sister and brothers had found the Lord. The pastor, at that time, was Dr. P. H. Anderson, a returned missionary. He organized the examining presbytery, composed of 37 Baptist pastors and denominational leaders in Georgia, and at eleven o'clock that morning the presbytery made its report to the church in conference. Dr. Aquila Chamlee had been asked to examine my doctrinal fitness for the ministry. "Can you, and do you give your assent to the following Baptist beliefs?" he asked me:

"We believe in the only one true and living God, and that there is a trinity of persons in the God-head—the Father, the Son, and the Holy Spirit—and yet there are not three Gods, but one God.

"We believe that the Scriptures of the Old and New Testaments are the word of God, and that they are the only rule of faith and practice.

"We believe in the fall of Adam, in the imputation of his sin to his posterity, in the corruption of human nature and the inability of man to recover himself from his lost estate.

"We believe in the everlasting love of God to His people, and in the eternal and particular election of a definite number of the human race to grace and glory; and that before the world began there was a covenant made between the

Father and the Son, in which the salvation of the redeemed is made secure.

"We believe that the righteousness of Christ imputed to sinners is the only ground for their justification before God.

"We believe that the Spirit and the power of God will effectually call, regenerate, sanctify and support those who were chosen in Christ so that they will persevere in grace, and so that not one of them will be finally lost.

"We believe that good works are the fruits of faith—that they follow justification, and are evidences of a gracious state.

"We believe that there will be a resurrection of the dead and a general judgment, and the happiness of the righteous and the punishment of the wicked will be eternal.

As for Gospel Order

"We believe that a visible church is a congregation of professed believers in Jesus Christ, who enjoy Christian fellowship with each other, have associated themselves together with a view to keeping public worship and a Godly discipline agreeably to the rules of the Gospel.

"We believe that Jesus Christ is the great head of the church and its only lawgiver; but that the administration of the laws on earth is vested in each church for itself; and equal share in the administration being the privilege of each member; and that discipline is intended for the purity of the Church and for the reclaiming of members who may be disorderly, either in principle or practice, and those should be faithfully kept for the glory of God.

"We believe that baptism in water and the Lord's Supper are the only ceremonial ordinances of Jesus Christ and are to be continued until His second coming."

Dr. John D. Mell, President of the Georgia Baptist Convention at that time, preached the sermon, taking for his text Philippians 3:8: "I count all things but loss for the excellency of the knowledge of Christ Jesus my Lord." The prayer of ordination was led by Rev. H. J. Arnett, the veteran preacher of Screven County who had meant so much to my life. Following the prayer, the members of the presbytery, led by Pastor Anderson, placed their hands on my head. The congregation sang *Blest Be the Tie That Binds Our Hearts in Christian Love.*

My father and mother insisted that everybody at the ordination service must come home with them for dinner. My brothers and other friends agreed that it would be so. They arranged long tables under the trees in front of the house, and on those tables they placed platters of chicken, beef, ham, venison and fish. And with the meats went salads and bread. Steaming coffee and iced tea, buttermilk, and sweet milk were poured from pitchers. Cakes and pies and fruits and nuts finished off the menu of country viands. Several hundred guests partook. A group of people from Druid Hills accompanied us to Screven County that day, and about mid-afternoon I gave the signal that we had better start the journey of 265 miles to Atlanta. We ate supper in Macon, and arrived in Atlanta about eleven o'clock, Saturday night. Mrs. A. B. Brown wrote the story, with photographs made by Mr. Walton Reeves, one of our deacons.

A Jewish friend in Macon came up to our table in the restaurant that Saturday night, asking what it all meant—where had we been, and what for? When told, he turned to Mr. Smith, and said: "But how could this be? Didn't you have to get the consent of the Bishop, or the Archbishop, or whoever runs the Baptist church? You mean you made a Rabbi out of this young layman who used to be a teacher out here at Mercer? I don't understand." Brother Ches answered: "Brother Jacob, your trouble is in not knowing about Baptists. You see, we do not call it the Baptist Church, but Baptist churches. A local Baptist church is independent of all other Baptist churches. No bishops, no synods, no episcopacy, no papacy, no Sanhedrin, no creed but the Bible, no ecclesiastical hierarchy. Each individual is responsible directly to God, through Jesus Christ our Great High Priest forever. We call it the priesthood of believers, and we believe in the equality of all believers before God. That is why Druid Hills Baptist Church could call a layman as its pastor, and that is why we could request Mr. Newton's boyhood church in Screven County to ordain him." The Jewish friend stood there, looking at us, wondering about it all.

When a Presbyterian pastor called on me the following week to welcome me into the fellowship of the evangelical ministers organization in Atlanta, he said: "There's one point that I want you to explain to me. Haven't you been baptizing the people there before you were ordained? How could that be?" I explained that Dr. McConnell had asked the church to adopt a resolution, requesting me to baptize the people, since his physical condition in the fall of 1928 would not permit him to do so—that the same resolution authorized me to baptize the friends who came on profession of faith after his death, and prior to my ordination. "Then you Baptists practice what you preach about the autonomy of the local church. You amaze me," he said. I explained that I could not have performed a wedding, prior to my ordination, since that act implied ordination in the eyes of the civil authorities.

We moved from Bonaventure to 1011 Oakdale Road in Druid Hills in 1931, and through the subsequent years we have enjoyed the larger yard, the patch, which has now been converted into a pasture for the sheep and cows, the gardens for vegetables and flowers, the fish and lily pools, the chickens,

ducks, guineas, birds, trees, grasses, and all the rest. We had
set our hearts on owning our home from the day we married,
and when the church graciously offered to buy 1011 Oakdale
Road and make it the pastor's home, we earnestly protested,
declaring our purpose to pay off the rest of the notes, and
enjoy the sense of belonging. Being outside the city limits,
we could join with neighbors in freedoms disallowed urban
dwellers. We had almost forgot about the stars and moon
until we got out there where the sky is open to those who
have eyes. And to go in one's garden and gather fresh vegetables is good for the soul as well as the body—to watch apples
grown from lovely blossoms to reddened goodness. I have
kept a record of bird nests in our trees and shrubbery and
bird houses, and I am about to agree that birds, like flowers,
know when they are loved and wanted. Blue birds, red birds,
mocking birds, threshers, wrens—they all appear at home. The
sparrows and jay birds are ever with us. We have enjoyed the
privilege of sharing the place with the young people in our
church, and it is rewarding to feel that they, too, are at home
when they come to 1011.

I was busy, day and night, trying to meet the opportunities of the pastorate. Funerals, weddings, counseling, visiting
in homes and hospitals—these and many other opening doors
kept me hustling every waking moment. I continued to edit
the paper until the end of 1929, when Dr. O. P. Gilbert relieved me of that delightful but taxing responsibility. I was
keenly aware of the need for planned study, and I set to work
on a schedule that would provide at least four hours each
day with my books.

Thirty-seven years old—half of life behind me—and a
totally new flight pattern to master! I knew what it was to
meet three classes of college students each day; and I knew
what it was to prepare two to three thousand words of editor-

ial copy per week, plus unlimited reportorial copy, daily columns for newspapers, and examining unlimited manuscript for the paper; and I knew what it was to speak, as a layman, in pulpits here and there over the state, using basically the same message with appropriate adaptations. But two sermons each Lord's Day to the same congregation, plus a devotional message at the midweek worship hour, plus an early morning radio broadcast every Sunday morning—that was something new for me, and far and away the toughest assignment of my life. What, I asked myself, would I have done, had I fully realized what was involved in the final great decision of my life? But such questions lingered for only short visits in my mind. Something in my heart enabled me to say: "I can do what He wants me to do, if I cleave trustingly unto Him."

I gave a flock of books to young teachers, making room for a working shelf of books on preaching. The first volume I bought was *The Preparation and Delivery of Sermons,* Broadus. That prompted me to get his *History of Preaching,* and from that book I moved on to master Dargan's volume by the same title, then Stalker's *The Preacher and His Models.* Before too long I had Ker, Dods, Pattison, James, Armitage and other such authors—all of them convincing me that preaching the Gospel was all that my old Negro friend had said: "God calls you to preach, but He 'spects you to do your part—to keep your axe sharp." I had sat in Dr. John Dewey's class at Columbia University, listening to his lectures on "How We Think," but I was now discovering that preaching is thinking, plus. Somewhere in that first year of study in exegesis and homiletics, I came upon a reference that introduced me to Alexander Maclaren's *Expositions of the Scriptures.* I had bought this set of books during my editorship of *The Christian Index,* chiefly for use in teaching the Sunday

School lessons, but I had never really got into the gold mine which Maclaren has provided for students of the Bible. I owe more to Broadus and Maclaren than any other authors in trying to master the unmasterable art of preaching.

Somewhere in those formative years of my preaching experience I resolved to tackle the so-called masters in the art of preaching. I worked on Enoch, Noah, Elijah, Elisha, Joel, Micah, Isaiah, Jeremiah, John the Baptist, Peter, Paul. I then moved on to Hippolytus, Origen, Clement, Cyprian, Irenaeus, Polycarp, Ignatius, Justin Martyr, Gregory (Wonderworker), Chrysostom and Augustine. In that first general period of preaching, following the Apostles, A.D. 70-430, one must not become too much engrossed in councils like Nicea and Constantinople, but search for the prophetic accent in preachers who were held in the grip of great convictions, and who were concerned for the moral stamina of the people. The tragedy of that first period, of course, was the union of church and state, under Constantine. Appearing then as a cloud, the size of a man's hand, that tragic admixture of church and state has steadily spread its shadow across the world.

In my study of the preachers of the early Christian era, Origen, Chrysostom and Augustine impressed me most. Augustine's *De Civitate Dei* must be accounted one of the great works in Christian literature, and as I go back to it, again and again, I find much there that helps me in today's frustrated, changing world. I was specially struck by the general admission that there was a decline in preaching in the fifth and sixth centuries. Why, I asked myself? Why should there ever be a declension in preaching? Rothe tells us that the general corruption in morals affected the lives of the clergy as well as the laity. That reminded me of certain passages in the Old Testament. It reminded of what Gibbon

said in the *Decline and Fall.* Also, it was pointed out that
the growth of liturgy and forms of worship lessened the power
of preaching. That reminded me that Baptists have ever
sought to avoid formalism in worship, and I again underscored my Baptist convictions. I read some of the sermons
by John of Antioch—simple, powerful preaching—and I
wondered why the later preachers would be trusting in harness rather than Christ-centered messages.

Alaric sacked Rome in 410. Genseric and his Vandals
pillaged the city in 455, and the pitiful remnants of empire
were surrendered to Odoacer at Ravenna in 476. In this
state of affairs, Leo I and Gregory I founded the papacy—Leo
boldly claiming pre-eminence on the assertion of "Peter's
primacy." His success at Chalcedon added to his stature in
dealing with Attila and Genseric, but these political and military stratagems failed to make him a great preacher. Whether
Leo or Gregory was actually the first pope is a debate that I
leave to those more interested than I am in the history of
the papacy. I was searching for preachers, not ecclesiastical
hierarchies, and I found very few impressive preachers until
I reached the "Voices in the Night," in the ninth, tenth and
eleventh centuries—Ansgar, Rabanus, Anselm, Damiani,
Aquinas—but how could these men be free to preach with
popes and kings and generals trading them like goods on a
shelf? Growing weary of the search for great preachers, I
jumped over to John Huss, and felt the glow of a great heart
and a great conviction. And that led me on to Wiclif, Colet,
Savonarola. I read every sermon by Wiclif I could find. What
a preacher!

And then Huss. I followed Huss through all the stages of
his persecution, and seemed to feel the scorching flames of
1415 by which they thought to silence his witness for soul
liberty. Savonarola's last sermon at San Marco, March, 1498,

will live on as one of the truly great sermons of all time. On the 23rd day of May, 1498, they burned the great preacher in the Piazza della Deignoria in Florence, and as I have several times stood and read the plaque, marking that spot, I have thanked God for a preacher whose simple, heartfelt message helped to reveal the dangers of man-made creeds and the curse of ecclesiastical tyranny.

Martin Luther, Zwingli, John Calvin, Peter Waldo, Balthasar Hubmaier, John Knox, John Wesley, George Whitefield, Hugh Latimer, Thomas Cranmer, and other preachers of the Reformation and subsequent centuries held me for many and many an hour. I had touched these men in my study of general history, particularly Luther, but I had to go to their record as preachers to really know them. I dare not allow myself to extend my remarks on what these preachers accomplished. Where will you match their contributions?

Then Spurgeon. Charles Haddon Spurgeon, like John Wesley, had much to do with the strengthening of British life, at home and throughout the world. We like to claim him as one of our great Baptist preachers, but he was, indeed, a catholic man—preaching the timeless message of the unchanging Christ to all men. I find his sermons hard reading, but rewarding, always.

Moving to America, I quickly discovered what every student of Baptist history well knows, that in order to interpret and understand Baptist preachers and preaching in early American life, you have to go back to certain men and movements in Britain and Europe—back to John Rippon's concepts of religious liberty and Christology, back to John Milton's plea for freedom, back to Thomas Helwys and John Smyth, back to Balthasar Hubmaier, back to J. G. Oncken, back to William Carey's missionary vision and zeal, back to John Bunyan's imprisonment and *Pilgrim's Progress,* back to the impulse of Roger Williams, back to the controversy between Richard Bernard and John Robinson in Nottinghamshire—back to the conditions that produced in the minds and hearts of these men the hunger for freedom to preach the Gospel of Jesus Christ. The ecclesiastical tyranny that had hailed Paul and Silas into court in Philippi, burned Huss and Savonarola and Hubmaier, strangled Tyndale, and in various ways martyred uncounted others, bore heavily upon these men of the sixteenth and seventeenth centuries, and they turned their faces to the New World across the Atlantic in hope of religious liberty, leaving behind, they fondly dreamed, the persecution of the Vatican and the established churches.

Thomas Carlyle's oft-quoted statement that: "The history of the world is but the biography of great men," helps one to appraise the influence of certain Baptist preachers in the formative years of our country—Roger Williams, Isaac Backus, John Smith, John Leland—to mention but four of these mighty men. I studied Roger Williams from his days at Cambridge, Archbishop Laud's decree that he must leave England because of his dangerous ideas of religious liberty, his declination of the prized Anglican pulpit in Boston, his ministry at Plymouth, then Salem, his controversy with Cotton Mather, and his final contribution in Rhode Island. I read his books and his sermons. I went on to read the influence which his writings exerted upon Thomas Jefferson, James Madison and the other founding fathers as "the pattern of the Republic" took form, to employ the fine phrase of Dr. John Martin Dawson in his *Baptists and the American Republic,* Broadman Press, 1956, a book which reflects more fully and accurately this saga of Baptist influence upon the American way of life than any single volume I know. It documents its every assertion on such authorities as John Adams, Clinton

Rossiter, Charles A. Beard, George M. Brydon, Ralph Barton
Perry, William Warren Sweet, Evarts B. Greene, Rufus M.
Jones, Anson Phelps Stokes, James Truslow Adams, John M.
Mecklin, George E. Ellis, Rufus W. Weaver, James Hastings,
William A. Muller, Oscar S. Straus, Perry Miller, Roland H.
Bainton, James Ernst, George Bancroft, William Thompson
Hanzsche, Claude G. Bowers, Richard Hofstadter, John Dos
Passos, A. H. Newman, R. G. Torbet, Robert B. Semple,
R. B. C. Howell, Thomas Armitage, Thomas F. Curtis,
Phillips Brooks, Henry Wilder Foote, Charles Small Long-
acre, Alvah Hovey, Walter Rauschenbusch and numerous
others. I did not have access to all these books at the time I
was first studying American Baptist preachers, but I have
examined them all in subsequent years, and I respectfully
submit that any unbiased student of the American scene will
agree that what Roger Williams, Isaac Backus, John Smith,
John Leland and other early Baptist preachers began was
faithfully continued by Baptist preachers and laymen in the
succeeding generations, holding ever aloft the banner of religious liberty—a free church in a free state. I need not pursue
the story in detail. The point I am here wishing to under-
score is that in the first years of my ministry, dating from
1929, I got the impact of men like Williams and Backus and
Leland, who, though deeply grateful for the contributions
of reformers like Luther, Calvin and Knox, were neverthe-
less mindful of the failures of the Reformation—failure to
completely sever church and state—failure in adopting the
fallacy of infant baptism—failure to rid the local church of
centralized controls—and who resolved, at whatever cost to
themselves, to give their witness always and everywhere to
separation of church and state, and the priesthood of all believers, based on the competency of the individual soul to

deal directly with God through Jesus Christ our great High Priest forever.

While this is not a book on Baptist history, it may not be amiss to record, at this juncture, a few of the earliest Baptist events in the New World. The first Baptist church in America was constituted at Providence, Rhode Island, in March, 1639, by Roger Williams, Ezekiel Holliman, and others. Later in the year of 1639, John Clarke and others constituted a Baptist church at Newport, Rhode Island. John Clarke was the first pastor at Newport. He was succeeded by Obadiah Holmes. Both Clarke and Holmes were arrested for preaching the Gospel and opposing infant baptism. Clarke was fined twenty pounds. Holmes was "whipped unmercifully" in the streets of Boston, according to Bancroft. Henry Dunster, president of Harvard College, was forced to resign because he stoutly opposed infant baptism. In 1663 a Baptist church was constituted at Swansea, by John Miles and seven other brethren, and in 1665 a Baptist church was constituted in Boston. In 1682 a Baptist church was constituted at Kittery, Maine, but it was so harried by fines and imprisonment that in 1683 Pastor Screven abandoned Maine and brought the little band of Baptists to South Carolina, constituting on the banks of the Cooper River the first Baptist church in the South, now the First Baptist Church of Charleston. By 1784 there were one hundred and fifty-one Baptist churches in New England with four thousand, seven hundred and eighty-three members. "The first Baptist minister to labor in New York City was Rev. William Wickenden, of Providence, sometime before 1669, and for these labors he was incarcerated four months," declares Vedder in his *Short History of Baptists,* 1891, p. 159. A Baptist church may have been constituted in New York City in 1669, but persecution soon ended its feeble life. The effort was revived in 1702, and by

1712 Rev. Valentine Wightman, of Groton, was preaching regularly in the small village which was to become the world's largest city. A century later, 1812, there were two hundred and fifty Baptist churches in the state of New York. The First Baptist Church, Philadelphia, was constituted in 1746. The Philadelphia Baptist Association was organized in 1707. The Charleston Baptist Association was organized in 1751.

An event of far-reaching significance for Baptists was the meeting of thirty-six delegates from eleven states in Philadelphia, May, 1814, and the organization of the General Missionary Convention of the Baptist Denomination in the United States of America for Foreign Missions, which afterward became known as the Triennial Baptist Convention, from its meeting once in each three-year period. The organization of this first general Baptist body in America stemmed from an awakening missionary impulse, dating from the Williamstown haystack, 1810, when Adoniram Judson, son of a Congregational minister, and several other young men, including Luther Rice, petitioned the General Association of Massachusetts to form a missionary society for the propagation of the Gospel throughout the world. Baptists were already at work in home missions, seeking to win the Indians to Christ, and they were raising money for foreign missions, chiefly for Carey's work in India. Judson was a graduate of Brown University and Andover Seminary, and along with his friend, Luther Rice, had become seriously concerned about certain doctrines, including baptism. The newly organized American Board of Commissioners for Foreign Missions, 1810, appointed Judson and his wife, Ann Haseltine Judson, and Luther Rice as missionaries, and they sailed immediately for India.

On the long voyage to India, Judson spent much time

studying the Scriptures, and he was convinced that the only baptism recognized in the New Testament was immersion. True to this conviction, he was immersed by Rev. William Ward in Calcutta, September 6, 1810. Ward had gone out to Burma with William Carey, pioneer Baptist missionary of Kettering, England. Carey had arrived in Burma in 1792. Rice was also convinced that immersion was the only mode of baptism taught in the New Testament, and he, too, was baptized. Finding themselves as Baptists without any supporting Board back at home, Rice proposed to Judson that he and his wife remain in India while he returned to America to arouse support on the part of Baptists. That accounted for the organization of the Baptist General Convention in Philadelphia in 1814. Rice travelled from New England to Georgia along the seaboard, appealing to Baptists to establish Baptist colleges in which preachers and missionaries might be trained. Turning inland from Georgia, he carried the crusade into Alabama, Tennessee, Mississippi, and Kentucky. Tracing the steps of Luther Rice, one finds college after college in Virginia, the Carolinas, Georgia, Alabama, Kentucky, Tennessee and Mississippi, dating from the 1820's and '30's. Able leaders joined Rice in this pioneer work of laying the foundation for Baptist life in America, including Adiel Sherwood, Jesse Mercer, Richard Furman, Samuel Wait, Robert Ryland, Richard Fuller, William T. Brantly, W. B. Johnson and others too many to mention.

Organization of the Triennial Convention in 1814 had insured support for Adoniram and Ann Haseltine Judson in their work in India, though differences with British civil officials forced the Judsons to transfer their base of operations to Rangoon. In 1819 the heartening word came to America that Judson had baptized his first convert, Moung Nau. Joining hands with Dr. George Boardman who had established a mission to the Karens, Judson and Boardman enjoyed great triumphs in missionary work in Assam, Siam, Hindustan, China and Japan.

The Triennial Convention met every three years from 1814 to 1844, but a deep and grievous wedge was sinking deeper and deeper into the fellowship of that pioneer Baptist body in America—the issue of slavery. After prolonged conferences and prayerful concern, the session in 1844 broke up in final agreement to disagree, and the Triennial Convention was dead. Luther Rice had died in 1836, and other great leaders were already dead, or were soon to follow. Judson died in 1850. It was a time of deep and frightening disturbance for Baptists and for everybody. In this hour of conflict, Baptists held true to their basic doctrines, even if their fellowship was ripping at the seams. They had the Philadelphia Confession of Faith, adopted by the Philadelphia Association of Baptists in 1742, and printed by Benjamin Franklin in 1743; they had the New Hampshire Confession of Faith, adopted in 1833; they had their local church covenants; and they had their New Testaments, which they declared then, as we do now, to be their all-sufficient rule and guide for their faith and practice. But American Baptists were breaking apart on the issue of slavery—a break which has not been repaired through more than one hundred years!

The work of foreign missions was conducted by the Triennial Convention from 1814 to 1844. In 1845, Northern Baptists organized the Foreign Missionary Society. The American Baptist Publication Society had been organized in 1824, and the Baptist Home Mission Society in 1832. The American and Foreign Bible Society was organized in 1837. Rhode Island Baptist College had opened its doors at Warren in 1765. It was removed to Providence in 1770, and the name changed to Brown University. The Newton Theological Institution was founded in Boston, 1825. Waterville College was opened in Maine in 1818, changing its name to Colby University in 1867. Worcester Academy in Massachusetts, and Suffield Literary Institution in Connecticut provided many of the early students at Brown University. New York Baptists had a school as early as 1820, which in 1834 developed into the Hamilton Literary and Theological Institution, finally becoming Madison University. Rochester Theological Seminary was an outgrowth of this original institution at Hamilton. Other early Baptist institutions of learning were Columbian University, Washington, D. C., 1821; Denison University, Granville, Ohio, 1832; Bucknell University, Lewisburg, Pa., 1846; Richmond College, Richmond, Va., 1832; Georgetown College, Kentucky, 1824; Mercer University, Penfield, Georgia, 1833 and Wake Forest College, North Carolina, 1834.

In my study of preachers and preaching, principally Baptist preachers, I came upon A. M. Poindexter, described by Dr. Broadus as one of the ablest men in the Baptist saga in America. I am convinced that he belongs in that category, but the men who impressed me most in the first two hundred years of Baptist life in America were: Roger Williams, Isaac Backus, John Leland, Thomas Baldwin, Richard Furman, Richard Fuller, Shubael Stearns, Daniel Marshall, Adiel Sherwood, Basil Manly, Sr., William B. Johnson, Jesse Mercer, William Jewell, James P. Boyce, R. B. C. Howell, Luther Rice and William M. Tryon. This list cannot include them all, but it is typical of the great, really great preachers of the first two centuries of American Baptist life.

And as I studied these men, my assurance in being a Baptist deepened and deepened. Yes, I am a Baptist because of an assurance.

We come on to 1844, and the division of American Baptists, due to the issue of slavery, as I have before pointed out. What was to be done? Dr. William B. Johnson, who had suggested to Luther Rice the organization of the Triennial Convention in 1814, and had pled so earnestly for the continuing fellowship in the Triennial Convention, now turned to his Baptist brethren in the South with the proposal that a fellowship be established among Southern Baptists. His was not the only voice in this call. In *The Religious Herald,* April 10, 1845, appeared a call to "The Baptist Churches of Virginia and the Baptist Denomination in the United States Generally" which began with these words:

"You will perceive by the accompanying resolutions of the Executive Committee of the Georgia Baptist Convention, that they have acceded to our proposal to hold in Augusta, Georgia, on Thursday before the second Lord's Day in May next, a Convention . . ."

This call from Virginia Baptists was signed by James B. Taylor, President, and C. Walthall, Secretary. The Virginia resolution specified that the proposed meeting in Augusta would consider how Southern Baptists would carry on their foreign mission work, and suggested that other subjects would need attention. Dr. W. B. Johnson, President of the South Carolina Convention, in an address to the Convention at Edgefield, the week preceding the meeting in Augusta, said:

"I invite your attention to the consideration of two plans. The one is, that which has been adopted for years past, namely, separate and independent bodies for the prosecution of each object. Your familiarity with the plan renders any remark upon it unnecessary. The other proposes one Convention, embodying the whole Denomination together with separate and distinct Boards for each object of benevolent enterprise, located at different places, and all amenable to the Convention."

Leaders in Kentucky, Tennessee and Mississippi advised delay, but the resolution of Virginia Baptists had crystalized the conviction that there must be immediate action, and on Thursday, May 8, 1845, three hundred and twenty-seven messengers from eleven states met at Augusta, Georgia, and organized the Southern Baptist Convention. Dr. W. B. Johnson was chairman of the committee to draw up a constitution, which was adopted Saturday, May 10. The preamble to the constitution reads:

"The messengers from missionary societies, churches and other religious bodies of the Baptist denomination in various parts of the United States, met in Augusta, Georgia, May 8, 1845, for the purpose of carrying into effect the benevolent intention of our constituents by organizing a plan for eliciting, combining, and directing the energies of the denomination for the propagation of the Gospel, adopted rules and fundamental principles which, as amended from time to time, are as follows: . . ."

They elected Dr. W. B. Johnson as the first President of the Southern Baptist Convention, with Rev. Jesse Hartwell, Alabama, and Rev. James C. Crane, Virginia, as the first Secretaries. Dr. Richard Fuller, Maryland, preached the sermon at Augusta. On Sunday, May 11, the Convention adjourned for worship in the First Baptist Church, where the messengers from eleven states joined with the members of the First Church in observance of the Lord's Supper. The Convention ended Monday, May 12, to meet in Richmond in 1846, when Dr. W. B. Johnson preached the sermon.

Two boards were established at Augusta—the Foreign Mission Board, located in Richmond, Virginia, with Rev. James B. Taylor, Pastor of the Second Baptist Church, Richmond, as Secretary; and the Home Mission Board, located at Marion, Alabama, with D. P. Bestor serving a few months, succeeded

by Rev. Russell Holman. In 1859 the Southern Baptist Theological Seminary was established at Greenville, South Carolina, with a faculty composed of James P. Boyce, chairman,
John A. Broadus, Basil Manly, Jr., and William Williams,
and twenty-six students. The Seminary was closed for a
period during the war, but reopened in Louisville, Kentucky,
1877.

Why am I a Baptist? Because of an assurance—an assurance,
deepened and confirmed beyond any serious question as I
trace the experiences of Baptists, preachers and laymen alike,
from the far distant scenes and centuries, to the conflicts and
struggles of the formative years of Baptist life here in America—even to the present hour.

I could write a full chapter on what happened to Baptists
after the War Between the States—the story, for example, of
our Negro brethren who, prior to the war, were members of
the white churches. Now that the war was ended, the question
arose, should the Negroes have their own churches? An ex-
ample might be cited here in Atlanta. The First Baptist
Church of Atlanta, constituted in 1848, had a number of
Negro members, among them a young man named Edward
Randolph Carter, born a slave in Athens, and brought to
Atlanta through the kindness of Henry W. Grady, Editor of
The Atlanta Constitution. Young Carter felt the call of the
Holy Spirit to preach the Gospel. He talked with Dr. H. C.
Hornady, pastor of the First Church, and, along with other
interested and concerned brethren, white and colored, agreed
that the Negro members of the church should have their
own church, so that Friendship Baptist Church was constituted, with a man named Quarles as its first pastor. Dr. Carter,
encouraged and aided by his white Baptist brethren, received
his theological training, and became pastor of Friendship
Church in 1882, serving until his death in 1944.

As a matter of fact, there were some separate Negro Baptist churches before the abolition of slavery, notably in Savannah, Mobile and Richmond. The three such Savannah churches had Negro pastors, but in the Anthony Street Church, Mobile, Rev. Keidor Hawthorne, pastor of Mobile's oldest white Baptist church, "presided also as pastor of the Anthony Street Church," and in Richmond, Dr. Robert Ryland, President of Richmond College, served for twenty-five years as pastor of the First African Baptist Church. (See *A History of Baptists in the Southern States*, B. F. Riley, American Baptist Publication Society, 1898, p. 319).

The story of our Negro Baptist brethren is one of the thrilling chapters in American church history, and I rejoice to observe the fellowship which has steadily grown between the churches and conventions of white and colored Baptists here in the South and throughout the Nation. I shall refer to the present strength of our Negro Baptist brethren, along with other Baptist bodies throughout the world, in the next chapter. My sense of assurance as a Baptist has been strengthened by the fellowship I have had, direct and indirect, with some of the notable Negro Baptist preachers and lay leaders of America—Rev. George Liele, Rev. Andrew Bryan, Rev. Cary Lot, Rev. John Jasper, Dr. W. J. White, Rev. Edward Randolph Carter, Dr. P. J. Bryant, Dr. E. K. Love, Dr. W. G. Johnson, Dr. Charles T. Walker, Dr. Benjamin Brawley, Dr. Booker T. Washington, Major R. R. Moton, Dr. Lacy Kirk Williams, Dr. John Hope, Dr. D. D. Crawford, Rev. J. B. Borders, Rev. D. V. Jemison, and Rev. G. L. Prince.

Turning back now to my more personal experiences of assurance as a Baptist in the unfolding years of my pastorate at Druid Hills, beginning in 1929, may I cite two situations that helped me to know anew that I was in the will of the Lord.

The economic tremor through which we passed in 1929 brought its inevitable grief to every strata of society, including the churches and all of the denominational activities. We passed through deep waters, but every passing hour taught me that God is able, if only we let go and let Him have His way. I learned to sing with understanding:

> When through fiery trials thy pathway shall lie,
>   My grace, all-sufficient, shall be thy supply;
> The flame shall not hurt thee, I only design
>   Thy dross to consume, and thy gold to refine.

There was more than mere satisfaction in our hearts as Southern Baptists, when, in 1943, Dr. J. E. Dillard, who had led us so valiantly in the Debt-Paying Campaign, announced that the last dollar, with interest, had been paid on our denominational obligations. It was that very year that we paid the last dollar on our building debt at Druid Hills, and that same year I handed Mrs. Newton the cancelled note on the final payment for our home at 1011 Oakdale Road in Druid Hills. Meeting economic disaster in honor was a wonderful triumph in Christian assurance.

The other situation occurred in 1931. The telephone rang, and a friend in the Atlanta AP Bureau was asking: "Are you going to take the job in Richmond?" He was surprised that I knew nothing about the story released by the Foreign Mission Board, announcing that I had been elected Executive Secretary. Then a long-distance call from Dr. R. E. Gaines, President of the Board, telling me that I had been elected, and asking if his committee might come to Atlanta the following day. Yes, I would be glad to see them, but I certainly could not be understood as implying any impression that I would accept. The Board had not approached me about this important matter before taking action.

Dr. Gaines was Professor of Mathematics in the University of Richmond, and one of the most delightful gentlemen I ever knew. He came with his committee, at ten o'clock the next morning, and we settled down in my study for the ordeal. The morning paper had carried the story, and my telephone had been ringing since sun-up. Professor Gaines took the floor, and literally so, striding back and forth as he marshalled his argument in mathematical sequence and logic, introducing powerful interludes, as, for example:

"We know that you volunteered for missionary service when you were an undergraduate at Mercer. We have examined the correspondence between Dr. Willingham and you. We feel that this is the Lord's way of guiding us and you to the fulfillment of that impulse in 1910."

As the whistles signalled high noon, I suggested that we adjourn for lunch, and we started down stairs. At the foot of the stairs we were met by a group of deacons who had been, as I later learned, in a prayer meeting. In the group were two former students of Professor Gaines—Mr. H. W. Stephenson and Mr. Z. A. Snipes. "What are you boys doing here?" he inquired. Being told, he turned to his committee, and said: "No wonder we are making so little headway with their pastor." The deacons took over, and after lunch, I convinced the committee that I could not encourage them to go on with their argument—that I felt I was in the will of the Lord at Druid Hills.

I shall keep the letter Dr. Gaines wrote me upon his return to Richmond. He made some argument for further consideration, but what impressed me about the letter was his acknowledgment that I was concerned only in finding and following the will of the Lord. Reviewing this situation took me back to the 1931 files, and I was impressed, as perhaps I was not at the time, with the many letters and telegrams, assuring me of the prayers of my friends. I think I know now why my decision was so much easier than otherwise it might have been. Reading this file again, I was specially impressed by letters from several veteran missionaries, and from such cherished friends as Drs. R. H. Pitt, Solon B. Cousins, A. T. Robertson, L. R. Scarborough, George W. Truett, W. L. Pickard, Rufus W. Weaver, Spright Dowell, Aquila Chamlee, J. H. Rushbrooke, John D. Mell, J. C. Wilkinson, T. B. Ray, W. D. Powell, and others too many to mention. We prayed, and the answer seemed clear, and on October 24, 1931, I sent this telegram:

Dr. R. E. Gaines, Pres't
Foreign Mission Board
Southern Baptist Convention
Richmond, Virginia
Having earnestly sought the guidance of the Holy Spirit in arriving at an answer to the gracious invitation of the Foreign Mission Board, I believe that I am in the Lord's will in my present work. I shall join with you and the Board and our Baptist people everywhere in unceasing prayer that our Father's will and way shall be found in this crucial hour.

LOUIE D. NEWTON

It was a crucial hour, due to the large indebtedness of the Board and all the other agencies of the Convention at that time, but it was not the burdensome debt that entered into my decision. We were all in the same boat regarding the debts. It was the feeling deep in my heart that I was where the Lord wanted me. It was assurance, if I may return again to the title of this chapter.

There were several invitations to consider other pastorates, but none of these bothered me for a moment. The people at Druid Hills were patiently moving along with me, upbearing me in their prayers, and I was supremely happy. Dr.

J. H. Rushbrooke, then General Secretary of the Baptist World Alliance, wrote me frequently about developments in Europe, holding to his well-known conviction that we should go on with plans for the Congress in Berlin in 1934. He came over in 1933, and while in Atlanta, he talked about future plans of the Alliance, urging me to consider taking over his duties, either at Berlin, or by the meeting of the next Congress, in 1939. We could never get beyond the discussion stage of the suggestion. It was Druid Hills for me.

Assurance! What a word! I say it humbly, but I knew, from 1929, that I was in the Lord's will. With Paul, I could say: "I know." And with Samuel Johnson, I could say: "He is no wise man that will quit a certainty for an uncertainty."

SEVEN

BECAUSE OF A PROGRAM

And Jesus came and said to them: "All authority in heaven and on earth has been given to me. Go therefore and make disciples of all nations, baptizing them in the Name of the Father and of the Son and of the Holy Spirit, teaching them to observe all that I have commanded you; and lo, I am with you always, to the close of the age," Matthew 28:18-20.

"Heal the sick," Matthew 10:8.

"But you shall receive power when the Holy Spirit has come upon you; and you shall be my witnesses in Jerusalem and in all Judea and Samaria and to the end of the earth," Acts 1:8.

"And behold, I send the promise of my Father upon you; but stay in the city, until you are clothed with power from on high," Luke 24:49.

I AM A BAPTIST because of a program of action for the individual, the local church, the district association, the state convention, the regional convention and the world fellowship of Baptists. I am convinced that this program of action is just as surely and soundly based on the teachings

189

of the New Testament as are the doctrines which we believe and teach and preach.

If there is a better word than "program," I'm for it, but I have not yet found it. I like to think that Abel had a program, else he would not have been at the right place at the right time with the right offering. Enoch, evidently, had a program —walking with God. Noah had a program, God-given. So did Abram, Isaac, Jacob (after much struggle with himself), Joseph, Moses, Joshua, David, and on and on across the cen· turies we come upon men and women who, at long last, yielded their wills to God's will, seeking first the Kingdom of God and His righteousness. The patterns of action varied, but these yielded men and women honestly sought to serve their day and generation by the will of God—in the will of God—until Paul could say: "Brethren, I do not consider that I made it my own; but one thing I do, forgetting what lies behind and straining forward to what lies ahead, I press on toward the goal for the prize of the upward call of God in Christ Jesus."—Philippians 3:13-14.

The Baptist program of action to which I gladly and resolutely commit myself has been an unfolding process. John the Baptist appears to have worked alone—"The voice of one crying in the wilderness"—to quote Isaiah. I fancy that John the Baptist would have welcomed cooperation, had there been even one other preacher who would have joined him in the open-air evangelistic meetings in Jerusalem, Judea and all the region round about Jordan. Even so, he had a program, and he stuck to it until it cost him his head. As I study the New Testament, I am strengthened in the belief that men and women who are honestly striving to find and follow the will of God will discover the formula of joined heads and hands and hearts, even as the cedars of Lebanon link their limbs in multiplied strength.

What I have just said may well raise the question, Why have Southern Baptists, in their program of action, declined the gracious invitations to membership in the several ecumenical movements? Perhaps the answer of the Southern Baptist Convention, Baltimore, 1940, to the invitation of the World Council of Churches to membership, would state the situation as well as any single record I might cite:

To the World Council of Churches
Dear Brethren:
The invitation to the Southern Baptist Convention to accept membership in the World Council of Churches was received by the President of the Convention at Oklahoma City in May, 1939. A special committee of thirteen was appointed to consider the invitation and to make recommendations as to the answer that should be made by the Convention to your invitation.
First of all, we would express to you our sincere and grateful appreciation for the courtesy and Christian spirit expressed in your communication. Directly replying to your invitation, permit us to advise that the Southern Baptist Convention is a voluntary association of Baptists for the purpose of eliciting, combining and directing the energies of our denomination in missionary activity at home and abroad, and in educational and benevolent work throughout the world. Our Convention has no ecclesiological authority. It is in no sense the Southern Baptist Church. The thousands of churches to which our Convention looks for support of its missionary, benevolent and educational program, cherish their independence and would disapprove of any attempted exercise of ecclesiastical authority over them.
In a world which more and more seeks centralization of power in industry, in civil government, and in religion, we are sensible of the dangers of totalitarian trends which threaten the autonomy of all free churches. We wish to do nothing that will imperil the growing spirit of cooperation on the part of our churches in the work of giving the Gospel of Christ, as we understand it, to all men everywhere. In the light of these considerations, we feel impelled to decline the invitation to membership in the World Council of Churches.

In conclusion, permit us to express the sincere desire of our hearts
that the followers of Christ may all be one, not necessarily in name
and in a world organization, but in spiritual fellowship with the
Father and the Son. If Christ dwells in all our hearts by faith,
we shall be brought into a spiritual unity that cannot be broken.
We invoke the blessings of the Triune God upon all who name
the Name of our Lord Jesus Christ.

This statement, submitted by Dr. George W. Truett, chairman, was unhurriedly discussed, with every messenger ac-
corded time for his opinion. In the course of the discussion,
nineteen brethren asked that a written statement of their
views be read—their views being at variance with the committee's recommendations—and that a standing vote be taken
on their statement. When the full and frank and fraternal
discussion ended, the Convention voted overwhelmingly to
approve the committee's recommendations. (See SBC *Annual,*
1940, pages 99 and 100).

What, the reader may reasonably ask, has happened since
1940 in the thinking of Southern Baptists regarding membership in the World Council of Churches, and other ecumenical
movements? I would answer that our position today is, apparently, substantially what it was in 1940. There are a few
local churches in our Convention that have definite commitments to the National Council and World Council, which
they are entirely free to do, but I do not know of any Baptist
organizations within the Southern Baptist Convention, such
as state conventions or district associations, that are affiliated
with the National Council or World Council.

On the other hand, it is generally true that our pastors and
churches in the South Baptist Convention cooperate with
other denominations in many ways, as, for example, resistance
to the alcoholic beverage menace, gambling, desecration of
the Lord's Day, lawlessness in every form, and any and all

encroachments upon the cherished principle of religious liberty. We gladly work with all fellow-Christians in support of such agencies as the American Bible Society, Scouting, ministries to war-ravaged peoples, prisoners, the Red Cross, the YWCA and the YMCA, Protestants and Other Americans United for Separation of Church and State, and in countless other fields of acknowledged Christian responsibility. This we gladly do, and we rejoice in the fellowship of kindred minds and hearts.

Back to the Baptist program, with emphasis upon the fact that it has been and continues to be an unfolding pattern. I have previously traced the effort toward a nation-wide Baptist program of action, leading to the organization of the Triennial Convention in Philadelphia, 1814. That pattern was rent by the issue of slavery, resulting in the disbanding of the Triennial Convention in 1844, and the organization of the Southern Baptist Convention in 1845.

Before pursuing the pattern of Baptist belief and action in the South, occasioned by the regrettable disbanding of the Triennial Convention in 1844, it may prove interesting to cite the statistical record (See Cathcart's *Encyclopedia,* page 1324), from 1770 to 1840:

"Baptist churches in the United States, 1770, 77; 1784, 471; 1792, 891; 1812, 2,164; 1832, 5,320; 1840, 7,771."

It is interesting to observe that there were 571,291 Baptists in the United States in 1840. By 1880, forty years later, there were 2,296,327 Baptists in this country.

Northern Baptists did not organize a convention following the disbanding of the Triennial Convention, as did Southern Baptists, but carried on their work through their Foreign and Home Mission Societies, their Publication Society, and Education Society. It was not until 1907 that the Northern Baptist Convention was organized.

Our Negro Baptist brethren organized their first state convention in North Carolina, 1866, with Alabama and Virginia following in 1867. As early as 1866, they held a southwide meeting in Richmond, but it was not until 1880 that they organized the National Baptist Convention, Incorporated, in Montgomery, Alabama. In 1915, there was a second nationwide convention organized—The National Baptist Convention of America. Latest published statistics (1955) indicate 4,557,416 members of the National Baptist Convention, Incorporated; and 2,645,789 members of the National Baptist Convention of America. The National Baptist Convention, Incorporated, has the following agencies: Foreign Mission Board, Philadelphia, Dr. C. C. Adams, Secretary; Home Mission Board, Milwaukee, Dr. T. T. Lovelace, Secretary; Sunday School Board, Nashville, Dr. A. M. Townsend, Secretary; Baptist Training Union Board, Nashville, Dr. Roland Smith, Secretary; *The National Baptist Voice,* Chester, Pennsylvania, Dr. Joseph Barber, Editor.

The American Baptist Convention (formerly the Northern Baptist Convention) reports 1,564,210 members (1955). Other 1955 statistics of Baptist bodies in the United States: Baptist General Conference of America, 49,981; North American Baptist General Conference, 45,121; Seventh Day Baptist General Conference, 6,259; Southern Baptist Convention, 8,474,741. Estimated number of Baptists in the world, 1956: Africa, 237,788; Asia, 714,321; Australasia and Oceania, 45,617; Central America and West Indies, 98,455; Europe, 1,122,948; North America, 18,967,251; South America, 138,-098. Total, 21,324,478. (Figures released by Baptist World Alliance, Washington, D. C., October, 1956).

Reviewing the program of our brethren of the American Baptist Convention, I am obliged to Dr. R. Dean Goodwin,

Department of Literature and Press Relations, New York City, for the following facts:

Dating from 1639, the First Baptist Church, Providence, Rhode Island, Baptists moved on to organize the Philadelphia Baptist Association, in 1707, the first such organization in America, including churches from Virginia to Connecticut. The Warren Association, 1767, was the second district association of churches. In 1802 the Baptist churches in Massachusetts organized a state missionary society, and in 1814 the General Missionary Convention of the Baptist Denomination in the United States for Foreign Missions was organized, in Philadelphia, with Adoniram Judson as the first missionary, and India his field. The Baptist General Tract Society was organized in Washington, D. C., 1824, later becoming the American Baptist Publication Society, 1888, Philadelphia. The Home Mission Society was organized in 1832, the Baptist Historical Society in 1853, the Woman's Foreign Mission Society in 1871, the Woman's Home Mission Society in 1877. When the Northern Baptist Convention was organized, 1907, with Governor Charles Evans Hughes as President, the work of all existing societies was coordinated. Later agencies organized were: Board of Education, 1912; Ministers and Missionaries Benefit Board, 1913; General Board of Promotion, later called Board of Missionary Cooperation, 1924, and now called Council on Finance and Promotion. In 1934 the Convention enlarged the work of its Executive Committee, and called it the General Council. Other Councils: National Council of American Baptist Men, 1922; National Council of American Baptist Women, 1951; Ministers Council, 1936; Council on Christian Social Progress, 1941. The American Baptist Assembly was established at Green Lake, Wisconsin, 1944. The work of the American Baptist Foreign Mission Society and the Woman's American Baptist Foreign Mission

Society, the American Baptist Home Mission Society and the
Woman's American Baptist Home Mission Society, were in-
tegrated in 1955. The budget of the American Baptist Convention (not including income from investments held by
the various societies) is $8,764,527. The American Baptist
Convention is affiliated with the Baptist World Alliance, the
National Council of Churches of Christ in the United States
of America, and the World Council of Churches. It was a
founding member of each of these organizations.

In addition to the information in the above paragraph,
kindly furnished by Dr. Goodwin, I must add my appreciation of the monthly ministry of *The Crusader,* the American
Baptist Newsmagazine, 152 Madison Avenue, New York City,
Dr. George Moll, Editor and Publisher. I have spread out
on my desk, as I write, the January, 1957, issue, with a won-
derfully rewarding feature article on the Triple Anniversary
in 1957—250th Anniversary of the Philadelphia Baptist Association (1707) ; 125th Anniversary of the American Baptist
Home Mission Society (1832); and the 50th Anniversary of
the Convention (1907). This feature carries pictures of Benjamin Keach, whose son, Elias Keach, organized the Penne-
pack group into a Baptist church in Pennsylvania, 1688; of
the Keithian meetinghouse in which the Philadelphia Association was organized; of the famed meetinghouses at Middle-
town, Holmdel, Stelton, Cohansey; and of such cherished
leaders as John Mason Peck, Heman Lincoln, Jonathan Going, William Colgate, W. C. Biting, Charles E. Hughes, H. L.
Morehouse and Henry C. Mabie.

Please observe that it was the decision of Adoniram Judson
to become a Baptist, in 1812, that led to the organization of
the first cooperative program of American Baptists, namely,
the Triennial Convention, 1814. Luther Rice and Judson
went out to India as missionaries under the American Board

of Commissioners for Foreign Missions of the Congregational Church, in 1812, their decision to offer themselves as missionaries, dating back to the haystack prayermeeting, having been the occasion of organizing the Congregational Board of Foreign Missions. They sailed in 1812, and on the voyage they studied their New Testaments, becoming convinced "that the immersion of a professing believer is the only Christian baptism," which prompted them to request baptism at the hands of Carey, Marshman and Ward in Calcutta, British Baptist missionaries, in September, 1812. The Congregational Board in Boston was so notified, and Luther Rice hurried home to build the fires of Baptist missionary effort, while Judson and his wife remained in India to proclaim the Gospel in that far away land. Thus the American Baptist program of world missions was born. It was an unfolding program in this instance, just as it was an unfolding program when Abram went out from Ur, under the leading of the Spirit of God; just as it was an unfolding program when Paul and Barnabas went out from Antioch, under the leading of the Spirit of God. I am not here trying to prove by inference that Abram and Paul and Barnabas were Baptists, but I am trying to emphasize the fact that the program which they followed was an unfolding program of God's leading, and I am fully convinced that our Baptist program today is an expression of voluntary response to the leading of the Holy Spirit. It is not a perfect program, due to our imperfect response, but the program is clearly outlined and commanded in the New Testament—evangelism, enlistment, stewardship, benevolence, education, fellowship, and all the other blessed expressions of discipleship. "As My Father hath sent Me, even so send I you," said Jesus. And He reminds us: "Ye are My friends, if ye do whatsoever I command you. I am the vine, ye are the branches. He that abideth in Me, and I in him, the same bringeth forth much fruit; for without Me ye can do nothing."

It is, I repeat, His program, clearly outlined and commanded, ever unfolding to those who seek sincerely to do His will. He does not force His program upon us, but He tells us what it is and asks us, as His friends, to take His yoke upon us. It is His program, His authority, His power, His purpose, His grace, His glory. It may become our program, our purpose, our joy.

Voluntariness, then, is the word at this juncture—I may, if I will, be a fellow-worker with God. No assessments, no coercion—voluntary cooperation!

Why am I a Baptist? Because of a program of voluntary discipleship. I am directly responsible to God, and He has given me the power of choice—choice of receiving Jesus Christ as my Saviour—choice of enthroning Him as Lord in my life.

How does it work—this principle of voluntariness in our program of action as Baptists? Please keep in mind the doctrine of the priesthood of the believer. Paul says that the Law was a schoolmaster, bringing him to Jesus Christ—that as long as he was under the Law, he was a slave, but when he was set free by the grace of the Lord Jesus Christ, free from the law of sin and death, he could then walk after the Spirit. As Baptists, we rejoice in the principle of cooperation as priests, equal in rank, answerable only to our Great High Priest, the head of His church. So that the individual Baptist, working in his local church, has a voice in the program of his church, his district association, his state convention, his worldwide cooperation.

Southern Baptists, from the organization of their first district association at Charleston, 1751, sought a program of cooperation by which they might effectively carry on their missionary, benevolent and educational work. State conventions followed, and, in 1845, the Southern Baptist Convention. The first two agencies of the Convention were the Foreign Mission Board and Home Mission Board, both established in 1845. Then followed the first theological seminary, Southern Baptist Theological Seminary, 1859, Greenville, S. C. The war slowed down all Baptist cooperative work, reducing many local churches to the barest existence, but as the severe period of reconstruction tapered off, Baptists in the South began their long pull toward a balanced program of missionary, benevolent and educational ministries.

When the Triennial Convention was disbanded in 1844, the missionaries on foreign fields were notified that they might make their choice between affiliation with Northern or Southern Baptists. Rev. J. L. Shuck, who had been a missionary in China for eight years under the old Board, chose service under Southern Baptists, and Rev. I. J. Roberts, who had been serving in China under a separate society, asked to be supported by Southern Baptists. When the Southern Baptist Convention met in Richmond in 1846, the Foreign Mission Board announced the appointment during the preceding year of Rev. S. C. Clopton and Rev. George Pearcy as missionaries in China, and the ensuing year Rev. Matthew T. Yates joined the staff of Southern Baptists in China. Thus China became the first foreign mission field of Southern Baptists. Adoniram Judson visited the Foreign Mission Board in Richmond in February, 1846. There is evidence in the early records of the Convention and the Foreign Mission Board that Southern Baptists were deeply interested in the work in Africa and Japan, giving support to Rev. Lott Carey in Monrovia. They were also interested in the work in Jamaica and Liberia. They actually appointed three missionaries to Japan in 1860, but the Rohrers were lost at sea and the others never sailed. The Home Mission Board carried on work with the Indians, and sought steadily to open up the great Southwest for mission work. There were many difficulties in the program of Southern Baptists in the last half of the nineteenth century—the war, anti-missionary spirit, and conflicts with our northern brethren—but there was the will to find and follow the Great Commission.

In 1888, at Baltimore, Southern Baptist women organized their Missionary Union, and this organization has been one of the really effective agencies of cooperation in community, state, home and foreign missionary work. The women now have their headquarters in Birmingham. In 1891, the Sunday School Board was organized, with Nashville as its headquarters, and this agency has become one of the power houses in developing the program which we love. The program for Baptist laymen was organized in 1907, with headquarters now in Memphis, and known as the Baptist Brotherhood. The Southwestern Theological Seminary, Fort Worth, was organized in 1908, for a number of years now the largest Baptist seminary in the world. The New Orleans Seminary was organized in 1917, and the Relief and Annuity Board, Dallas, was organized in 1918. The Southern Baptist Hospital, New Orleans, was established in 1921. The Convention authorized a radio program in 1938, now the Radio and TV Commission, with headquarters in Fort Worth. In 1950 the Convention established two new seminaries—Golden Gate, Berkeley, California, and Southeastern, Wake Forest, North Carolina. Various commissions and standing committees were established, during the first half of the twentieth century. For example, Education Commission, Christian Life Commission, Historical Commission, Baptist Foundation, Public Affairs Committee, Denominational Calendar, Baptist Papers, Christian Vocations, etc. The Committee on Public Affairs conducts its work in Washington, D. C., in cooperation with other Baptist bodies. The other Commissions and Committees have their headquarters in Nashville.

These agencies and institutions of the Southern Baptist Convention reach down through the state conventions, through voluntary processes, to the district associations and the local churches. All programs are arrived at through conference and agreement. No convention or agency or institution or commission or committee has any authority over the local church, just as the local church has no authority to enforce cooperation on the part of the individual member. It is all voluntary. Dr. J. B. Lawrence, Emeritus Secretary of the Home Mission Board, used to say: "Tell the people and trust in the Lord." That says it very well, for Baptists. Tell the people what the needs are, and give them a "Thus saith the Lord" for your plan, and they will, in most instances, cooperate. But don't try to push a Baptist! He will not be shoved around.

This unfolding program of cooperation among Southern Baptists, dating from 1845, has brought forth an impressive movement. Keep in mind that there were only 4,461 churches in the South in 1840, with 2,543 pastors, and 323,518 members. Try to think of Southern Baptists without a church or preacher or member in Texas! That was the situation in 1840, but by 1880 there were 1,910 churches, 1,111 pastors, and 107,578 members in Texas. We are grateful in Georgia when we remember that men like W. M. Tryon went out to Texas in the 40's and helped organize the Texas Convention, Baylor University and the first Baptist paper in that empire; and men like J. S. Murrow who went to the Indian Territory in the 50's and helped establish the Baptist movement in that great area.

Keep the figures of 1840 in mind and compare them with

the figures of 1955, when there were 30,337 churches in the
Southern Baptist Convention, with a membership of
8,474,741. Remembering that there was not a Baptist church
in Texas in 1840, look at the 1955 figures, when there were
3,641 churches, 1,425,930 members!

At the local church level, where you must always go to
understand how Baptists work together, it is permissible, I
trust, to outline how the average church goes about the task
of building a program of cooperation amongst the membership—a cooperation in carrying on the work of the local
church, and in cooperating with sister churches in the total
program of the denomination.

The pastor is always the key to the situation. He has no
authority to impose, but he has unlimited opportunity to
lead. We who are Baptist pastors delight to keep ever before
us as the ideal of effective leadership the words of Paul, when
he said: "We persuade men . . ." II Corinthians 5:11. The
first step I undertook when I became pastor of Druid Hills
Church was to set up the Pastor's Cabinet, composed of the
heads of all the departments of the church life—Chairman
and Vice-Chairman of the Board of Deacons, Chairman and
Vice-Chairman of the Finance Committee, Chairman of the
Trustees, Chairman of the Board of Ushers, Clerk, Treasurer,
Chairman of the Relief Committee, Superintendent of the
Sunday School, Director of the Training Union, President
of the Woman's Missionary Society, President of the Brother-
hood, Minister of Music, Chairman of the Music Committee,
Chairman of the Guest Book Committee, Chairman of the
Youth Council, Librarian, and Members of the Church Staff.
This cabinet meets monthly for dinner, with reports from
every member of his or her department, and full opportunity
for discussion, so that every person charged with leadership

responsibility is familiar with what is going on in every other phase of the church's life.

From the monthly cabinet meetings, we go into the joint meeting of the Finance Committee and Board of Deacons, where written reports are heard from every department, and a detailed report of all gifts received and how expended. The annual budget of the church is arrived at after conference and agreement, and the monthly financial reports must show how the funds allotted have been used, together with a detailed report on all gifts for missions, benevolence and education, distributable and designated. All reports are sub-mitted to the church, in writing, at the monthly church conference, having been reviewed and recommended by the Board of Deacons. The Sunday School, Training Union, Woman's Missionary Society, Brotherhood, Youth Council, and other units of the church life have their own cabinets, hold their monthly meetings, and make their reports, in writing, to the Board of Deacons, and through the Deacons, to the church. All such reports, when approved by the church, are filed with the Clerk, and his Book of Minutes and Reports is kept in the church vault.

Stemming from this idea of the Pastor's Cabinet, all plans of evangelism, enlistment, stewardship and promotion are first discussed in this small, responsible group, then sub-mitted to the larger groups for questions and suggestions, and finally, after the widest possible conference and agree-ment, submitted to the church for approval or disapproval. All the while we constantly invite any and all suggestions from any member of the church by which we may do a better job.

With such approach to the local church program, Southern Baptists go on to make their program of cooperation in the district association, the state convention, and the Southern

Baptist Convention. And the same would be true, I believe, in all other Baptist groups.

Contributing to the total picture of cooperation are many important factors that must be mentioned. For example, the denominational paper. In Georgia, we have *The Christian Index*, to which I have referred in earlier chapters. Our church has had our paper in our church budget since 1921—the church paying for the subscriptions at $1.25 per home. We follow the same plan in placing *The Commission*, of the Foreign Mission Board, and *Home Missions*, of the Home Mission Board, both monthly magazines, in the hands of our people. Also, the church participates in circulating *Home Life*, monthly magazine published by the Sunday School Board. The Woman's Missionary Society promotes the publications of Woman's Missionary Union, Auxiliary to the Southern Baptist Convention. Every state has its Baptist paper, and through the church budget plan, the circulation of these papers is nearing the two-million mark. It is impossible to fully estimate the value of the denominational paper in the life of Baptists. When Baptists are informed, they become interested. When they read, week after week, about missions and benevolence and education, they are ready to give.

Another vital factor in this cooperative program of action of Southern Baptists is the denominational college, junior and senior. Indeed, I may cite the importance of Baptist academies as rendering a very real service. In the earlier years of our Southern Baptist development, before the days of the standardized high schools, our people provided educational ministries on the level of high school training, for which we are most grateful, and from which we reaped large dividends. We still have several Baptist Bible Institutes that are rendering needed service, though the trend more and more is toward the junior and senior college, since the public high schools are now reaching into almost every area.

Southern Baptists have thirty senior colleges and universities with an enrolment in 1956 of 37,672 students, of which number 5,363 were ministerial students. We have twenty-one junior colleges with an enrolment in 1956 of 7,757, of which number 1,085 were ministerial students. We have twelve academies and Bible Institutes with an enrolment of 2,825 in 1956, of which number 440 were ministerial students. Counting the 5,428 students in the seminaries, we had a total enrolment of 53,682 students in our Southern Baptist educational institutions in 1956, and of that number, 10,782 were ministerial students. It is interesting to add that 2,544 of these students were volunteers. With few exceptions, mostly among the academies and institutes, the denomination owns and controls its colleges, just as it does its seminaries. The total endowment of these seminaries and colleges amounts to $55,081,081. Endowment and property values amount to $198,896,062. One may reasonably ask how we maintain standard institutions with such relatively small endowment. The answer is found in the annual appropriations from the Cooperative Program and designated gifts. Here again is illustrated this voluntary program which may not look on paper as dependable as large sums in conservatively invested endowment, but, in the absence of adequate endowment, it is a demonstrable fact that our people are providing a steadily increasing support for Christian education. Best of all, God's favor seems to be upon our efforts in the fact that the Holy Spirit is calling out so many fine young men for the ministry and so many fine young men and women for missionary duty. Our people are committed to the idea and ideal of owning and controlling their colleges and seminaries, thus insuring that they shall fulfill the purpose of the founders and the unchanging purposes of God.

Answering to the command of Jesus, "Heal the sick," Matthew 10:8, Southern Baptists own and control thirty-six hospitals, in fourteen states, with a bed capacity of 7,786, representing a capital investment of more than $100,000,000 (1954 figures). Our people believe that they are rendering a vital Christian ministry in these hospitals, else they would not be interested. The ministry of the chaplains in our hospitals is one of our greatest joys. A high average of free and part free service is rendered by each of these hospitals. Special offerings are received in most states on Mother's Day for the charity work of our hospitals. They also share in the annual appropriations of Cooperative Program receipts. A feature of these hospitals is their teaching ministry for nurses and doctors.

Care of orphaned children is a cause most dear to every Christian's heart, and Southern Baptists rejoice to share in this blessed ministry. There were twenty orphanages in 1954, owned and controlled by Southern Baptists, caring for 5,588 children, with capital investment of approximately $30,000,000. In addition to annual appropriations through the Cooperative Program, these homes for children receive generous special offerings, usually at Thanksgiving, and it would be impossible to estimate the amount of food and clothing which the people gladly give. In Georgia we have a plan of loading freight cars with all sorts of farm products, much of it for the dairy herd, the pigs, chickens, etc., but also ample provisions for the children in such delectable viands as home-canned fruits and vegetables, hams, and other essential items for the table. The trend toward modern cottage homes for not more than twenty-four children, where they live as a family, with their own kitchen and dining room, recreation room, living room, guest room, and matron's room, is an improvement over the earlier plan of large dormitories. Every effort is made to afford these children the finest possible Christian atmosphere in which to live and go to school and play and worship. In most homes they have outstanding orchestras, choral clubs, athletic teams and all the other expressions of wholesome life which parents try to provide for their children. An exceptionally high percentage of the children accept Christ as Saviour when they reach the age of accountability. And they go out into life as stable, Christian men and women. I do not know a deeper well spring of Christian life than the love of our Baptist people for little neighbors bereft of parental love and care.

Another expression of benevolent cooperation in the Baptist program is the Relief and Annuity Board, Dallas, Texas. Dating from 1918, this agency of Southern Baptists, through its several retirement and supplemental plans, is now serving, actually or prospectively, 36,523 pastors and their loved ones. The Board has paid out in benefits over $22,000,000 during its ministry. Present assets stand at $46,000,000.

The Sunday School Board, dating from 1891, is one of the largest agencies of the Southern Baptist Convention. This Board operates in four fields: (1) The publication of literature, books, and supplies; (2) the discovery and development of education and service programs for use in the churches; (3) the operation of Baptist Book Stores; and (4) the operation of summer assemblies at Ridgecrest, N. C., and Glorieta, N. M. Some idea of the scope of this agency may be gained from the fact that total net sales in 1955 amounted to $19,520,365. There are 1,133 persons employed in the work of the Board. There were 6,640,868 members of the Sunday Schools in the Convention in 1955, an increase of 284,379 over 1954. There were 2,223,502 members of the Baptist

Training Unions in the Convention in 1955, an increase of 160,550 over 1954. There were 681,194 Sunday School training awards in 1955, and 688,772 Training Union awards in 1955. In addition to the Sunday School and Training Union work, the Sunday School Board carries on the Departments of Baptist Student Union, Music, Church Building, Audio Visual Aids, Broadman Press, Church Library Service, Church Recreation Service, Survey and Statistics, the Book Stores, Assemblies, etc. There were 65,855,363 copies of all periodicals published by the Board in 1955. The ministry of the Sunday School Board in the fields of Bible study, training for Christian service, evangelism, stewardship, Christian citizenship, and Christian culture is a constant inspiration to Southern Baptists.

The Foreign Mission Board, dating from 1845, is now at work in thirty-eight foreign countries, with an active staff of 1,113 missionaries. The ministry of this great agency cannot be outlined in the limits of this report. It reads like a modern Book of Acts, and one may confidently say that Southern Baptists are today concerned as never before in trying to make every church a base for world missions. The ministry of the Foreign Mission Board is expressed in evangelism, education and benevolence—winning lost souls to Christ and to church membership, indoctrination, Christian education, and medical ministries. In every time of war, famine, or other pestilence, the Board channels the response of our people to refugees, prisoners, the wounded and the lonely. We pray that the day may come when every Baptist will be a missionary, in spirit. The Foreign Mission Board received $12,076,816 for its work in 1956.

The Home Mission Board, dating from 1845, is now at work in more than half the states of our country, with strong

stations in Cuba, the Canal Zone and Alaska. Its work is
carried on under the general divisions of Evangelism, Direct
Missions, Cooperative Missions, Negro Work, Jewish Work,
Missionary Education, Editorial Service, Promotion, Chap-
lains Commission, General Field Work, Church Building
Loans, and other services. In 1955 there were 1,493 full time
workers, 1,105 of them missionaries. It is impossible to fairly
estimate the reach of the ministry of the Home Mission
Board. The importance of its work grows with every passing
day. The Home Board received $3,758,281 for its work in
1956.

I cannot close this section without a word of appreciation
of the Executive Committee of the Convention, with headquarters in Nashville. Having served for more than twenty-
five years on this committee, under the Secretaryships of Drs.
Austin Crouch, Duke McCall and Porter Routh, I can say
that the present pattern of Baptist life in the South owes
more than any of us can ever express to the dedicated leadership of these three men, and Drs. McCall and Routh would
join me in saying that Dr. Austin Crouch, more than any
man, dead or living, has brought into being the Cooperative
Program—the touchstone of every forward movement among
Southern Baptists in the last four decades.

Why am I a Baptist? Because of a program—a program that
recognizes the basic Baptist principle of voluntariness. And I
thank the Lord upon every remembrance of the way we have
come and the direction in which we are now going. Truly we
may say with Samuel: "Hitherto hath the Lord helped us,"
and with the writer to the Hebrews: "From henceforth expecting . . . let us draw near with a true heart in full assurance
of faith . . . looking unto Jesus, the author and finisher of
our faith, who for the joy that was set before Him endured

the cross, despising the shame, and is set down at the right hand of the throne of God."

"Now the God of peace, that brought again from the dead our Lord Jesus Christ, that Great Shepherd of the sheep, through the blood of the everlasting convenant, make you perfect in every good work to do His will, working in you that which is well-pleasing in His sight, through Jesus Christ; to whom be glory for ever and ever. Amen."

EIGHT

WHY WE ARE BAPTISTS

WHEN I FINALLY AGREED to undertake this book, one of the first thoughts that came to my mind was to ask a few widely representative Baptists from widely representative Baptist communities throughout the earth to join me in this assignment in brief answers to the question, Why I Am a Baptist. I could wish, of course, that any one of these friends might have been asked to do the book. Grateful for their response to my request, I am listing their replies, alphabetically:

* * *

I became a Baptist because I was born in a Baptist home, reared by a Christian father and mother. I accepted Christ as my Saviour and Lord in a revival meeting in the Baptist

211

church in a western college town where my father was the Pastor. As a boy it seemed perfectly natural and normal for me to become a member of the church he loved and served so well. The faith I found in that home and that church has carried me through more than half a century, and I am increasingly grateful for the spiritual heritage that was mine. Later, I was educated in a Baptist college, trained in a Baptist seminary, and privileged to share in a Baptist world fellowship.

I am a Baptist now because of conviction. After mature thought and study, I am convinced that the Baptist concept of Christian faith and work is true to the New Testament and that Baptists have a distinctive contribution to give to Christian life and work around the world.

I expect to continue through life as a Baptist, though I have a very deep appreciation for other Christian faiths and for the great Christian souls of other denominations. I have a growing appreciation of the worth and need for the precious principles Baptists have stood for through the years, often at great sacrifice. I think of such basic beliefs as our conviction that the New Testament is our sole and sufficient basis of faith and fellowship, salvation by grace through faith, the importance of a regenerate church membership, the church as a fellowship of believers who have been baptized by immersion on profession of faith in Christ as Saviour and Lord, the competence of the individual soul before God, and the priesthood of all believers.

I am especially glad to be a Baptist because of our witness through the years for religious liberty, soul freedom, and the separation of church and state. I quite agree with Thomas Jefferson when he said, "No man shall be compelled to frequent or support any religious worship or ministry or shall otherwise suffer on account of his religious opinions or beliefs, but all men shall be free to profess and by argument to maintain their opinions in matters of religion."

I like the Baptist emphasis on the autonomy of the local church, democracy in church government, and on the other hand, the importance of cooperation with others of like faith in the world mission entrusted to us by our Lord. I am a Baptist because I believe in these principles and am happy to join with others who cherish these same convictions to proclaim and practice them. I feel that this is the best way in which I can serve the Lord Christ in my day and generation.

> THEODORE F. ADAMS
> Pastor, First Baptist Church
> Richmond, Virginia
> President, Baptist World Alliance
> 1628 Sixteenth Street, N.W.
> Washington, D. C.

*   *   *

The beginning of my life in Clay County, North Carolina, among the majestic mountains and amidst family and friends who were fervent in worship, simple in manner of life, Baptist members for generations, gave me a heritage that would necessarily influence my religious life.

When my parents moved to Atlanta, Georgia, where I was reared, I gained religious impressions from my school teachers. Each of them read the Scripture and we repeated the Lord's Prayer daily, except for my sixth grade teacher. She was a Christian, but her belief in creeds and ceremonies confused me, and she was constantly telling us that her church was misunderstood by non-members. Being of an inquisitive nature, I began to search the Scriptures to find answers to some questions that were forming in my mind.

It was my custom to spend the summer with my grandparents where I was born. My grandfather, Rev. John T. Platt, was a successful farmer, a veterinarian, and a preacher. On Saturdays and Sundays he hitched up the buggy and let me go with him to fill his appointments. He served five churches near Young Harris, Georgia, and Murphy, North Carolina. He could say with Paul, "for the preaching of the cross is to them that perish foolishness, but unto us who are saved, it is the power of God," I Cor. 1:18. He was most hospitable! He lived at a time and in a place where strangers had to be cared for since there were no hotels near. He was a good steward of all his possessions. He was truly a missionary in whose home family prayers were observed regularly with the light of faith illuminating the faces of the circle gathered there. He quoted Scriptures fluently, and could answer my endless questions with Scripture passages. He was truly an example of all he preached, which greatly affected my decisions.

Baptist churches must be New Testament churches in belief and practice. The Bible is the Word of God given to us through inspired writers and it is the final source and complete authority for us in all matters pertaining to our faith and practice. By the grace of our Lord Jesus Christ, through faith, we can be saved eternally. This precious gift inspires believers to follow Him in conduct, witness and devotion. The two ordinances of the Baptist churches as instituted by Christ, namely: baptism, the symbol of the death, burial, and resurrection of Christ; and the Lord's Supper, symbolizing the broken body and spilled blood for the atonement of our sins by Christ, have no saving power, but are done in obedience to His command. These Baptist fundamentals were instilled in me during my childhood. Reading, particularly the trials and courage of Baptists, strengthened me.

My convictions are such that I can only be a sincere member of a church with a democratic form of government that holds to the belief that every individual has equal rights with others, and is able to go to God directly through Christ who is the only recognized Head of the Baptist churches. Religious liberty, the autonomy of each Baptist church, yet the voluntary cooperation of most of these churches in associations and conventions to combine efforts for mission endeavor, Christian education and other needs challenge my best efforts to be a part of the great movement that seeks "to make known to the sons of men His mighty acts and the glorious majesty of His Kingdom." Psalms 112:12.

Mrs. John I. Alford, Sr.
President, Woman's Missionary Union
Georgia Baptist Convention
Atlanta, Georgia

*   *   *

Chief among my reasons for holding membership in a Baptist church is the freedom which I enjoy there. Each local church is a fellowship of people each of whom has responded to a personal encounter with God in Christ by accepting Him as both Saviour and Lord. This relationship through Christ is so direct and immediate that it precludes dependence upon any human institution or office as a means of entrance into the presence of God. The freedom which each individual secures through faith in Christ predicates a spiritual competence which an all-wise Creator fixed as a quality of the human soul. In turn the individual must accept responsibility for this competence by a voluntary choice, because in the ultimate sense every person stands alone before God and there makes the decision which determines his eternal destiny.

Within the Baptist fellowship one finds a company of redeemed witnesses who are confident that the revelation of God in Christ is the effective Gospel for people of faith everywhere, and that is the basis for a world mission which requires self-dedication by every Christian disciple. In sharing the Christian mission with others, I readily acknowledge the right of everyone to respond in his own way to the Gospel message.

Spiritual competence requires that all people shall be protected in the right to express their religious convictions and that every man shall be free to worship God in a manner that satisfies his understanding and need. With other Baptists I strive to guarantee this freedom to others with a zeal equal to that which I show in cherishing and guarding my right to approach God.

Within this freedom lies a sacred opportunity for everyone to study the New Testament which contains the inspired Word concerning the redemptive love which God manifested for the world through Jesus Christ his only Son. The sayings and deeds of Jesus of Nazareth fully and completely reveal God in all concepts by which the human mind can appropriate truth. Since human capacity for truth is infinitely less than God, no individual or group of individuals can comprehend the full meaning of Jesus Christ. Many doors to truth stand open. Each man under the leadership of the Holy Spirit will find Jesus as the Christ who satisfies every need. Every man starts from where he lives in his search for God, and everyone finds abundant satisfaction through faith.

Because no human institution is good enough or wise enough to be entrusted with the challenge and nurture of an eternal soul, Jesus established His Church which is the fellowship of all disciples who have dedicated themselves to the cross. In keeping with my profession as a faithful disciple, I strive to perform fully the obligations of citizenship to the State. In doing so I freely submit to the superior authority of Christ as Lord. As the individual is competent by faith in Christ, so the Church as the Body of Christ is competent in itself to meet all the requirements of its mission. The Church and the State are different in composition, in nature, and in purpose, therefore the Church and the State must remain separate.

REUBEN E. ALLEY
Editor, *The Religious Herald*
Richmond, Virginia

*   *   *

I am a Baptist because I am in harmony with these beliefs:

1.   Baptists believe in the Bible as the all-sufficient guide of faith and practice. Each individual claims the right to interpret the Bible for himself under the guidance of the Holy Spirit. He refuses to be bound by another's interpretation, either in the form of creed or confession of faith. Resolutions and statements of conventions have no authority over his conscience. He makes his appeal straight to the Bible.

2.   Baptists believe in the competency of the individual soul in its dealing with God. This belief rules out infant baptism and all forms of proxy religion. Each individual must repent and believe for himself, without the intervention of parent, priest or sacrament.

3.   Baptists believe in the autonomy of the local church. They reject ecclesiasticism in all its forms. The local church is sovereign and independent, answering to no authority except that of Christ. All denominational progress must be accomplished through voluntary cooperation. Any form of coercion is unthinkable.

4. Baptists believe in the democracy of believers within the local church. Church officers are not rulers, but servants holding office by virtue of the vote of the congregation and answerable to the whole congregation for every act. Members of the church are brethren in Christ, standing upon a plane of spiritual equality, regardless of wealth or intellectual attainment. The possession of unusual talents, whether of wealth or culture, is the sign of added responsibility for service.

5. Baptists have preserved the beautiful symbolism of baptism. Immersion in water is an acted picture of the believer's death to the old life of sin, his burial in the watery grave, his resurrection to walk in newness of life. The ceremony recalls to our minds the immersion of Jesus in the Jordan, His death, burial and resurrection. It also points the finger of prophecy to the time "when the dead in Christ shall rise and the glory of His resurrection share."

6. Baptists are the outspoken champions of religious liberty. Their belief in separation of church and state leads them to the conviction that the state should not interfere with matters of religion except to protect every man in his right to worship God according to the dictates of his conscience, or not to worship him at all. "Our fathers chained in dungeons dark" bore testimony to this faith. Now that we have come into full enjoyment of the rights for which our fathers suffered and died, we should be zealous to see that, in communities where Baptists are in the majority, these rights are enjoyed by those of different faiths.

These six statements summarize the distinctive beliefs of Baptists. It is immediately apparent that this is no attempt at a complete statement of Christian doctrine. The great fundamental truths of the Christian religion concerning God, Jesus Christ, the Holy Spirit, man, sin, salvation, etc.,

we hold in common with other Christian groups. We cherish
the bonds that unite us in Christian fellowship with all who
love our Lord Jesus Christ in sincerity. We rejoice in the
larger unity of belief with all true Christians. The only
thing here attempted is a brief summary of those beliefs which
distinguish us as a people and which constitute the bond of
doctrinal unity among Baptists.

WALTER POPE BINNS
President, William Jewell College
Liberty, Missouri

* * *

I am a Baptist because I was born in a Baptist home. My
father was a Baptist preacher. I was baptized in a pond at
the age of twelve. I was taught that Baptists were right, that
the Bible was a Baptist Book, especially since John the
Baptist baptized Jesus in Jordan. During this early period
I was never taught the basic tenets of my denomination. I
accepted in credulity that Baptists and right were synony-
mous. For years I held to this position with absolute certainty.

As I grew, I learned more about other denominations. I
came to know more about their history, doctrine and Biblical
support. My position was altered to the point of entertaining
profound respect for other denominational positions, but
never to the point of changing.

While my respect for other denominations has grown to
be profound, I have never found enough outside a Baptist
fellowship to cause me to want to swap. Why then am I still
a Baptist?

I believe in Religious Liberty. I believe that one of the
most risky acts of God was to make man free. It was dangerous, exceedingly dangerous unto death. As dangerous as it
was, God made man free. Such freedom is God-given. No

system, no government, no ruler, no power of any kind can interfere or be allowed to take away the liberty and freedom of any soul.

This leads to another closely related belief. I believe in the Priesthood of all Believers. By way of contrast, Catholics have a doctrine of sacerdotalism, which means, without the Priest there can be no church. The Priest intercedes. He is the "Go Between" man and God. Recognizing some truth in the position of sacerdotalism, also the necessity of the preacher, I believe that every man can go to God for himself.

As a Baptist, I believe the Bible is the inspired word of God. There are other inspired words of God—spoken and written by poets, philosophers, scientists, historians and even simple souls—but in a peculiar, significant sense, the Bible is the word—not *a*, but *the* word of God. I believe the Bible is the best progressive revealed word of God, with Jesus Christ the best revelation of the Eternal God.

Why am I a Baptist? I believe the New Testament as a trustworthy guide is sufficient. It claims religion in its cry for help to be a prayer; in its life after death, immortality; in its sociology, a brotherhood; in its worship, inspiration; in its insight, prophecy; in its upward reach, God; in its ordinances, baptism and the Lord's Supper; in its ethic, the good life; in its preaching, revelation, information and power.

These are found more specifically in Jesus. He is Lord, Master and Saviour. He administers to every soul. The experiences above become rock-ribbed bottom stones of reality. For them there can be no substitute.

I am Baptist because I was born in a Baptist home. I am Baptist because after growing up and learning of other denominations, I have found none better. I am Baptist because I believe in religious liberty. I am Baptist because I believe God-given freedom to every soul should not be blocked by

anything on earth. I believe the Bible in a particular sense
is God's word. I believe Jesus is the supreme revelation of
God—He thereby is the Lord, Master and Saviour. I believe
the New Testament is the final blue print for our lives.

WILLIAM HOLMES BORDERS
Pastor, Wheat Street Baptist Church
Atlanta, Georgia
President, Georgia Baptist Missionary
and Educational Convention
Atlanta, Georgia

* * *

Having become a Baptist by choice rather than by family
association, and having made the choice at the age of 26, it
means that serious and deep convictions had been formed in
me.

It began one day when I asked the mother of a great
Baptist preacher, "What is a Baptist?" I did not know. Since
my conversion three years before—which did not take place
in a church—I had avoided discussing denominations for it
generally led to argument. The silver-haired saint answered
me, "Would you really like to know?" I replied, "Certainly!"
Then she said, "Have you ever studied your New Testament
to find out what kind of church member a Christian is supposed to be?" I answered, "No, I read my Bible every day
but never thought of looking for that." She said, "Well, suppose you do." "But," I said, "do you not have books?" "Oh,
yes," she replied, "but we prefer you to get the truth this
way."

So I studied the New Testament for several weeks with
this object in mind. As I did, certain principles stood out
clearly and I adopted them.

I returned to this dear woman and reported what I had

found. She said, "Do you believe that?" I answered, "Most assuredly." "Then," she said, "you are a Baptist."

The principles I found at that time have remained with me and I hold them more firmly and understandingly today. To list these principles is to best state why I am a Baptist. There may be others added since, such as training, fellowship, privilege of service, investment of life and stewardship in the work of the Baptists but these really stem from the principles I derived from the Word of God. They are as follows:

1.   The *New Testament* is a sure guide to Christian faith and practice.

2.   The *Church* is a living body of believers indwelt and empowered by the Holy Spirit. It is not the Church because of hierarchical order, privileged priesthoods, organic disciplines and maneuvering partisans. It is a nonpolitical, nonsectarian, voluntary connection on the ground of New Testament faith and practice between believers and their Lord. It is, therefore, a creation of the Spirit and not the result of organic ambition.

3.   The *ordinances* of the Church are two—baptism and the Lord's Supper. They are ordinances in the sense of witnessing divine grace, not as a means of receiving it; that no one has a right to the ordinances who has not already received the grace of our Lord Jesus Christ, that those baptized in the New Testament were voluntarily immersed, and those who partook of the Lord's Supper were known to be steadfast in the apostles' doctrine.

4.   The *ministry* of the Church is the Lord's appointing, as its Head. The apostles were all men whom the Lord called personally.

5.   The *rule* of the Church is by lot, or vote, after its members have inquired of the Lord in prayer. This is in

contrast to ecclesiastical orders which in practice take the government of the Church out of the hands of the Lord and His people and lead the people in a carnal struggle for power.

6. In *civic* or *social matters* the Church is the conscience of God for society, demanding freedom for all men for the purpose of obeying God rather than men, knowing that whoever practices such freedom will never use it to do harm to any but will perform the highest moral duty.

7. The Church, being God's instrument for channelling His mercy to mankind, is obligated to bear the Gospel of Christ to all nations.

8. The assembled Church is the moral representative of the Kingdom of God, its ambassador, to keep before the world the eternal purpose of God in Christ.

Since I have never changed from these concepts which I obtained from the New Testament and since, in my humble judgment, the Baptists in their freedom, devotion, and sincerity most nearly approximate these positions by common, voluntary, noncreedal agreement, therefore I am a Baptist.

JOHN W. BRADBURY
Editor, *The Watchman-Examiner*
New York City

*   *   *

I am a Baptist because Baptists emphasize the spiritual over the formal in religion.

Baptists base their beliefs on the Bible. They have no other authoritative creed. They accept it as inspired of God. They conceive it the obligation of every person to "search the Scriptures" that he may know God's will and way for his life. They believe the Holy Spirit to be the Divine Interpreter of the Bible to all who will read and heed. It is our one standard of faith and practice.

Baptists believe in a triune God-head, one God manifested to man as Father, Son, and Spirit.

Baptists insist on the essential Deity of Jesus Christ, God manifest in the flesh.

Baptists accept the Bible statements concerning Man. They believe man was created in the image of God; that he was endowed with freedom of choice; that he wilfully sinned; fell under condemnation of God; and that he is utterly unable to save himself.

Baptists believe that through the vicarious atonement of Christ upon the Cross the Holy God is reconciled to sinful man who accepts that redemption.

Baptists believe that because Christ fully atoned for sin, salvation for man is all of grace and wholly apart from any worth or work of man, and wholly apart from any ecclesiastical rite. Christian service is the expression of gratitude for the salvation already given. When sinful man believes in his heart on Christ, he is "born again," becomes a new creature, and is assured of eternal security.

Baptists have what we hold to be a Scriptural conception of the church. We believe Christ founded the church upon His divine self as the "Rock" and not upon Simon Peter. The church has no saving power. It should be composed of only regenerated individuals. We believe in the equality of all members. A Baptist church is a divine democracy. We recognize no spiritual overlords. We believe in the local autonomy and independence of every Baptist church. We believe in the absolute separation of church and state. We believe it the privilege of every Baptist church to voluntarily associate itself with other Baptist churches in forming Associations and Conventions for the purpose of more effectively proclaiming the Great Commission of Christ.

Baptists accept the two ordinances given by Christ to His church as significant symbols that portray the central saving truths of Christianity. The Lord's Supper, with its broken bread and poured out wine, is a picture of Christ on the Cross. Baptism by immersion is the symbol of the burial and resurrection of Christ. These ordinances have no soul-saving efficacy. They are for believers only. To change the mode of administration of either is to destroy its significance.

Baptists believe the Bible teaches an eternal hell for all who reject Christ as Saviour and an eternal heaven for those who accept Him.

Baptists believe in the coming of the day when Christ shall return as conqueror of Satan and sin and "the kingdoms of this world are become the the kingdoms of our Lord, and of His Christ, and He shall reign for ever and ever."

Because these are Baptist tenets, I am a Baptist.

   T. F. CALLAWAY
   Past President, Georgia Baptist Convention
   Thomasville, Georgia

*　　*　　*

I became a Baptist because I was reared in an earnest Baptist home. The earliest memory I have of hearing my father's voice was as he prayed for his family. My mother taught Sunday School and was faithful to her responsibilities in the church. When I was only six years of age, I felt my need of Christ, trusted Him as my Saviour, and united with the church.

I am a Baptist now by conviction. For thirty years I have served as a minister, both in this country and as a missionary. The longer I serve, the deeper my conviction grows.

I am a Baptist because of the doctrines of grace. I fully believe that man is in a tragic lost condition as a sinner, but that salvation for any person is available by the grace of God through faith in Jesus Christ.

Doctrines of grace are believed by many people. Among Baptists they are so characteristically proclaimed, that one finds himself in an atmosphere of spiritual comradeship because of these deep convictions.

Baptists are vitally interested in all types of humanitarian service. In our labors at home and around the world millions of dollars are expended in Christian education, medical services, goodwill centers, welfare undertakings, and other types of social service. It is our deep conviction, however, that the basic needs of mankind are met only when individuals are led to repent of sin and place their trust in Jesus Christ for salvation. Transformation of the individual by personal faith is the hope for a better society and the whole world.

I am a Baptist because of the principle of soul competency. I believe that when an individual turns unto God by faith in Jesus Christ, he has direct access to the grace of Almighty God without dependence upon any intermediary, whether priest, ceremony, organization, or creed.

The distinctives of Baptist life are best understood in light of this principle. It is the reason why Baptists resist all trends toward sacramentalism and church authority. Any trend that places minister, ceremony, or organization between a believer and his Lord is from a Baptist point of view an encumbrance that ought to be removed. Only when an individual comes to a personal experience of faith in Christ is he prepared for baptism and church membership.

I am a Baptist because of the Scriptures. We believe that every Christian is under obligation to his Lord to study the Bible and know what God has commanded. We believe that churches must pattern their lives and ministries after the teachings of the Bible. We believe that the Scriptures are adequate as a standard of faith and practice. It is our conviction that God through the leadership of His Holy Spirit will enable believing hearts to grow in their understanding of the Scriptures so that there is constantly a widening horizon of Christian understanding of truth. Baptists insist upon baptism of believers by immersion because we believe it is the teaching of the Bible.

I am a Baptist because of the New Testament pattern of church life and government. A New Testament church ought to be the purest example of democracy to be found in the world. Baptists believe in the universal priesthood of believers. We believe that all who put their trust in Christ are children of God and are brethren. In churches they have equal rights and privileges. We believe in a simple, democratic organization of church government, with each New Testament church standing alone in its relationship to God, but joining in fellowship with other churches in mutual efforts to extend Christ's Kingdom through the world. We believe that no convention, council, or central authority can exert government over any local church because Christ is the Head of the church.

I am a Baptist because of the witness borne by Baptists to religious freedom. We believe no coercion should ever be placed upon any person in matters of religious faith. We desire the same freedom for others as we claim for ourselves. We believe in absolute separation of Church and State. We believe every man ought to be free to believe and practice his own faith without any interference or coercion from any source. Baptists have suffered very severely in their history to make our witness to religious freedom. We are, therefore, very cautious about any centripetal tendency in which a potential threat to religious freedom exists.

I am a Baptist because of attitudes toward others. Baptists

in no sense feel that only Baptists are children of God. It is our conviction that every sincere believer in Christ is a child of God. We regard all who put their trust in Jesus Christ as our brethren. We are united with them in love and hope. As Baptists we acknowledge our debt to our brethren of other denominations. We have received great benefits from them, and we trust others have received blessing from the convictions and efforts extended by Baptists.

I am a Baptist because of a deep conviction concerning world missions. With all my heart I believe Christians are responsible to give the Gospel to every person in the world. Convictions held by Baptists lead in clear line toward worldwide evangelization. The Gospel of Christ is a message of hope, salvation and strength for every human being regardless of circumstances, nation or race. It is imperative that we make it known wherever man is found.

> BAKER JAMES CAUTHEN
> Executive Secretary, Foreign Mission Board
> Southern Baptist Convention
> Richmond, Virginia

*   *   *

I am a Baptist by rearing and preference. At the age of ten, I publicly related my experience of grace—without benefit of prompting or questioning—to a revival congregation of a Baptist Church in North Georgia, and after baptism, was received into that fellowship. My first pastor was my father.

Baptist doctrines, though relatively unimportant to me at that age, were by no means unfamiliar, for I had been a listener, sometimes not a willing one, to discussions which centered around Baptist beliefs and practices. Our home was the meeting place of ministers of the Gospel, most of them Baptists, but often ministers of other faiths. My father's youngest brother was also a Baptist minister, and my mother's brother was a distinguished Presbyterian minister. I, therefore, at an early age, had something more than a casual interest in the fine distinctions which centered around the forms of baptism, that set apart foreknowledge from predestination and makes "falling from grace" contrapuntal to "saved once and for all." However, this early knowledge of Baptist "peculiarities" had little to do with that first decision to affiliate with a Baptist church. Loyalty and devotion to my father, pride in his high calling, and love for his flock dictated the early decision.

My preference for the Baptist Church developed as I grew older. Living in a small community where denominational zeal and rivalry were intense, I found myself compelled to defend my choice and my church. Thus I began to read books on church doctrines and comparative religions, with special emphasis on authors like Carroll and Sampey. The forty years which have passed since I first affiliated with a Baptist Church, all of which have been spent in or about a classroom, have afforded me opportunities for study of the fundamental principles, practices and doctrines of our religious bodies, and what is even more important, time for leisurely reflection.

As a teacher of history, political science and English literature, I know the pages which have been blotted with the record of cruelty, bigotry, and intolerance, all stemming from authoritarianism in religion and government. Thus my unswerving allegiance to the four freedoms in our Baptist faith: freedom from coercion of creed, freedom from the coercion of ritual, freedom from coercion of ecclesiastical authority, and above all the freedom to break through a thousand professional interpreters to see the Master Himself, to look upon His gracious and compassionate ministry and to hear Him speak His living word.

These freedoms extolled in the New Testament writings sum up what Baptists mean by the phrase "priesthood of the believer." They alone give complete and full dignity to the human being and make me a Baptist by preference.

G. B. CONNELL
President, Mercer University
Macon, Georgia

*   *   *

The obvious explanation is obedience to the testimony of Scripture. In his memorable defence before the Diet of the Empire of Worms on the 17th of April, 1521, Luther used the phrases, "My mind is taken captive by the Word of God. I can do no other." So it is with me, and it involves acceptance of believer's baptism.

True, other Christian groups would assent to Luther's position, but like Luther himself they do not accept the plain testimony of Scripture on the matter of baptism. They prefer the church's tradition (even though New Testament scholars are unanimous that baptism in New Testament times meant baptism of believers only, and that by immersion). Baptist loyalty involves acceptance of explicit New Testament teaching about baptism, and it is on that we take our stand.

The same principle applies to the question of the church. There are Christian groups that take special pride in what they call their churchmanship, and they sometimes assume that Baptists sit rather loosely to questions about the nature and function of the church. But this is quite a mistake. Baptists have very definite beliefs about the church, and the reason why these differ from those of other Christian groups is that Baptists base their conclusions entirely on the New Testament, not on the New Testament as interpreted in the light of long tradition.

An adequate exposition of Baptist views about the church would run to many hundred more words than this brief statement allows. But the following are points that can be mentioned:

1. Baptists believe that the church is a society of the converted only. Children are not made members by baptism, nor are older folk. The only people who can be members are those who definitely accept Christ for themselves and experience regeneration through His Holy Spirit.

2. Baptists believe that membership of the church involves total dedication, and that is why, like the New Testament, they baptize believers by immersion as emphasized in Romans 6:3-6, because the believer is totally united with the Lord in complete surrender to His will. "Lord," said Peter, "not my feet only, but also my hands and my head." Body, soul and spirit—all must be consecrated to Him.

3. Baptists believe that the ministry of the church is the ministry of the total community of believers. We have ministers set apart for the work of leadership, but that is a matter of expediency and good direction and it does not make ministers a class apart (a clerical caste) nor does it exempt believing men and women from their responsibility as ministers of Christ and His Word wherever they are. "Every member a missionary" was J. G. Oncken's demand in Germany, and the remarkable expansion of Baptist work on the Continent of Europe (including Russia and Rumania) is due to the devoted service of men and women of every class who daily as the Lord gives them opportunity, preach and teach the Word.

4. Baptists believe that the church is a society directly governed by Christ through His Spirit, and therefore they have always emphasized freedom—not simply their own free-

dom, but the freedom of Christ through His Spirit to guide
His people.

Baptists repudiate authorities of various kinds that restrict
the liberty of the Spirit—state control of the church for instance, and ecclesiastical control as well, exercised through
creedal formulas or fixed liturgical services or age-long practices which are regarded as binding everywhere and always
on the church of God. The Spirit is free to direct the church
as He Himself sees best, and the church that is true to its
Lord must keep itself free from all the entanglements that
would restrain its liberty of thought and action in Christ.

5. Baptists believe that all men must be free to think and
speak as they are led of the Spirit, and we must respect the
freedom of those who differ from us, even should they be
unable to accept Christ's claims. Only the freely surrendered
man can be the true servant of Christ, and we therefore refuse to compel any by force to accept a faith he does not
seriously believe.

For a world like this Baptists have a clear and consistent
message, grounded firmly in the Gospel and giving freedom
of action to Christ's believing community, and the longer I
live and think, the happier I am that I can wholeheartedly
preach the Baptist faith.

> HENRY COOK
> Associate Secretary in Europe
> Baptist World Alliance, London
> Past President, British Baptist Union

*   *   *

The reasons why I am a Baptist are so simple that I am
afraid they would seem too elementary and too obvious to
go in print.

You see, I am just a simple, plain, believing New Testament Christian. It has been my business as a preacher and teacher to try to keep in sight of the best that has been said and written from the yesterdays down through today in the field of Biblical studies and theology. When I think of the Baptists and the New Testament and my own experience and the faith into which I was born, always it is my heart that speaks, assuringly and convincingly.

I am reminded of one of Goethe's sayings, and it is this: "The highest cannot be spoken." That's the way I feel.

SOLON B. COUSINS
Department of Religion
University of Richmond
Richmond, Virginia

*   *   *

My being a Baptist had its genesis in a paternal ancestor who was a chaplain in the American army of the War of the Revolution. It was fostered by a childhood spent in a small three-church community where without compromise we attended each other's services and each in respectful firmness sought to prove his doctrines to be based on the Scriptures. In early youth the Gospel I had learned brought me to a deep sense of sin's guilt and persuaded me to a personal acceptance of Christ as Saviour. This created the experience of a new birth.

What I had learned and what its persuasion generated in me brought me assured confirmation that the Scriptures as I understood them sustained my developing beliefs. Through the passing years the study of the curricula of our Baptist culture progressively increased my conviction that our faith is of God. This faith was explored in contrast with the doctrines and history of the other Christian groups. This comparative quest measured the beliefs of others with Baptists and mine. Better than fifty years of such enquiry have increasingly confirmed the conviction that a true Baptist and I belong to be in the same church.

One who has studied the psychology of religion cannot fail to be impressed by the reaction of religious beliefs on the personality of such a believer. Presbyterians, Episcopalians, Lutherans, Methodists, Baptists, Catholics and the others are stamped by their distinctive elements of faith. These spiritual cultures create in their adherents a recognizable variation from the members of different Christian communions. This similarity to each other and dissimilarity to their neighbors is manifest in their subjective perceptions, thinking and reactions in a way that conditions their concepts and attitudes.

This, therefore, constitutes an affinity that creates the conditions that form adherence to fellowships. It generates forces that stimulate denominational devotion. These forces are fed by elements that usually overcome opposing ideas. All of us go back to the Bible and to Jesus and get some identical things. However, we carry to them some things we have derived from our heredity and environment that cause us to find in the Scriptures and in Christ something distinctively different. What we find fits us. It moves us to seek partnership with those who are possessed by similar convictions.

Baptists are dominated by the principle of voluntariness in their religious thinking. With them the area of their freedom of choice has no limitations except those imposed by the Scriptures, the spirit of Christ and the laws of their country that are not contrary to the Word of God. This characterizes the several aspects of their faith, life and service.

There are those who cannot understand how a people who are thus self-regulated can ever have any unity of spirit, faith and action. The answer lies in the fact that Baptists recognize their obligation which they have voluntarily assumed to limit themselves by the discipline of the Scriptures, the mind and spirit of Jesus Christ. Therefore, they practice co-operation with each other in the ventures to which their responsibility to Christ commits them. This has created varied diversities, but their basic thinking has developed in them an extraordinary unity and efficiency. They are paradoxical radicals who stand at attention before their Lord Christ. They would be as unchangeable as He and are ready for new ventures at His command. This attitude furnishes them a sustained sense of message and mission.

> Norman W. Cox
> Executive Secretary, Historical Commission
> Southern Baptist Convention
> Nashville, Tennessee

* * *

I am a Baptist because I believe the Baptist views on the ordinances, that immersion is essential to baptism, and that baptism is for believers only . . . and give reasons why Baptists do not practice infant baptism. The Lord's Supper is a memorial of Christ's death, it is not a means of grace, it is not a means of salvation. It symbolizes that through which salvation comes, namely, the sacrificial death of Christ.

I am a Baptist because I believe in the congregational form of government.

I am a Baptist because I believe in the Baptist principle of equality of members . . . and without orders in the ministry.

I am a Baptist because I believe in religious liberty and in the separation of Church and State.

AUSTIN CROUCH
Executive Secretary Emeritus
Executive Committee
Southern Baptist Convention
Nashville, Tennessee

*   *   *

I am a Baptist because I believe that Missionary Baptists more nearly follow the teaching and practice found in the New Testament than any other religious group. Baptists believe that the New Testament is the sole and sufficient rule of faith and practice in all matters of religion; that the Bible "surpasses all other books in wisdom and greatness, just in proportion as its Author is wiser and greater than all other authors." The Bible needs no defense; it speaks for itself. In Acts 1:16; 2 Peter 1:19-21; 2 Tim. 3:16 the Bible claims to be divinely inspired.

I am a Baptist because Baptists believe in individual responsibility to God for the performance of duty. This means that the individual is removed from all dependence on family, friends, government, and he is brought face to face with his maker. "To his own Master he standeth or falleth . . . and so then every one of us shall give an account of himself to God." Freedom to read and interpret the Bible for himself, freedom to approach God for himself. Baptists believe in the competency of the soul under God to do business with God without any human intervention, and would not, for any consideration, baptize unconscious infants or force their own children into their churches.

I am a Baptist because Baptists believe "that a church is a body of baptized believers, equal in rank and privileges,

administering its own affairs under the Headship of Christ."
Christ condemned the custom of giving one member superior
authority over others. Read Luke 22:25-26; Matt. 23:8-10.
The ranking officers are the pastor and deacons, who were
ordained, not for lordship but for leadership; not for dictation but for service. In a Baptist church all members, young
and old, rich and poor, male and female, are entitled to a
voice and a vote. The only thing that holds Baptists together
in our local churches, in our district associations, and in our
state and Southern Baptist conventions is the cementing force
of brotherly love, and an abiding interest in the kingdom of
Christ. According to Matt. 18:17; 1 Cor. 5:3-5; Acts 15:22;
2 Cor. 5:19; 2 Thess. 3:6; Gal. 1:6; Acts 1:15-26 and Acts
6:1-7, churches of the New Testament were cosmopolitan in
their makeup, and they were democratic in their delibera-
tions. It is unthinkable for anyone to read the New Testament
and to say that a church has the Scriptural right to vote members out of the church if the church has not the right to vote
them into the church.

I am a Baptist because Baptists believe that salvation is
by grace through faith, and faith alone. Baptists stand almost
alone in their belief that the two ordinances, baptism and the
Supper of our Lord, are wholly symbolic, and that they do
not confer, nor subtract grace, and are no part nor parcel of
salvation. We believe that they are church ordinances, and
must be administered by the church. Custom has made it
the duty of the pastor to administer these ordinances, and in
case the church has no pastor, it is the duty of the church to
designate someone to administer these ordinances. Both baptism and the supper are church ordinances, but in the New
Testament the Lord's Supper is more strictly a church ordinance than baptism; however, the New Testament locates

the ordinances in the church. In 1 Cor. 11:18-20 we read,
"First of all when you come together in the church I hear
that divisions exist among you; For there must be also fac-
tions among you ... When therefore ye assemble yourselves
together it is not possible to eat the Lord's Supper."

G. J. Davis
Retired Baptist Minister
Atlanta, Georgia

*   *   *

Upon making an early Christian decision, I naturally
joined the church of my parents. It happened, however, that
in my environment I soon met stiff challenges to my faith
from associates which induced first-hand study. Years of
diligent study have made me deeply aware of weaknesses in
my denomination, but convinced me that I belong where I
want to be, so I do not hesitate to give the reasons why.

I am a Baptist because I hold with Thomas Helwys,
founder of our first church in England, in giving primary
emphasis to the recognition of the individual, one's direct
responsibility to God and one's absolute soul liberty. I am a
Baptist because I agree with Roger Williams, founder of
our first church in America, in his enunciation of the doctrine of separation of church and state which along with his
democracy and full religious liberty furnishes the pattern
for the American Republic.

I am a Baptist because I believe in the unlimited Lordship
of Jesus Christ, whose explicit word is supreme over all
things in the church. Like our Walter Rauschenbusch, I believe Jesus Christ should also govern the individual and
society. Still again, I believe with our great colonial leaders
Isaac Backus and John Leland in the spirituality of the

church, composed of conscious, regenerated, baptized believers.

I believe with our John Bunyan and sufferers for freedom's sake that the Baptist democracy is both Scriptural and preferable to all other systems of church government, because it asserts that the people are sovereign and all ecclesiastical powers are conferred upon the congregation of believers.

It gives me satisfaction that my church strives earnestly to carry out the program of service inaugurated by Jesus as described in Matthew 4:23 and termed now as missions, education and benevolence, in which fields of Christian service Baptists have furnished illustrious leaders such as William Carey, Adoniram Judson, Luther Rice and the galaxy of preachers of the program like Charles Haddon Spurgeon and George W. Truett.

> JOSEPH MARTIN DAWSON
> Former Executive Secretary, Public Affairs
> Committee, Baptists of the United States
> Washington, D. C.

*   *   *

God has entrusted to us Baptists certain great and vital truths, for which we have to bear witness to the world and to our fellow Christians of other confessions. I would like to mention four such Baptist distinctives.

1. Authority of the Bible

The first of these historic Baptist convictions is our insistence upon the authority of the Bible as a trustworthy and all-sufficient rule of faith and conduct. As we study Christian history we can readily see that again and again the renewal of the church began with the question: "What say the Scriptures?" And we believe that a true renewal of the Christian church today can only come from such a return to the authority of the Bible.

From this emphasis has come our traditional Baptist reluctance to establish any creeds and impose them as coercive upon our people. Creeds have certain values as banners of the faith to proclaim to all the world the beliefs of the Christian fellowship. But wherever they are laid on men's consciences by ecclesiastical command, or by any other form of human authority, there they become instruments of coercion.

2. Regenerate Church Membership

A second great Baptist distinctive is a regenerate church membership. All through the pages of the New Testament we find that at the beginning of true discipleship stands an experience of personal conversion, personal commitment, personal confession of faith. And the church is the fellowship of people who have had this experience. It is in this basic conception of the church as a gathered fellowship of committed believers set apart from the world, that we Baptists may well be called the most consistent and radical Protestants.

3. Freedom of Conscience

The third Baptist distinctive that we must emphasize in these days is freedom of conscience, or, as Baptists have liked to call it, soul liberty. From the beginning of their history, Baptists have been champions of religious freedom.

Out of this insistence on religious liberty comes our rejection of infant baptism. We refuse to join a child to the church before he can utter his protest or give his consent. We regard infant baptism as an intolerable invasion of the sphere of man's own most sacred religious rights.

From this principle of freedom of conscience, we Baptists also derive our traditional insistence upon a free church in a free state. The marriage of church and state which has a long and tragic history in Christianity has never been a happy one, especially for the church. It has always had in itself the seed of spiritual tyranny. Whether the state tries to subordinate and use the church for its own ends, or whether the church tries to use the state as an intrument for its purposes, Baptists must resist and reject either attempt.

4. Evangelism

The fourth Baptist distinctive is Evangelism. This is, of course, the unfinished task of every Christian and every church. But it is especially vital and indispensable for us Baptists. For we do not replenish the membership of our churches through the birth-rate; we can only replenish and expand it through evangelism. Therefore, a Baptist church which does not believe in evangelism condemns itself to death.

That is why Baptists have stood in the forefront of the world-wide missionary cause. The new missionary movement really began when a handful of Baptists in England, after listening to William Carey preach his historic sermon: "Expect great things from God, attempt great things for God," founded the Baptist Foreign Mission Society and then sent Carey out as their first missionary to India.

These then are some of our basic Baptist convictions, four sturdy pillars undergirding our fellowship. The authority of the Scriptures, a regenerate church membership, freedom of conscience and evangelism. But each of them presents a challenge to every new generation of Baptists. For only as each new generation puts its sweat and toil and, if necessary, its blood and tears into the work of holding these truths aloft, will they be maintained. The world today needs the Baptist witness; may we be ready, by God's grace, to give it, un-ashamed and unafraid.

HERBERT GEZORK
President, Andover Newton Theological School
Newton Centre, Massachusetts

*   *   *

I am a Baptist because I was born to parents who were Baptists. Under their guidance and by their example, I accepted Jesus Christ as my personal Saviour and united with a Baptist church. My father and mother were both deeply religious. In the home we read the Bible and had family prayer every day. My parents encouraged all of us and insisted that all of us read and study the Bible for ourselves and that we study it with open mind, reverent heart and dedicated will.

I am a Baptist because in my study of the Bible, and particularly in my study of the New Testament, it became the conviction of my soul that the Baptists more nearly approximated the New Testament pattern of the church than any other denomination. The New Testament emphasis on the local church, its autonomy, its self-government, is the pattern for church government. It is my conviction that the local church, under the Lordship of Christ, directed by the Holy Spirit, cooperatively planning its program, making its witness for Christ, is to be followed by the followers of Jesus.

I am a Baptist because the Bible teaches me that there is a great fundamental principle which is to govern our relations as Christians in the church. We call it the principle of voluntariness which binds men and women of the same mind together to accomplish common goals. We voluntarily join the church and enter into the many aspects of its ministry at home and abroad. We voluntarily associate ourselves in the area where we live with other Baptist groups and to an association for the furtherance of the Kingdom of God in that place. We voluntarily associate ourselves with churches in a state to form a state convention which will enable us to promote together what we believe to be the chief objectives of our Lord. We follow this same principle on a southwide basis. The association, the state convention, and the Southern convention have no legislative or judicial power. All of these Baptist bodies are deliberative bodies. We cooperate together because we are of the same mind and heart in these vital matters pertaining to the Kingdom of God, and not because of coercion. We believe that a church should have the right to cooperate, or not to cooperate, as it is led by the Holy Spirit. It is my conviction that this is the New Testament pattern and that Baptists come nearer than any other group I know conforming to this pattern.

I am a Baptist because we do not look to a man as the founder of a local church, but to Jesus Christ as the founder and as our Saviour and Lord.

I am a Baptist because I believe in the competency of the individual soul before God, that all Christians are priests of God and all are on equal footing before God.

I am a Baptist because I believe in the separation of church and state. The state should not control the church and the church should not control the state. They should supplement one another. The church should give to the state its great and vital spiritual and moral principles by which good and wise government is possible. The state should recognize the moral foundation upon which it is built and should see that there is no establishment of religion by the state and therefore give all who would follow their Lord the opportunity to follow Him as they feel and are guided by the Holy Spirit.

I am a Baptist because I believe in the two ordinances of

the church: the Lord's Supper and baptism by immersion. These ordinances are symbols; they have no sacramental value, but they symbolize great spiritual and eternal truths for God's people.

HOWARD P. GIDDENS
Pastor, First Baptist Church
Athens, Georgia
President, Executive Committee
Georgia Baptist Convention
Atlanta, Georgia

*   *   *

Originally I became a Baptist because my mother took me from my earliest childhood to a Baptist church. The Baptist doctrine was the only doctrine that I knew and I did not know much of that. When I became a Christian the normal thing for me to do was to join the church which I had always attended.

Having now been a Baptist minister for more than 35 years, I still remind myself that it is exceedingly hard for any one to be completely objective in his thinking, and that many people of equal sincerity and of greater mental powers, are fully as convinced as I that the doctrines of some other church are more nearly correct.

However, having always maintained that I would willingly join another denomination if I could be convinced that that denomination more nearly followed the Scriptural teaching than did my own, and having tried to study very carefully the doctrines of all other Christian denominations, I am now a thoroughly convinced and loyal Baptist.

Many of the doctrines which we hold are cherished by other denominations. However, I believe that the sum total of Baptist beliefs is nearer to the Scriptural teachings, and I believe that Baptist churches are more like the first churches of Christendom than are any others.

I am a Baptist because I believe that the Holy Bible is our sole and adequate authority for faith and practice.

I believe that salvation is by grace through faith, and that not of works lest any man should boast. (Ephesians 2:8-9). If baptism or good works, knowledge or character, church membership or denominational approval were a part of the saving process, just that much would be taken from the efficacy of the Cross of Christ. I believe that only those who have consciously and without duress exercised faith in Christ, believing that He is the son of God and trusting Him and Him alone for salvation, have a right to be baptized into the fellowship of a church. I believe that this baptism must be a burial in water. (Romans 6:3-11).

I believe that every soul is competent to find and to fulfill the will of God, by going directly to God in prayer, having made a careful study of God's word, and this without needing the direction of any other human being.

I believe that a local church, made up of such competent and consecrated baptized believers, is capable of administering its own affairs and of demonstrating and presenting the Gospel to all who are in reach of it.

I believe that our Baptist plan by which local churches associate themselves with other like churches for fellowship and the propagation of the Gospel, has proved itself in that Baptist churches are bound together in bonds of fellowship and in mission enterprises as closely as the churches of other denominations, and our mission program stands well by comparison with those of centralized denominational authority.

I am a Baptist because Baptists have always stood for absolute separation of church and state. We believe that the tithes and offerings of any local congregation are sufficient to carry on the work of that congregation and to help to send the Gospel to all the earth, without regulation or assistance from any civil authority.

I am a Baptist because true Baptists are just as anxious that others have the rights and privileges of free worship as that they shall have these rights themselves.

DICK H. HALL, JR.
Pastor, First Baptist Church
Decatur, Georgia

* * *

Like the watermark in a good grade of paper the word freedom is impressed on our Baptist life and practice. An evidence of quality, an assurance of substantiality, it is our most distinctive characteristic. It cannot be eradicated without destroying the fabric itself. Our denomination has put to work the concept of freedom in four areas.

First, there is the church. Membership is a matter of free choice. A person joins by the free exercise of his will—that is, when he receives Jesus Christ as Saviour and Lord. No one is born into the Baptist church.

Too, the churches themselves are free, each one a unit by itself. All local churches are related to other similar bodies only on a voluntary basis. No ruling of any association or convention is binding upon a local church unless the members of that congregation make it so.

A second area in which Baptists apply their principle of freedom is in relation to the state. Religion and government are obviously very closely associated in the lives of men. If there are no boundaries between the church and the state and the loyalties due each one, these two great supports of society may well set themselves against each other in a struggle for supremacy. Baptists were among the earliest pioneers in leading Protestantism to belief in the complete separation of church and state. We do say, however, that Christian ethics and morality should and must lie at the very foundation of the state. But we also believe that no one denomination's expression of religion should have preferential position over any other.

Another place where our Baptist principle has been applied is with reference to the Bible. This we believe to be the word of God. It is the handbook of faith, the guide to conduct, the authority in religion and morals. The Bible belongs to all Christians, to no one group more than to another. But it is apparent that this Book needs careful interpretation.

Down across the years it has been interpreted in three ways —by church direction, by creedal agreements, by individual decision. Baptists have largely followed the third pattern. That is, they have insisted that every individual is competent, under the guidance of the Holy Spirit, to read his Bible and interpret it in the light of his background and in the face of his needs. This does not, of course, throw out all the help and assistance that can be secured from the stored-up wisdom and scholarship of the past and present. But in the final analysis, the individual church member has a right to decide for himself what God is saying to him through the Bible.

And finally our Baptist principle applies in our relationship to God. No man, nor church, nor priest, nor parent, nor teacher (institution or individual), can stand between a human being and his God. Many may give us guidance, encouragement, and help, but no one may stand between us and the Divine object of our worship. The individual soul is competent to do business directly with the eternal God.

This is our Baptist watermark. It is this principle of freedom, which undergirds and pervades our Baptist polity and

practice. Rightly understood and properly used, it insures
a blessing.

V. CARNEY HARGROVES
Pastor, Second Baptist Church of Germantown
Philadelphia, Pennsylvania
Past President, American Baptist Convention

* * *

I am a Baptist because I was nurtured by dedicated Baptist
parents in our faith. But there are aspects of that faith and
loyalty which give me much satisfaction. This feeling of pride
is compatible with a higher loyalty to the Christian Gospel
which transcends all denominational lives. While our most
important Baptist principles are now embraced by some
other religious communities we are historically distinguished
for a pioneering service. Our emphasis upon liberty, our
insistence upon congregational government, our exaltation
of democracy, our appreciation of sovereignty of the individual, and our growing sense of responsibility for projecting
the ideal of love into all human relations—these are the elements in our Baptist policy and tradition that appeal to me.

Our denominational program is *of, by, and for* the people.
We may forget it momentarily, but, basically, our whole
concern is for *people,* not budgets or buildings or statistics,
and I like that quality in Baptist life. And the same exhorta-
tions for individual self-examination and critical judgment
are directed often enough to the denominational policy-
makers to strengthen my confidence that we will not succumb
to errors that inevitably affect all popular government, ecclesiastical as well as political.

I take pride in the world-mindedness of our Baptist people.
Our mission program is not window dressing, it is a serious
commitment, and I could not be happy in any society which

renounced it. I think my father's profound religious convictions had a lot to do with the example he set for me as a lawyer. My first lessons in the science of government were from him and I do not think he would have been quite as effective in imparting some of the essentials had he not seen the relationship between the church and our assumption of moral responsibility as members of the legal profession. My mother also had a part in interpreting our Baptist beliefs and practices.

BROOKS HAYS
U. S. Congressman, Fifth District, Arkansas
House of Representatives
Washington, D. C.

* * *

I cannot claim, as some do, that I am a Baptist entirely by choice. My father, who died when I was only two and one-half years old, was of another persuasion. Subsequently, since my mother was a Baptist, I attended a Baptist church from early childhood. I was reared in its atmosphere and under its teachings.

However, *I am a Baptist by conviction*. Had I been reared under other circumstances but had had occasion to study Baptist beliefs in comparison with others, with an unbiased mind, I am certain that I would have been a Baptist *by choice*.

Why am I a Baptist? Because Baptists have no creed but the New Testament. While we accept the Old Testament as the inspired word of God, we regard the New Testament as the fulfillment of the Old.

Resultant is the belief in the essential worth and dignity of the individual before God. Under the guidance of the Holy Spirit he may interpret the Scriptures for himself. Every believer is a priest before God. As such he may come to the throne of grace boldly, there to present his confession and to receive forgiveness for his sins. Without benefit of ordinance or institution, through the one Mediator, Jesus Christ, he is a child of God, not by his works of righteousness, but by the merit of the atoning death and resurrection of the Son of God. Since his redemption in its beginning depends not upon what he does but upon what Another has done for him, so in its endurance his salvation resides in the constancy of God rather than in the inconstancy of man. The Holy Spirit seals us unto eternal life, and by His abiding presence develops us in grace, knowledge, and usefulness in the service of the Lord.

Furthermore, from the New Testament Baptists derive their conception of ecclesiology. Under the absolute Lordship of Christ every church is a unit unto itself with no organic connection with or authority from or over any other body. Baptists are an independent people who express their independence through voluntary cooperation. They have ever been the primary exponents of the absolute separation of church and state and of freedom in religion. Repudiating all excursions into the Old Testament for the significance attached to the ordinances and other institutions of the Christian faith, Baptists adhere to the symbolisms and administrations which are peculiar to the New Testament alone. While to them the redemptive work of Christ is the final covenant of which others were but shadows, the Christian fellowship and practice within the churches are unique and apart— definitely Christian without derivation from the rites and institutions of the Old Testament.

Finally, growing out of their insistence upon the New Testament as the one rule of faith and practice, Baptists are not extremists or literalists in that regard. Without the narrowness of a binding creed, yet they are remarkably united in those elements of faith growing out of the message of the New Testament. Few Baptists ride a hobby. They are slaves neither to tradition nor to that which is new. Gauging everything by the teachings of the New Testament they are a steadying force in the field of theology. Granting to every man the right to believe as his heart dictates, they, in love but with strong conviction, demand the same right for themselves. Following no man blindly, they seek always to find the will of the Lord.

In such attitude they accept gladly the Commission of Christ to make disciples of all nations. Daily expecting the return of their Lord, Baptists, in the large, place their emphasis upon the present task committed to His disciples. To them the field is the world, the harvest is ripe, and their Lord has thrust them forth into the harvest field. In their task of evangelism they seek not only to win the souls of men but to develop and enlist their minds and bodies as well. To them the cause of Christ has its here-and-now social aspect as well as its then-and-there spiritual culmination.

As a Baptist, therefore, I seek to blend my life with all those of like faith and order, and, insofar as I can do within my convictions, with all other of those who love the Lord, to proclaim Christ as the one hope for all the world, that the Kingdom of God may come in the hearts of men.

HERSCHEL H. HOBBS
Pastor, First Baptist Church
Oklahoma City, Oklahoma

* * *

I am a Baptist because Baptists believe completely the New Testament account that Jesus Christ is the son of God who came to give eternal life to all who will accept Him as Saviour.

We accept the New Testament as the only authority of

faith and practice. The teachings of Jesus Christ are our guide. Man can neither add to nor take from those New Testament teachings.

Baptists know that "whosoever believeth" (John 3:16) in Christ has salvation. We seek to follow Him in all ways. Convenience has not led us to substitute sprinkling for immersion. Neither has false teaching caused us to transform the memorial of the Lord's Supper into a sacrament.

I love the Baptist emphasis upon the worth of the individual, just as in Jesus' day. Jesus stepped across racial and religious barriers so that all might come before Him. Just so, Baptists seek for Him the soul in the bowery with as much eagerness as they do the one on Fifth Avenue.

I love the responsibility that Baptists give to the individual. Each prays directly to God and is accountable to Him. Each person is his own priest and Jesus Christ is the one and only intermediary. Anything different is contrary to the New Testament. In the words of the Apostle Paul, "There is one God, and one mediator between God and men, the man Jesus Christ" (I Tim. 2:5).

Baptists know they have the Truth. Yet, any thought of forcing it on another is repugnant to their love of freedom. Baptists hate tyranny whether it be in the political or religious realm. They demand the same rights for others that they claim for themselves. That is the example of Jesus who could have knocked down every earthly restriction to His ministry.

I love the simplicity of Baptist worship. Chant and ritual would, for me, curb the communion with God which comes in a Baptist service. This democracy in worship emphasizes the individual responsibility to God for all who have reached the age of accountability.

I am a Baptist, too, because love for Christ demands expression. I find that expression by joining hands with other Baptists to carry out His commission that we go "into all the world, and preach the gospel to every creature" (Mark 16:15). All else is secondary in the Baptist program.

We believe that soul-winning is as much the business of the pew as it is of the pulpit. Each Christian should be a witness to others. Too, our Baptist organizations permit cooperative endeavor in missions, Christian education and benevolence far more effective than would be possible under enterprise.

I am a Baptist because I believe Jesus Christ would have me be a Baptist. As a Baptist, He is my one example.

JOHN JETER HURT, JR.
Editor, *The Christian Index*
Atlanta, Georgia

* * *

As a Christian, I have respect for the religious views of other believers who have not been reared or nurtured in the denominational tradition in which I have spent all my religious life. I have the greatest appreciation for the high values of other religions and other denominations; but when I speak of personal religious experience, I must refer to my reaction to the teachings, doctrines and values that have come through the Baptist denomination.

Why I was born into the family of a Baptist preacher, and reared by a Baptist mother, and why Providence so ordained that I should be converted and baptized into a Baptist church, I know not, and hence have no answer. But having studied the doctrines of the Baptist church, I have arrived at some reasons why I am a Baptist.

I am a Baptist because I believe profoundly in freedom: the freedom of the individual, the freedom of conscience, and the freedom of men in a democratic society.

I appreciate the fact that every individual has access to God. Each person, however weak or depraved, can go directly to God in prayer, and be heard and accepted. This not only implies the worth of the individual in the sight of God, but it is a testimony to the sacredness of every human personality.

I am a Baptist because I believe in the way of salvation as provided through the redemptive act of Jesus Christ. The coming of Christ into the world is not only a revelation of the nature of God, but is a concrete demonstration of God's love and concern for mankind. This doctrine of redemption is the only constructive answer to the sinful nature of God's human creatures.

I am a Baptist because I believe in the ultimate victory of justice, goodness, truth and righteousness. The explicit doctrine of immortality as set forth in the Baptist church, is in harmony with the idea of spiritual victory over all the other forces in the universe. This faith keeps one moving forward through the dark shadows of the great unknown, and gives one courage to walk with hope through the darkness, ever looking for the dawn of eternal things.

> J. H. JACKSON
> Pastor, Mt. Olivet Baptist Church
> Chicago, Illinois
> President, National Baptist Convention,
> U.S.A., Inc.
> Chicago, Illinois

*   *   *

Baptists are a peculiar people, but their peculiarities are not what some may think they are. Paul wrote to Titus and said, "Christ gave Himself for us that He might redeem us from all iniquity and purify Himself a peculiar people, zealous of good works." Some Baptists have misread it and think he said, "A peculiar people, jealous of the good works of others."

I am not a Baptist because I think they are the only Christian group in the world. Beyond a doubt, many others belong to Christ. Baptists are not the only Christian group; but they are a Christian group, and I could wish every Christian were a Baptist. They are not the only people doing good in the world, but they are doing good. They do not stand alone in soul winning, but they do win souls for Christ. They are not the sole possessors of power in prayer, but they do rejoice in prayers answered.

Baptists do not stand alone in holding to convictions; but they do have convictions, and most of them believe they are based on the Scriptures. They are not a perfect people. Their efforts are not errorless. Their personnel is not perfect. Their projects are not all practical. They are not the most missionary-minded, nor are they the most faithful givers. Therefore, I am not a Baptist because I think they have a monopoly on God. Then why am I a member of this group?

My parents were Baptists, but when I joined this church I did so with the understanding that I would change churches if in my Bible study I found them to be wrong and some other group more nearly right in their interpretation of the Scriptures. For 35 years I have studied with this in view, and I have never yet found any other Christian group conforming to the whole New Testament pattern. On the other hand, I have never found a single principle in the belief, practice, or policy of Baptists that does not seem to be in accord with what Christ and His apostles taught. Regardless of all other considerations for or against any Christian group, to me this must be the determining factor as to the church to which I must belong.

This is why I became and remain a Baptist. However, there

are certain other factors that keep me happy in this church. I am happy that from all available historical information this Baptist people seems to be more able than any other group to trace its origin to the first church which Christ established. I am happy that they have always stood firm for the cardinal doctrines of the new birth, salvation by grace alone, immersion only for baptism, security of believers, and democracy in church government.

History says that Baptists in Colonial America refused to be the state church in at least one colony, and that they refused to allow any other group to be such. They have always been more responsible than others for the separation of church and state. Yet they have always supported both with men and money.

As a Baptist I am happy that according to the records Baptists have made the most astounding growth of any religious body in the lands of democratic freedom. They have never prospered in countries controlled by dictators and monarchs. They believe in freedom, and freedom is absolutely essential to their well-being as a denomination. They do not hesitate to oppose a national evil, and most of them will put principle above their politics in support of the right. It is good to be a Baptist where in the light of the Scriptures one may decide for himself what is Christian and what is not.

E. S. JAMES
Editor, *The Baptist Standard*
Dallas, Texas

* * *

To begin the discussion of this important subject, one must be perfectly honest and say that it stems from the fact that my father and mother were Baptists, though my mother did not become a Baptist until I was a good-sized lad. This influence cannot be ignored, but if one must depend upon that for his reason for being a Baptist, then he may find himself drifting and being tossed about with every wind of doctrine.

So, I must find some reasons of my own as to why I am a Baptist. In the first place, I accept the Bible as the Word of God, and its teachings as our rule of faith and practice. This is very important in the life of a Baptist who has no priest, bishop, or authoritative church to interpret the Bible for him. So, I believe that the inspired word of God is the source of the ultimate conviction we have on such questions as this.

In the second place, from this book, our source book, for all matters of theology and religion, I find that Baptists believe in the dignity of the individual. This is of great importance. There are others who believe this, but Baptists have always felt that every individual stands before God equal. As someone has said, "The ground before the Cross is level." Believing in this conviction, I have found that anyone, to become a Baptist, must be old enough to receive and believe the message of Scripture. It is at that point that I have been drawn away from many other Christian people.

I want to be a Baptist because of the right of the individual to choose Christ as his Saviour.

In the third place, I am a Baptist because the teaching of the Scripture is clear on the necessity of the immersion of the body of a believer in water as a symbol of personal renunciation of sin, and the acceptance of Christ's death on the Cross as our Saviour and Lord. Being thus willing to be buried with Christ, I also purpose to live for Him and with Him.

In the next place, I am a Baptist because I believe in the democratic procedure of the activities of the church. I could not and cannot accept that any individual or group of individuals have any authority over the soul of another individual.

I am convinced that every man or woman and child, old enough to receive Christ, must be free to express himself, his conviction, his belief, and his desires. For that I thank God and rejoice that in the Baptist fellowship of a Baptist church, I find this freedom and this right of self-expression.

In the last place, I am a Baptist because I find in that fellowship a wholesomeness and an urgency in evangelism akin to the church when it began in Jerusalem, and I am frank to say that more than any other group of believers I know, I feel that Baptists are most like the early church as we have its record in the Acts of the Holy Spirit recorded in the Book, usually referred to as Acts of the Apostles.

For these main reasons, I am happy to call myself a Baptist, and I have a particular fellowship with those who share these simple beliefs with me. As a Baptist I recognize every believer in the Lord Jesus Christ as his personal Saviour as a fellow Christian. But in carrying out the implications and teachings of the Gospel, I can do that happily and freely only through my Baptist relationship.

> C. Oscar Johnson
> Pastor, Third Baptist Church
> St. Louis, Missouri
> Past President
> American Baptist Convention
> Past President
> Baptist World Alliance

*   *   *

This writer joined a Baptist church when he was a boy fourteen years old because he had just become a Christian and believed that one should belong to a church. His choice of a church was made with little difficulty because there was no other church in the community, and he had never attended any other! But that is not the only reason for his being a Baptist now; it was only the beginning of a process of development in Christian experience, a process which is still continuing.

After more than forty years of church membership and thirty-two years as a minister, he would call himself a Baptist by conviction and not merely a member of a Baptist church. These years of study (mostly in Baptist schools), preaching, teaching, writing, and mingling with people have tended to clarify his convictions as to what constitutes the true principles of the Christian faith and of the church. He, therefore, believes that the position which Baptists generally take is consistently Scriptural and sound and that it includes the principles which he regards as essential. He mentions five of these principles in simple declaration, using the first personal pronoun, singular.

I believe that every person has a right to be free to choose his own religion, and I believe every person is responsible for his own choice and his approach to God.

I believe that the Bible is the sole and sufficient authority for all Christian belief and practice. Furthermore, I believe that every person has the right to read and interpret the Bible for himself, and that no person should be bound by any man-made or ecclesiastical creeds, but that all opinions should be respected as such.

I believe that every local church should be composed of Christian people who have voluntarily united with the church upon their own personal profession of faith in Jesus Christ and have been baptized (immersed) as a symbol of their religious experience and the basic teachings of the Christian faith. I believe also that every local church should be free to govern its own affairs without any ecclesiastical authority over it.

I believe that every church should be on an equal basis with all others in relationship to the state and that state and church should be kept separate. In no case would I approve the support of any church or church-controlled agency or service by government funds.

I believe that Jesus Christ commissioned His followers to go into all the world and preach, teach, and serve the needy people according to His command and that the Holy Spirit guides, teaches, and empowers them in doing so. I believe also that carrying out that commission requires cooperation among the churches on some such plan as that used by the Southern Baptist Convention.

For these and other reasons, I am a Baptist, of the kind more definitely known as those who belong to the Southern Baptist Convention churches. By conviction, and with as little prejudice as possible, I am glad to be a Baptist.

S. H. JONES
Editor, *The Baptist Courier*
Greenville, South Carolina

* * *

I thank God that I am a Baptist. However, I do not consider the Baptists as the only Christians among other denominations. We are living in an age of ecumenism, therefore our eyes should be open upon everything that is good in other churches of the world. One should remember that Methodism has saved England from the spiritual death. Moody and Torrey, Congregationalists, were used by God for a great revival in America. Pastors Eugene Borsier and Adolf Mono, of the Reformed Church, preached the Gospel with much blessing in France, while Lord Radstock, a darbist of England, was the apostle of revival among the rich and poor of Russia.

Why then being a Baptist do I consider myself a happy man? Why did I choose to be a member of the Baptist church?

My first reason. Because the teaching of Baptists is the closest to the Gospel of Christ. I have before me the Baptist church's doctrine. I meditate upon each part of it. How truly they are based upon the Holy Scripture! Here is the Person of God—the Scriptures—the man's nature—his salvation—the church—baptism—the second coming of Christ—the Lord's Supper—the last judgment—everything is a complete harmony with the Gospel. Indeed, in this regard the Baptist faith is the last word of the Reformation. Martin Luther, J. Calvin, H. Zwingli performed a great task. They gave the people the Bible and stressed the great teaching of the justification by faith alone, in the redeeming sacrifice of our Lord Jesus Christ on Calvary's Cross. However, they did not bring the Reformation to the very end. The baptism of infants was left untouched. Only Baptists solved this vital question according to the teaching of the Gospel and thus brought the work of Reformation to an end.

Second reason. The order and life of the Baptist churches reminds me of the Apostolic church. The same simplicity of the services, absence of the pomp and rituals. The Holy Scripture is the only foundation of the faith. Pastor-presbyter is deriving the same grace from God for his ministry to his people, he is the first one among equal ones. This simplicity and mobility, lost from the days of Constantine the Great, has been restored in the Baptist churches, helping them greatly in the blessed and successful Gospel work for the Kingdom of God. The world Christianity has departed too far from the simplicity of faith and service of the Apostolic church. The task of the Baptists should be to call them back to the ideals of the first centuries' Christianity.

My third reason. In the Baptist churches nothing separates me from Christ. On the contrary, everything in the sermons, songs, prayers is drawing me nearer to Him. Christ is in the center of the Baptist churches. This pleases me indeed! There are no cults in them but one—that of Jesus Christ. In the Baptist churches He is Alpha and Omega, beginning and end. He is the center. The faith and order of Baptists resolve around Him.

Fourth reason. The priesthood of believers is precious unto me. A great peril lies in the division of the church into two groups: the priesthood and common people. This happily does not exist in the Baptist churches. "Each Baptist a missionary!" said J. Oncken of Germany. However, we can say that he also is a shepherd of the sheep intrusted with by God. This conviction, preserved in the Baptist churches, of the spiritual priesthood of the believers made of Baptists an aggressive spiritual army. Each Baptist—a soldier!

My fifth reason. I am glad that I am a Baptist because in the Baptist churches especially the spirit of witness about Christ is so vividly alive. The spirit of witness is a true sign of a church which is alive. Where this spirit lives, many are being added by the Lord to the church. In no other denomination do I see this passion to help souls to get saved, to bring them to Christ, as in the Baptist churches. The spirit of testimony is a great treasure that has been lost by many a Christian. It should be carefully guarded if it is not lost yet. No great evangelistic campaigns can take place without the spirit of witness living in the church—living in each member.

The final, sixth reason. I am a Baptist because only the Baptists hold the true doctrine about the baptism of the believers by immersion, as the expression of a conscious promise unto the Lord to live for Him and serve Him. This satisfies my heart. My whole being protests in me against the teachings of the Pedo-Baptists about the regeneration through baptism. There is no indication in the Scriptures about the baptism of the infants that are unable for themselves to give a promise to God. I am glad that Baptists are holding the banner high of baptism of believers that are able to confess their faith in their Saviour. This is the only baptism based upon the Holy Scripture.

> ALEXANDER KAREV
> General Secretary of the Baptist Union
> in USSR, Moscow

*   *   *

I became a Baptist because my family was Baptist. My grandfather, W. L. Kilpatrick, was a Baptist minister and his brother, J. L. Kilpatrick, was also a Baptist preacher. My great-grandfather Kilpatrick was a Baptist minister. My father, R. Addison Lansdell, was reared a Methodist but felt called of God to become a Baptist and a Baptist minister. I grew up in Baptist churches and had little acquaintance with other groups. Perhaps it is also true that I would not have remained a Baptist if I myself had not found the Baptist way congenial to my interests and convictions. I am enough of an individualist to like the Baptist way and I believe in democratic procedures. Also I like the simplicity and dignity I have found in the worship services of Baptist churches.

> MISS EMILY LANSDELL
> President
> Carver School of Missions and Social Work
> Southern Baptist Convention
> Louisville, Kentucky

*   *   *

My people have been Baptists for generations. However, I am a convinced Baptist through a half-century of Bible study and church experience. Baptist doctrine and polity may be illustrated by the hand which unifies and coordinates the five fingers. Individual responsibility to God is like the hand, from which stem five great Baptist principles.

The thumb of the hand is belief in the Bible as the only Baptist creed, and the inalienable right of the individual to read and interpret it as the Holy Spirit of God leads his conscience. For this I like the Baptist way. An enlightened Baptist conscience is superior in authority to any ecclesiastical council or *ex cathedra* edict from a church potentate. My individual liberty to interpret the Bible and my open mind lead me to contend for believer's baptism only and for immersion. I can find only the symbolic meaning of the Lord's Supper, no saving or sustaining grace. All other doctrines must be tested by the individual conscience and the teaching of the Word of God.

The forefinger upon the hand of individual responsibility is religious liberty. Liberty has been the foremost word in Baptist history. They have been the first propounders of absolute, equal and absolute freedom of the individual soul to worship as his conscience is led of the Spirit of God. Baptists demand this liberty for those who differ as well as for themselves. Religious liberty demands separation of church and state. It demands that no church ordinance be imposed upon a child until he is old enough to accept it voluntarily or to refuse it. If Congress should compel everyone to become a Baptist, and use the U. S. Army to enforce the law, Baptists would be the first to go to war against that armed power. I surely would.

Third, my profound belief in the competency of the individual soul to approach God without human or ecclesiastical mediation makes me a Baptist. To me, a human priest is an impertinence. Saving grace in baptism and sustaining grace in the Lord's Supper are unthinkable. Saving grace must be reserved for Christ, the Saviour. Proxy religion is swept away. Scriptural salvation must be found always through the individual's sincere repentance for sin and trusting faith in Christ.

The fourth finger on the Baptist hand of individual responsibility is the equality of all believers. Absolute equality and equal authority of believers along with lack of gradations in the ministry all appeal to me as being both Biblical and Christian. Christ alone is Lord; we are brethren. Any humble pastor can greet the President of the Baptist World Alliance as "Brother," and both will like it.

Lastly, I like the democracy, autonomy and independence of a local Baptist church, free in doctrine, polity, worship and practice, free from outside overlordship from a pope, bishop, synod, council or convention.

The Baptist hand with its five principles, exalting the worth of an individual, holds me within its friendly clasp.

ROLAND Q. LEAVELL
President
New Orleans Baptist Theological Seminary
Southern Baptist Convention
New Orleans, Louisiana

*   *   *

Originally, I presume that I am a Baptist by heredity! I was born into a Baptist home. My father was for 44 years a Baptist minister. Until I entered college I seldom attended any church other than that of my father. My religious education was acquired in a Baptist Sunday School. Thus, during the early formative years of my life, I was surrounded by

Baptist influences and became familiar with Baptist beliefs and practices.

My remaining a Baptist for the rest of my life is due to other factors. One was education. During five years at Yale University, including one year in graduate study in comparative religion, and through regular attendance at Yale University's Battell Chapel, I became acquainted with members of other churches, listened to other preachers, attended other than Baptist communion services, and thereby acquired an understanding of the beliefs, dogmas, principles, and practices of other churches. During this educational process I became aware of no convincing reason for leaving the Baptist denomination. Following my graduation from the Colgate Rochester Divinity School in 1913, and for the next 40 years, until my retirement in 1953, I was employed in journalistic and editorial service at Baptist National Headquarters. Thus I remained a Baptist.

Here entered the third factor in my remaining a Baptist. It was *conviction*. My editorial responsibilities brought me official connections with boards and committees of other churches, with the National Council of Churches, and with the World Council of Churches. Through these contacts I developed within myself an intelligent ecumenical-mindedness that distinguishes between unachievable organic church union and the imperative necessity of cooperative church unity in a world so disastrously torn asunder by class, race, color, politics, and ideologies.

In the basic Christian doctrines, concerning God, Jesus Christ, sin, salvation, I do not find myself as a Baptist far apart from Methodists, Presbyterians, Congregationalists, Lutherans, and the rest. I can worship God, receive blessing, experience spiritual satisfaction, obtain moral guidance, and express my allegiance to Jesus Christ in any of these churches.

In one realm, however, the Baptists are different. This is the realm of freedom. As understood and proclaimed by a Baptist, religion is a free, personal relationship between the human soul and God. Into this realm nothing may intrude— no church, no hierarchy, no governmental decree, no established creed, no sacrament, no preacher, no priest. The mercy of God and the grace of Christ are freely available to all. No mediation by any person, priest or preacher, or by any ritual or ceremony is required. This freedom applies also to dogma and organization. Liberty of conscience, no creedal bondage, freedom of doctrinal interpretation, local church independence—these constitute Baptist ecclesiastical democracy as compared with hierarchical totalitarianism and church authoritarianism. Such freedom a Baptist insists on not only for himself but grants to and demands for all others. Throughout their history Baptists have contended for full religious liberty for all, whether Protestants, Catholics, Jews, pagans, infidels, so long as in the profession of their own faiths and practices they do not interfere with the rights and privileges of others.

That principle of religious freedom I would not surrender for any consideration. To that I give my unqualified assent and enthusiastic support. And that is why I remain a Baptist.

WILLIAM B. LIPPHARD
Former Editor, *Missions*
American Baptist Convention
Executive Secretary,
The Associated Church Press

* * *

I was not born into a Baptist home. My parents and their children became members of a Baptist church on conviction, and the central point in that conviction concerned the nature of the church. I would emphasize this because the view is sometimes erroneously expressed that Baptists have created a special form of churchmanship because of an eccentricity. But so far from its being an eccentricity the central principle in Baptist conviction is fundamental to our understanding of the church as the New Testament presents it.

Who is the Head of the church? The New Testament answers not any man, however noble or exalted, but Jesus the Lord, as Paul wrote in Ephesians 5:23. Who are the members of the church? The New Testament answers clearly: those who repent of their sins and confess their faith in Christ by baptism.

We believe that in New Testament times baptism was the baptism of believers by immersion. Historically Baptists have emphasized the meaning and value of baptism by immersion on the ground that, in addition to its being an obedience to the command of Christ, it safeguards the following principles: (1) The right of every human soul to immediate access to God. This great Reformation principle focusses attention not on priests or any other human intermediary, but on our Lord Himself as the true and living way. (2) The individuality and necessity of conversion. No other person can make up our minds for us or make our own response to God through Jesus Christ. (3) The true nature of the church as composed of converted people who accept Jesus as their Saviour. In our view baptism practiced on the New Testament pattern and restricted to those who can make a personal decision safeguards those essential principles as the baptism of infants can never do. It emphasises the spiritual and moral nature of the ordinance, excluding anything in the nature of baptismal regeneration or magical power. The whole symbolism of baptism is that of union with Christ in His saving and risen power. The corollary of our Baptist emphasis on personal and individual dedication to Christ and obedience to Him is the emphasis on liberty, both in Church and in State, which has always been a conspicuous feature of Baptist witness.

Dr. E. Y. Mullins summarized our Baptist position in words which Baptists all over the world would accept. He wrote:

The Biblical significance of the Baptists is the right of private interpretation of and obedience to the Scriptures. The significance of the Baptists in relation to the individual is soul freedom. The ecclesiastical significance of the Baptists is a regenerated church-membership and the equality and priesthood of believers. The political significance of the Baptists is the separation of church and state. But as comprehending all the above particulars, as a great and aggressive force in Christian history, as distinguished from all others and standing entirely alone, the doctrine of the soul's competency in religion under God is the distinctive significance of the Baptists.

I would add that our evangelistic and missionary fervor, shown throughout our history has exemplified Oncken's dictum "Every Christian a missionary."

F. Townley Lord
Pastor, Bloomsbury Baptist Church
London
Former Editor, *The Baptist Times*
London
Former President, Baptist World Alliance

* * *

I am proud to be called a Baptist! Baptists did not choose their name. It was given to them by their enemies. The name "Baptist," like the name "Christian," which was first applied to the followers of Jesus at Antioch, was intended to distinguish those people who lived and worshipped differently. I am proud to be called a Baptist!

I am proud of our Baptist heritage. I am grateful for men like Statler who, before his tongue was torn out and his body burned, wrote his confessions in which he demanded for himself and for all others the right of a free conscience.

I am proud to be a Baptist because of what we have done in the field of education. I am proud of Baptists like Henry Dunster, the first president of Harvard; of John Clarke, who was among the first to advocate a free public school system. I am proud that it was a Baptist college, Brown University, which first provided "full, free, uninterrupted liberty of conscience."

I rejoice that Baptists have been in the forefront of religious education with men like Deacon William Fox, who stands at the head of the Sunday School movement.

I am proud of Baptist pioneering in missions. William Carey, an English Baptist, rediscovered Christ's Commission and became the father of modern missions.

I am proud to be a Baptist because of what we believe. We accept the Bible as our all-sufficient guide to faith and practice.

It is reported that at the Council in the Vatican when the College of Cardinals had at last passed the doctrine of the infallibility of the pope, in 1870, Cardinal Manning, in the excitement of that moment, jumped upon a table and swung that document around his head, crying, "Let all the world go to pieces; we'll reconstruct it on this paper." Without denying anyone else the right to believe what he pleases and to act as he pleases, we Baptists say, "The whole world will go to bits unless it is constructed on the revelation of God in his Holy Word."

I am proud of our Baptist faith in the Word of God and in the power of the Spirit of God to guide men into an understanding of the truth. We have no ecclesiastical hierarchy to enforce uniformity. We need no creed to coerce the faith of men. Our unity is not that of artificial uniformity in the acceptance of humanly prescribed dogmas but of loyalty to divine revelations.

I am proud to be a Baptist who believes in the authority of the Bible and the competency of the soul of man in matters of religion. I am proud to be a Baptist who not only demands for himself but also recognizes for others the right of a free conscience and the responsibility for personal decision to trust Jesus Christ as Saviour, Redeemer, and Lord. I am proud to work with my fellow Baptists who recognize the necessity of uncoerced cooperation in the spread of the Gospel to save a lost world.

> DUKE K. McCALL
> President
> Southern Baptist Theological Seminary
> Louisville, Kentucky
> Former President
> New Orleans Baptist Theological Seminary
> New Orleans, Louisiana
> Former Executive Secretary
> Executive Committee
> Southern Baptist Convention
> Nashville, Tennessee

* * *

I am a Baptist because I am a Christian, and because a Christian must, in fidelity to New Testament tradition, be found within the "household of faith"—the church. Christian experience is liable to wither and die apart from the stimulating and sustaining action of "fellowship with the brethren." The Apostle did not counsel "the assembling of yourselves together" for the sake of the church, primarily, but for the sake of the believer. So, because I am a Christian, I am a church member.

As a church member I am a Baptist. There are many branches of the Christian church, and I could belong to any one of them. I am a Baptist, to begin with, because my parents were Baptists, and because their brand of Christian experience commended their church to me. Moreover, I am a Baptist out of gratitude for all that Baptist churches have done for me and meant to me. I was found by Christ, the Good Shepherd, in a Baptist church. I have been faithfully taught and led by Baptist pastors and teachers. I have grown spiritually through services rendered, and leadership given, with the encouragement of Baptist churches. My own experience validates the claims of Baptists to a sure knowledge of the way of salvation and to faithfulness in making it known to men.

With maturing years I have found my Baptist convictions deepening. They become increasingly reinforced by Biblical and theological studies, and through an increasingly pragmatic understanding of what Baptists stand for within the Christian tradition. The Lordship of Christ delivers me from ecclesiastical tyranny of any kind, from state presumptions, from deceptive self-reliance, from creedal rigidities, from a religion which is deadened by traditionalism rather than enlivened by an ever-contemporaneous Holy Spirit. The sufficiency of Scripture gives authority to our pulpit, buoyant confidence to our pastors and people, constant standards for our individual behavior and for our church practice (such as baptism by immersion with its indubitable Scriptural authority). Our principle of regenerate church membership is precisely defined by the New Testament practice of adding unto the church "such as were being saved" (Acts 2:47). It repudiates the ancient evil of equating citizenship with church membership; it exposes the pretentions of those who claim to mediate salvation by sacramental acts; it provides a valid standard by which people are both admitted to, and rejected from, the church of Jesus Christ. The priesthood of all believers makes personal faith the means of access to God in Christ, and makes every Christian responsible for making the Gospel known and for being an "under-shepherd" to seek the lost and to restore them to the "fold." Thus every believer becomes a "co-worker with Christ," and each may experience the surpassing joy of being an ambassador of Christ, of entreating men in His name.

As a Baptist I can hold in balance freedom and responsibility, churchmanship and evangelical ardour, conviction and response to the contemporary action of the Spirit of Truth, tolerance towards others and fervent devotion to the loyalties which Christ has committed me. In no other church body could I find in a greater measure this satisfying balance of essential beliefs and practices. And the amazing growth of the Baptist fellowship around the world in this century confirms me in the denominational views I hold, and in the compelling Baptist loyalties that hold me.

T. B. McDormand
General Secretary-Treasurer
Baptist Federation of Canada
Toronto, Ontario

*   *   *

Two questions follow a man through life. With the interrogative "How" he investigates the nature of a thing or an event. With the interrogative "Why" he looks into the inner relationships and motivation. To the question why I am a Baptist, I give a three-fold answer.

The aged Apostle Paul reminded his young fellow-worker Timothy of the sincere faith which dwelt first in his grandmother Lois and in his mother Eunice and then filled his own heart (II Timothy 1:5). The influence of my resolutely Christian parents, their personal example, their loving care, and their persistent intercession made a lasting impression upon my sisters and me. In their manifold difficulties I came to the realization that fellowship with Jesus Christ was at the center of their lives. Daily family prayer, regular attendance at worship, and diligent collaboration in the Lord's work, all awakened in my young heart the first signs of spiritual life. As growing children we became convinced that for our dear parents there could be no greater joy than to see that Jesus Christ was the foundation and the substance of life for us.

My second reason is suggested by the personal experience which the Apostle Paul described in Galatians 1:16, "It pleased God to reveal His Son in me." A Damascus hour came in my youthful experience. The mystery of this hour of God in my life can be indicated only inadequately with words. On a lonely summer afternoon, far from home, God met me as sovereign Lord and through the Holy Spirit let the sublime figure of His Son Jesus Christ shine in my innermost being. God's goodness and God's severity, as they are revealed supremely and uniquely on the Hill of Golgotha, overcame me and became the object of my personal religious experience and the occasion for my entrance upon Christian discipleship and into His church. As indicators of the way I am indebted to my parents, Sunday School teachers, and preachers, but my chief debt is to God Himself, for whom

I love and whom I serve, not because of tradition but because of the personal experience of salvation.

Since I have come to believe in Jesus Christ as my Saviour and Lord, God's Word has proved itself a source of strength and a plumb-line for my natural and spiritual life. I have been a member of Baptist churches for more than half a century. My service has involved several changes in field of work and therefore in local church membership. On bright peaks and in dark valleys, in the midst of the changes and trials of life and of time, I have with many fellow-believers proved the present effectiveness of the eternal Word of God, which gives the best and most trustworthy guidance for the immediate situation and task. The Holy Scriptures alone, of the Old and New Testaments, remain binding upon individual believers, the Christian family, and the church—also in relation to baptism and the Lord's Supper. I acknowledge myself as a Baptist because with the Apostle Paul I declare, "For we cannot do anything against the truth, but only for the truth" (II Corinthians 13:8).

JAKOB MEISTER
Former President
Baptist Union of Germany
Now residing in Zurich, Switzerland

*   *   *

When I accepted Christ as Saviour at ten years of age I *became* a Baptist because of home environment and parental influence.

Now I *am* a Baptist because of deep conviction that in matters of faith, practice, polity and interpretation the Baptist position is in harmony with New Testament teachings.

Specifically, I accept and cherish the spirit and practice of

Christian democracy to which Baptist churches subscribe and adhere. The principle of the independence and autonomy of local Baptist churches makes a strong appeal, as does the doctrine of the competency and responsibility of the individual, led by the Holy Spirit, to personally approach God through Christ for reconciliation, divine guidance and spiritual strength.

I am in full accord with the prevailing practice among Baptists of voluntary cooperation between churches in all denominational ministries, including the work of evangelism, missions, benevolence and education. Baptists recognize Christ as the sole authority over individual churches and only His commands as their marching orders and unifying force. I believe this to be in accord with New Testament teachings, just as I accept this same authority for the Baptist concept of the equality of all believers.

Among the great doctrines which are accepted by Baptists generally and which challenge the response of my mind and heart are the virgin birth, the deity of Jesus, the atonement, salvation by grace, the new birth, baptism of believers only, the Lordship of Christ, the authority of God's Word as the unquestioned guide for faith and practice, and many others.

While I am a Baptist by conviction, conviction that the Baptist position meets the test of fidelity to Bible teachings and truth, I am strengthened in this conviction because of the blessing and favor of God upon the work and witness of those who are bound together in this fellowship through Christ.

Finally, I am a Baptist because I believe in the principle of the separation of church and state, the freedom of worship, the right of every individual to worship God, or not to worship, according to the dictates of his own conscience, and because Baptists have been and continue to be militant champions of these and other great foundation principles of truth and freedom.

JAMES W. MERRITT
Baptist Layman, Gainesville, Georgia
Former Executive Secretary-Treasurer
Georgia Baptist Convention
Former President
Georgia Baptist Convention
Senior Recording Secretary
Southern Baptist Convention

* * *

Let it be understood now and always that the basic doctrine of Baptists is the dignity, sanctity, and competency of the individual believer. I do not mean by that that we put this doctrine ahead of our belief in the sovereignty of God which we share with the Presbyterians, or justification by faith which we share with the Lutherans, or the necessity of a religious experience which we share with the Methodists, but it is this belief in the dignity, sanctity and competency of the individual which through the years Baptists have felt compelled to emphasize. It is out of this basic conviction that our other Baptist principles grow.

Take, for instance, our insistence on baptism by immersion. Our belief in immersion is based not only on the fact that this was the way in which Jesus was baptized, and not only because it is set forth in the New Testament as a church ordinance, but because it symbolizes an essential Christian experience in the life of the believer.

Why do we refuse to baptize infants? Because we feel that we have no right to commit a helpless child to any doctrine or church. Believing in the dignity, sanctity and competency of the individual believer, we hold that each person must act and speak for himself when he becomes of age. No man is to act as a proxy for another in matters of religion.

Why do we not have a priesthood? Because a priest is one who approaches God for another, and we hold that there should be no intermediary between God and man. Every man can, and must, approach God for himself without the interference of official, sacrament, ritual, or anything else. God, speaking through His Son, said, "Come unto me all ye that labor and are heavy laden, and I will give you rest," and in order to respond to this invitation one does not have to do so through the ministrations of a priest. We believe in the priesthood of believers. Whenever and wherever an earnest Christian gets down on his knees before God, there you have a priest, an altar, and an acceptable sacrifice.

Why do we not have bishops and church courts? Because we do not believe that any man is set in authority over another, or that any ecclesiastical body is competent to dictate to a local church.

Why do we believe in religious liberty and the separation of church and state? Because we feel that the individual should be left free to worship God according to the dictates of his own heart without any interference from the state, and that the truth of God is sufficiently compelling within itself, not requiring legal recognition or compulsion in order to commend it to the minds of men.

EDWARD HUGHES PRUDEN
Pastor, First Baptist Church
Washington, D. C.
Former President
American Baptist Convention

*   *   *

I. *A Scriptural Conception.*

I am Baptist because of a Scriptural conception of truth which distinguishes Baptists from other denominations. These doctrines are expressed by Dr. B. H. Carroll in his *Baptists and Their Doctrines* as "six distinctive Baptist principles which have distinguished Baptists from other Christian denominations: namely, (1) The New Testament—The Law of Christianity; (2) Individuality; (3) Freedom of Conscience; (4) Salvation Eessential to Baptism and Church Membership; (5) The Doctrine of the Church; (6) God's Order in the Gospel of His Son."

By these distinctive principles Baptists have been a peculiar people not in the sense of being odd, but in the sense of being different in what they have believed. For these conceptions Baptists have stood through the ages and for them they have been persecuted and by them they have been identified.

Because they have been a peculiar people Baptists have been a persecuted people in the life of yesterday and have left a glorious heritage through much labor and many hardships.

Baptist principles in the life of yesterday call for Baptist principles in the life of today and must be preserved in the life of today.

Baptists have become a great people not through superior natural abilities. They have had no monopoly of mind nor of method. Others have had men of great minds and great abilities. Others have had their share of sense and sentiment and sincerity.

Baptists have become a great people through superior Scriptural conceptions. They have had a heritage of distinctive doctrines. They must not be less Baptist now than their heroic fathers who passed on to them their Scriptural conception in distinctive Baptist doctrines.

It would be good if we could drink deep draughts of Baptist belief that the New Testament is the Law of Christianity —all the Law of Christianity—always all the Law of Christianity—and refresh ourselves with the truth that the New Testament fulfills the types of the Old Testament and sets the pattern of our living in this day of the grace of the Lord Jesus Christ. We would be freed from all proxies in religion and take our place as priests able to approach God for ourselves.

It would be good if we could linger with our Baptist belief of individuality—of responsibility to God when we must each stand face to face with God without any sponsor but Christ.

It would be good if we could give time to our Baptist belief of freedom of conscience—freedom to serve God not by constraint of man or government but by conscience.

It would be good if we could refresh our minds with Baptist belief that salvation is essential to baptism and church membership—salvation rather than sacramentalism or sacerdotalism.

It would be good if we could consider our Baptist belief of God's order in the Gospel of His Son and hear again His accent of the Great Commission and the subordination of going and baptizing and teaching to the main business of making disciples.

It would be good if we could rejoice in Baptist belief that the church was built by Christ and not by man—a particular congregation not an organized denomination—a pure democracy with all of its members equal.

II. *A Scriptural Conviction.*

I am a Baptist because Scriptural conception has given a conviction of Scriptural truth which compels me to be a Baptist.

III. *A Scriptural Conscience.*

I am a Baptist because Scriptural conviction has given a Scriptural conscience. Conscience is not enough in itself. Conscience must be Scriptural if it is to be right. The soul's clock must keep correct time set by a standard and not be left to haphazard direction.

I would not force another to my conception and conviction and conscience, but I would ask for myself and others the same right to be a Baptist as others have to differ with us.

GEORGE RAGLAND
Pastor, First Baptist Church
Lexington, Kentucky

*   *   *

My first memory of a religious service was the baptism of some converts in a creek near Calhoun, Missouri, where I was born. My mother was a Baptist and we attended the Baptist church there.

When I was six years old we moved to Oklahoma. The first Sunday Schools that I attended with regularity were Union Sunday Schools conducted in school houses near our home. I recall very little doctrinal or denominational emphasis in these schools, but I memorized many Bible verses.

During these early years I often accompanied my sister and others to the religious debates conducted in that pioneer country between the Baptists and the Campbellites. I decided then to study my Bible more carefully and to discover the truth relative to their doctrinal positions.

Later we moved to a farm near Lone Wolf, Oklahoma. My aunt and uncle who lived on the adjoining farm, went regularly to the Baptist church. Soon I was going with them. During those days, my sister, eight years older than I, was under deep conviction. She studied her Bible diligently and prepared a list of doctrinal questions with Bible Answers. This study interested me very much and I intensified my study of the Bible. We had no concordance or Bible dictionary. I did not know of such a book, but I realized the need for one so I spent hours finding scriptures on faith, love, salvation, baptism and other key words which appeared important to me.

My Sunday school teacher in those days impressed me with her faithful service and Christ-like life. She was a loyal Baptist and that placed the Baptists on the front row in my thinking.

At the age of twelve I was converted. For more than two years I had been attending the Baptist church regularly. The pastor took a personal interest in me. Those I most admired and loved were Baptists. I had read *The Little Baptist,* an interesting story which impressed me greatly. My Bible reading and study confirmed the conviction that the Baptist church more nearly conformed to the New Testament pattern than any other, so I asked permission of my parents to join the church. The permission was granted and I joined the church at Lone Wolf, Oklahoma.

That is the story behind my becoming a member of a Baptist church, but many subsequent factors have entered into my becoming a Baptist at heart.

Soon after my conversion I had a pastor who took a personal interest in me. He took me to the first associational meeting I ever attended. He asked me to use my horse and buggy to take him to schoolhouse revivals which he conducted near our little village. He spent hours talking with me about our Baptist faith and practice.

My study and participation in B. Y. P. U. were influential. Here I formed important habits of Christian living and began to express my limited knowledge of Bible doctrines in program participation.

After finishing high school I entered Oklahoma Baptist University where I met several splendid teachers and leaders that strengthened my faith and greatly influenced my life. Among them were Dr. W. D. Moorer, a wonderful Bible teacher; Dr. J. W. Jent, a real scholar and a great teacher; and Dr. J. B. Rounds, whose ministry as missionary, Sunday School Secretary and State Mission Secretary inspired me and gave me added assurance.

As a student in Missouri University I met the first real challenge to my doctrinal position. It came from two sources; the Bible critics and the advocates of the ecumenical movement. The attack served to strengthen my faith, helped me to better organize my own religious beliefs and made me keenly aware of the dangers of false teachings.

The privilege of serving with Dr. J. B. Lawrence as his assistant pastor and hearing him preach during our association for five years, added much to my faith and to my knowledge of Baptist doctrine and practice. My study in the Southwestern Baptist Theological Seminary under such men as Dr. W. W. Barnes, Dr. L. R. Scarborough and Dr. W. T. Conner enriched my life and gave me still further assurance in my religious convictions.

My recent association with Baptist denominational leaders has given me an ever-growing appreciation of our doctrinal position and of the integrity and sincerity of those who have led our Baptist forces through the years and who now lead in our program of advance.

I am glad that I am a Baptist and rejoice in the doctrines and church polity which seem to me to follow more closely than any other the teachings of God's inspired Word and the

practices of the early churches as recorded in Acts and the
Pauline Epistles.

COURTS REDFORD
Executive Secretary
Home Mission Board
Southern Baptist Convention
Atlanta, Georgia

*   *   *

My parents often remarked that they started taking me to
church when I was two months old. My earliest recollections
of childhood are with reference to our little Baptist church,
in which I was converted and baptized at the early age of
seven—which then was thought too young for a child to become a member.

If you had asked why I was a Baptist when I was ten, or
during my college days, my answer would have been, "Because I was reared a Baptist and my parents were Baptists."
The Baptist church of my youth was fortunate in having
pastors who were strong in teaching Baptist doctrine and what
Baptists believe. Most of this was taught on Wednesday evening at prayer meeting, which service we rarely missed.

Soon after I answered the call to preach, I was disturbed
considerably over the answer to this question, "Why am I a
Baptist?" If I should have been reared in a Presbyterian or
Methodist home, would I not belong to that church?

It was during my first year in the Seminary that these questions began to concern me, and I sought advice and help
from the beloved Dr. John R. Sampey. In his kind and con-
siderate way, he outlined for me a course of study to answer
this question.

At the end of many months of research, study, and prayer,
I had come to the conclusion I was a Baptist because I be-

lieved the people called Baptists follow out more nearly the principles and doctrinal truths of the New Testament church than any other denominational group. Twenty-eight years have passed since I came definitely to that conclusion.

Service these many years as pastor, and now in denominational work, has only increased my love and zeal for the Baptist cause. It is my firm conviction that Christ is the answer to the needs of the world today, and that the program of Southern Baptists is His program to meet the problems of a sin-sick world.

R. Alton Reed
Executive Secretary
Relief and Annuity Board
Southern Baptist Convention
Dallas, Texas

*   *   *

I became a Baptist by choice, not because of convenience or family ties. I remain a Baptist because I believe in the tenets of the Baptist faith.

Taken as a whole, I believe the doctrines accepted by Baptists are closer to those practiced by the early church than any other Christian group on the face of the earth. In making such a statement, I do not claim that Baptists have a monopoly on those beliefs accepted and practiced by early Christians. As a matter of fact, I doubt if Baptists have any so-called distinctive beliefs. Other Christian groups accept one or more of the basic tenets of the Baptist faith. However, taken as a whole, I believe Baptists stand closer to that which a New Testament group of people should believe than any Christian group.

Baptists have many doctrines which have notable and deep significance. However, three basic tenets accepted by Baptists were instrumental in attracting me to the Baptist faith. They are:

Competency of the individual: Embodied in this doctrine is the very bedrock upon which is built much of what Baptists believe and practice. Baptists say that each and every person has direct access to God through His Son Jesus Christ. No individual—be he prince, potentate, king, priest, or preacher—can stand between any person and his Creator. Also rooted in this doctrine is the Baptist belief concerning separation of church and state. Believing as they do in soul liberty and the competency of the individual, then it logically follows that church and state must ever be separate. The state must never come to the place that it will coerce in any way the religious rights of its citizens. Believing as I did in the priesthood of the believer and respecting each and every individual's right to believe as he wished was one of the reasons instrumental in causing me to embrace the Baptist faith.

Then, too, I am a Baptist because of what Baptists teach about salvation. Baptists teach that salvation is by grace, that it is a gift which cannot be merited in any way by works. Baptists base such a belief on God's Word. It can be readily seen that such a belief nullifies baptism and church membership as prerequisites for salvation. The roots of this doctrine as taught by Baptists go deep and in many directions. Among those roots which are imbedded in God's Word are such doctrines as justification through faith, perseverance of the saints, and security of the believer. These and similar doctrines teach us that our initial experience of salvation will stand throughout eternity. I accept such beliefs and stand with them because I have personally experienced salvation, and know that that which I have committed unto my Lord will stand forever.

Another reason why I am a Baptist is because of the form of government which they practice. Baptists are a democratic people. They are not controlled by a hierarchy. Among Baptists, those who lead are selected by the people they serve. The leaders have no authority or control over the churches. They issue no ultimatums. They create no dogma. Pursuing this doctrine, one becomes acutely aware of the fact that it is the individual that counts in the Baptist faith. I embrace this belief wholeheartedly.

Why am I a Baptist? Indeed, many pages could be devoted to answering the question. Let it be said once again, however, that I am a Baptist because of choice and because I believe in those things which Baptists teach. These doctrines mentioned above have assured me that my decision and faith have been well-founded. Consequently, I have cast my lot with this people who seek to live and practice those things which Christ expected His people to do when He established and commissioned His church on earth many centuries ago.

GEORGE W. SCHROEDER
Executive Secretary
Brotherhood Commission
Southern Baptist Convention
Memphis, Tennessee

* * *

It would be both trite and true to say that I am a Baptist because of conviction. None of my immediate forebears were Baptists; until the time of his death at the age of 84, my father was active in an official capacity in the Methodist church. My mother died when I was six years old; at fifteen I was making my own way in the world with no thought of anything other than my job as a range rider in Eastern Oregon, earning the standard wage of $35.00 per month, and board.

By a strange interposition of Providence, which I did not recognize as such then, and for which I have no natural explanation now, I became a Christian. Coming into Baker, Oregon, to replenish camp supplies which I was to take by pack horses up to our camps in the Blue Mountains, I wandered, without knowing what it was, into a church one night. At that time I was nineteen years old, and as "fiddle footed" as any carefree youngster in the world.

I found myself listening to a preacher who was reading a Scripture text—he said that's what it was—I did not know—which changed the whole course of my life, "What shall it profit a man if he gain the whole world and lose his soul?"

My whole world at that moment was a $50.00 saddle and a $25.00 pony, and to tell the truth that was all I knew, and all I cared about. But that night a new world opened to me—and I became a Christian by faith in the only begotten Son of God, who came to save me from my sins.

Now what about a church—for I had an instinctive desire to be one of those who lived with others and not by himself in Christian fellowship; what church? I bought a small New Testament, and took my way back to the camps. For several weeks I read my Bible—entirely on my own, and with no one to either advise me or interpret for me. If I had ever heard of Baptists, other than a general way, I do not recall it. But these things came to be very clear to me as I read my New Testament and have become increasingly so in the 51 years that have elapsed:

1. The New Testament teaches that salvation comes through repentance toward God and faith in Jesus Christ. Acts 20:21, 11 Cor. 7:10, John 3:14-19.

2. The New Testament knows only a regenerated church membership. John 3:3-8, Gal. 3:26-27.

3. Only believers joined the church, and were baptized. Acts 2:41, Acts 16:14-15, and the very command of Jesus to "make disciples" before baptizing them (Matt. 28:19-20) we cannot ignore.

4. Baptism means immersion. Mark 1:9, Acts 8:38-39, Romans 6:1-4.

5. The New Testament churches had only two classes of officers—pastors and deacons, Acts 20:28, Titus 1:5-7, Timothy 3:1-13. This church democracy has no place for ecclesiastical overlords.

6. The New Testament teaches the separation of church and state—Acts 4:19.

7. The New Testament teaches the eternal security of the believer—John 5:24, Romans 8:1, 31:39.

8. The New Testament teaches that both believer's baptism and the Lord's Supper are means of expressing salvation, not of procuring it. Col. 2:10-12, 1 Cor. 11:18-36.

As I read these scriptures, I asked myself, "What church most nearly conforms to them?" And the answer to that is why I became a Baptist.

J. W. STORER
Executive Secretary
Southern Baptist Foundation
Nashville, Tennessee
Former President
Southern Baptist Convention

*   *   *

Why I actually became a Baptist must have been determined largely by the church affiliation of my parents. Why I am now a Baptist finds its explanation in deep Christian convictions based upon a conscientious study of God's Word.

Baptists are a people of many qualities. They are by no means perfect. Certainly, they would be the last to lay claim to infallibility. At the same time, they point to a perfect Christ, have complete faith in the inerrant revelation of God through the Bible, and seek to exalt Him everywhere to the best of their ability.

While Baptists have not reached the ideal of perfection, it is my fixed conviction that they are more like the original New Testament church than any other religious group. On that premise, I state my preference and declare my loyalty.

There are many things about Baptists which I like very much.

I like their democratic spirit and processes. By temperament I am a commoner, and by disposition I am democratic in my approaches and relationships. A person of such temperament fits perfectly into the Baptist spirit and life. Baptists are made up of common people the world over. Though some of our members are exceedingly wealthy and others highly cultured and educated people, the rank and file of our Baptists are found in the middleclass group of people. They are men of the field, women of the factories, and young people in the classrooms of the consolidated school. I like that about Baptists. I like their love and concern for all people. Their spirit is New Testament; their love for souls is universal.

I like their requirement for a regenerated church membership. There is no other sound basis on which a spiritual church can be built. Spiritual programs cannot be erected on carnal men, but a redeemed church membership can be used of God to redeem the world. Unless men have experienced God's wonderful salvation, know "the language of Zion," and walk in the ways of deep consecration, they cannot do much toward lifting a world from its dire distress.

Baptists strive to make sure that every church member knows Christ experientially and individually in order that he might serve Christ understandingly as well as be saved eternally.

I like their emphasis on the Bible. In no other way can people know "the way, the truth" or "the life." God's Word is the infallible guide for life's highway and the most important book on the bookshelf of humanity. It is eternal in duration, complete in revelation, unparalleled in inspiration. Baptists exalt the Bible and delve into its pages constantly to discover truths about the ways of God in earthly life.

I like their loyalty to the ordinances. Feeling no authority to change God's instructions nor wanting any part in setting up ordinances of their own, Baptists take God at His word and administer the ordinances in the way that He did and commanded His followers to do after Him. As physical symbols of spiritual truths, the ordinances declare in an audio-visual way the eternal ways of heaven in human redemption. To change the symbols is to alter their meanings.

I like their program of work. It is intense, but it is rewarding. It calls for perennial evangelism, perpetual visitation, and unceasing instruction. It demands a training program that is never retarded. It has a place for every prospect and a task for every member. It is aggressive, dynamic and productive. No wonder Baptists are moving forward with such rapid strides of progress. They have planned and prayed for a spiritual and numerical advance and are laboring for it sacrificially.

I like their spirit of destiny. They have a high sense of holy calling and an awareness of a Divine mission. Baptists are anchored to the Book, but they are not bound to the many superfluous traditions that are not Bible-based. Their eyes are ahead. Their motto is not "Back to Christ" but "On to Christ." Knowing that He has never been reached, much less excelled, and that He is yet far ahead, Baptists are moving on to Him so His will can be fully done. I like that definite sense of holy calling and Divine destiny among Baptists in this hour. Baptists have an unparalleled opportunity to influence the world for God in this day and generation. They feel it and are dedicated to it.

Under God, we give Him our best in time and talents through a local Baptist church, because we believe that is His will for our lives and our glorious opportunity of close discipleship. Through our church we work with Baptists the world over to foster those doctrinal positions and denominational beliefs which are so clear in Bible teaching and so dear to our hearts.

> JAMES L. SULLIVAN
> Executive Secretary
> Sunday School Board
> Southern Baptist Convention
> Nashville, Tennessee

*   *   *

There are many reasons I might give about why I am a Baptist. Certain ones rise like great mountains on the island of my mind, and I am concerned in this article with these basic affirmations which have characterized the people called Baptists through the centuries. These principles constitute what might well be called a Charter of Soul Liberty.

The first article of this Charter of Soul Freedom concerns our interpretation of the unique position of man before God. This position is well expressed in two of the axioms of Christianity by Dr. E. Y. Mullins, namely, to be responsible the soul must be free, and all men have an equal right to access to God. As a great spiritual judgment, this principle is comparatively simple and arises out of our faith in the dignity and worth of man.

Such a conception endows human personality with great value and responsibility and vastly enlarges the horizons of the soul. No serious student of the Bible can believe in the divine right of rulers or make a fetish of blood and soil or surrender the rights of his soul to any priest or hierarchy.

Because of this insistence upon the competency of the soul in matters of conscience and faith, Baptists have rejected the practice of infant baptism. No person or institution has the right to deprive the individual of the blessing of doing business with God in his own way within the sacred precincts of his own soul. For this reason the membership of a Baptist church is composed only of those who have made the response of genuine repentance and personal faith in Jesus Christ as Saviour, and have followed our Lord in Christian baptism.

Baptists have always placed strong reliance upon the voluntary support of the individual for achieving the objectives of the Kingdom. This is another article in our Charter of Soul Liberties. The only possible way for Christianity to make good on its own assumption is on the basis of a spiritual response in the redeemed heart. Entangling alliances with temporal powers create attitudes of complacency and indifference which abort the dynamic processes of Christianity.

One of the great days of God's Kingdom came when our Baptist people declared their belief in a free church in a free state. This involved their assumption of the burden of self-support and the foregoing of all participation in public funds collected by taxes. The great protagonist of this idea in America was Roger Williams, who led the Baptist people of Rhode Island to follow this principle. Williams was ably supported in his position by Thomas Jefferson and other leaders in early American life.

The keystone article in our Charter of Soul Freedom is the doctrine of religious liberty. This is the bastion of spiritual Christianity. The beloved George W. Truett was fond of saying that "Religious liberty is the nursing mother of all other liberties." This is vastly different from religious toleration, for toleration implies the superiority of the group doing the tolerating. The Baptist interpretation of religious liberty simply means that any religious group anywhere in the world has the right for free and unhindered propagation of its message within the framework of the commonly accepted requirements of public welfare. This prohibits the establishment of any state religion and affords the same civil status and opportunity to all religious groups. Furthermore, the rights of the atheist, or non-believer, are secured in that he cannot be coerced in matters of conscience by the state.

These basic ideas have made Baptists what they are, and a fresh and vigorous application of these convictions today will keep us what we ought to be.

MONROE F. SWILLEY, JR.
Pastor, Second-Ponce de Leon Baptist Church
Atlanta, Georgia

* * *

In all candor and forthrightness, I became a Baptist because I was reared in a Baptist home and a Baptist church.

I shall ever be grateful that my mother, as a bride, was baptized into the fellowship of a Baptist church, my father's church, coming from a church of another denomination. The church always meant much to my parents, and their loyalty to the church made a great and lasting impression upon my young life.

Therefore, I learned to love the church that loved me, that taught me, that trained me, that won me to Christ, that received me, that baptized me, and gave me an opportunity for growth and development.

That man is fortunate whose mature study and convictions sanction his early training and enrich his youthful beliefs. I am a convinced Baptist because I accept for myself the fact that a Baptist church more nearly conforms to the pattern of the New Testament churches in doctrine and in practice.

As a Baptist I take pride in and endorse the position of my church on these several points:

The primacy of the Bible which has always evidenced itself in the beliefs of my people. I find altogether satisfying Paul's affirmation, "all Scripture is given by inspiration of God, and is profitable for doctrine, for reproof, for correction, for instruction in righteousness: that the man of God may be perfect, thoroughly furnished unto all good works." The Word of God, illuminated by the Holy Spirit, is a sufficient rule of faith and practice.

The doctrine that the individual has direct access to Christ through the aid of the Holy Spirit. I accept with my church that conviction, repentance, and faith in Christ result in salvation without the need of intermediary priesthood.

The outstandingly distinctive principle of Baptists, that of voluntariness on the part of the individual in all things pertaining to religious matters. Not by outward coercion but by a mighty compulsion within, the new man is motivated for Christian endeavor.

The conviction that the ordinances are not sacraments but acts of obedience symbolizing great religious truths dear to the heart of every believer. New Testament baptism pictures the death, burial, and resurrection of our Lord. And as a believer is baptized, it signifies that he has died to an old life of sin, is buried with Christ in baptism, and is raised up with Him to walk in the newness of life. The meaning and the method are of utmost importance. The Lord's Supper is a memorial symbolizing His meaningfulness to the individual to be observed in obedience to Christ.

The democracy of a Baptist church which gives me the privilege and a responsibility in the conduct of the affairs of my church.

Being a Baptist I appreciate my Baptist heritage, and I am challenged by the present and future. Holding to New Testament truths, with emphasis upon individual freedom, missions and evangelism have resulted in Baptists being the fastest growing of any of the major denominations. The reason is self-evident, and to that reason I subscribe.

CAREY T. VINZANT
President, Tift College
Forsyth, Georgia

*   *   *

To begin with, I suppose it may be correctly stated that I was a Baptist because my parents were Baptists. From the standpoint of religion, however, I realized early in life that I had to *be* something, because I was an "incurably religious being." Having been born and reared in a Godly home, an inescapable religious hunger was awakened in me and inspired my quest for the right kind of religion.

When I attained the age and ability to inquire for myself, I felt the need of a guide that I could unquestionably trust. Nothing I found satisfied my longings as did the Bible. Hence, a firm conviction gripped my heart that the Holy Bible was the sole, sufficient, and authoritative guide in all matters pertaining to religion.

Accepting the Bible as God's recorded revelation to man, I was convinced that God is a supreme personal spirit, one person with three personalities, Father, Son and Holy Spirit.

As I continued my study I learned the basic doctrines of the New Testament which have become the guiding principles of my life. Chiefly among these principles are that: Man's sin problem can be solved only through the redemptive purpose of God in Christ. Every individual is competent to approach God without the aid of a priestly intermediary. When a person truly accepts Christ as Saviour, he is saved forever from the penalty of sin, to work out that salvation through the process of sanctification or growth in grace. Jesus Christ was God incarnate, both deity and humanity. He lived a sinless Life. He was crucified, buried and rose again from the dead. Following His resurrection ministry, His promise was fulfilled in the coming of the Holy Spirit who has been and still is the administrator in New Testament church affairs. Baptism is by immersion and symbolizes death, burial and resurrection. The church is a democracy, an organized body of baptized believers, equal in rank and privilege, united in the faith concerning what Christ has taught, covenanted to do what He has commanded and cooperating with other like bodies in Kingdom movements. To the church was committed only two ordinances, baptism and the Lord's Supper. The church and state should forever remain separate. There are two permanent abiding places for the dead—Heaven for the righteous and Hell for the wicked who reject God's redemptive plan. Christ is literally coming back to earth for the final consummation of His Kingdom.

I am a Baptist, therefore, because I honestly believe that in the Bible we have God's pattern for our lives and the church. This pattern has stood the test of the ages. I believe that Baptists more accurately conform to the New Testament pattern than any other group on earth.

My convictions concerning what Baptists believe have deepened through nearly fifty years of study and experience and

I was never more certain in all my life than I am at present, that I am following the New Testament as an ambassador for Christ.

C. C. WARREN
Pastor, First Baptist Church
Charlotte, North Carolina
President, Southern Baptist Convention

*   *   *

Very seldom we are able adequately to give all the true reasons for what we are, what we think or what we aim at. Our motives are always mixed up with various interests, which we partly know and partly never think of, nor are capable fully to perceive.

With this reservation I am going to answer the question, Why I am a Baptist. I well understand, that my points of view today were not characteristic for the young man of 17, who once professed his faith, was baptized in the country chapel and joined the small Baptist church in the north of Sweden. But now I wish to summarize my statement in the following few points:

1. *My home.* I was brought up in a home where the revival type of religious life prevailed. With the Lutheran state church and her clergymen in the parish we had only few and occasional relations. Baptists and Congregationalists moulded our life by Sunday Schools and meetings of various kinds. My parents became Baptists, but it was not at all self-evident that we children should go the same way, as the Lutheran teaching in the school was pretty strict in those days and the "worldly" way of life prevailed in most of the homes in the neighborhood.

2. *The Bible.* When I became a Baptist at 17, the real reason must have been the simple Bible teaching in my home

and in the services and meetings in the chapel. Studying the Bible I one day got hold of a tract by the great C. H. Spurgeon regarding the Scripture teaching about baptism. In one column the Bible references were given in nine points, while the other column had been left empty for the reader to put in Scripture references, chapters and verses, which mention infant baptism. In my search for the latter I was not able to find any at all. This was then enough for me, and I acted accordingly.

3. *Theology and Church History.* Since then I have been studying theology many years, and I have been occupied by research work in several fields as Regius Professor of Church History at Uppsala University, Sweden. Having taught this subject in a quarter of a century I have had many opportunities to re-think my position as a Baptist in a State University connected with a national Lutheran church, but nothing in my studies in exegesis, patristic sources and church history of later centuries has upset my Baptist faith or has given me reason to alter my denominational affiliation. I am still profoundly convinced that the New Testament teaching is clear and can be summarized thus: Learn to know the Gospel, believe it firmly, repent and be baptized every one of you in the name of Jesus Christ for the forgiveness of your sins; and you shall receive the gift of the Holy Spirit (Acts 2:38). The model of a free church is to be found in Acts 2:42.

4. *The present situation.* In our days of scepticism and indifference it is very important that, regardless of later historical development and human traditions, we as Christians try to stick to the Apostolic teaching as it really is preserved in our New Testament, not as it is stated in later sources of the primitive church. I am glad to be in the Baptist line of believers through centuries, for whom the only accepted tra-

dition has been to read the Word of God in simplicity and
good faith. In a time of increasing alienation from church
life and Christian conception we must try to follow the
Apostolic teaching as faithfully as we ever can.

5. *History seems to me to give a sort of confirmation to
the Baptist witness* as being needed and also effective in wide
circles and in missionary enterprises. There is a chain of
Baptist heroes and martyrs, who teach the world that "it is
impossible to kill the truth." Such a living witness of spiritual
freedom through centuries under persecutions and martyr-
dom must be an important part of the work of God in history.
This fact has always strengthened my conviction that *for me*
the place among the Baptists is a call and a task from God
himself.

I well know the faults and shortcomings of the Baptist
movements in various countries. I know and regret the many
varieties and divisions in Baptist denominational life. May
these lines only be regarded as a humble attempt to give the
motives of my personal affiliation with one of these denominations, where we also are interested in the ecumenical cause.

> GUNNAR WESTIN
> Regius Professor of Church History
> Uppsala University, Sweden
> Past Vice-President
> Baptist World Alliance

*   *   *

In the first place, my family were Baptists. My father was
head of the deacons at the Dudley Street Baptist Church.

Secondly, I have seen no particular reason to adopt any
other faith or any other church, and

Thirdly, I feel quite certain that the particular church or

religious faith one belongs to has no important relationship
to his usefulness in life.

PAUL DUDLEY WHITE
Heart Specialist
Boston, Massachusetts

*   *   *

The paradoxical form of expression was used by our Lord.
It is highly appropriate in stating our Baptist position.

They believe in the competency of the soul under God,
but hold to the depravity of human nature. By competency
of the soul under God they mean that each individual can
and must approach God for himself, and that there is a certain crisis in which he must encounter God alone without a
human intermediary. By depravity we mean that he is wholly
disqualified and incapacitated to achieve salvation or the supreme purpose for which he was made. (1 Tim. 2:5; 1 Peter
2:9; Jeremiah 10:23; Eph. 2:1-3; John 6:44)

We believe that the soul of man is justified by faith without works, but that faith is justified by works. We know that
by the works of the law no flesh can be justified. The moral
and ethical teachings of Jesus are even more impossible for
human frailty. It must be by faith that it might be by grace.
However, we believe that a faith effective to save is effective
to produce works energized by love. (Romans 3:20-28; Ephesians 2:8-10; James 2:18; Galatians 5:6)

We believe that man must be saved by perfect righteousness, yet no man is capable of flawless goodness. Christ provides the perfect righteousness which is put to the credit of
the believer. (James 2:10; 2 Cor. 5:21)

We believe that the redeemed man has perfect status, but
not perfect stature in Christ. His standing or status in Christ
before God is perfect. His stature, however, is to be progres-

sively perfected unto full stature in Christ. Imputed right-eousness is to become imparted righteousness in life and ex-perience. (Hebrews 10:14; Philippians 3:15; Colossians 1:28)

We do not believe that the ordinances are essential to sal-vation, but we believe that salvation is essential to them. We believe that they help to save saving truth. For these reasons our apparent contradiction in fighting for their New Testa-ment place and purity resolves itself. Salvation is a death to the old life and a resurrection to a new life. This new life must be nourished, but it must first come into being. The symbols of these realities must portray this truth by proper form and order. Hence the nature of baptism and the Lord's Supper and their chronological and logical order. (John 14:17; Acts 10:47; Acts 18:8; 1 Cor. 11:1-2; 18-33; Romans 6:3-11)

We maintain that the church is committed to the primary task of seeking the lost but that no one is saved by church membership. He must be regenerated and redeemed as a qualification for church membership. (Eph. 2:1-6; Acts 2:47)

We hold that each local church is sovereign and autono-mous, yet is under the sovereign Lordship of Christ. As to other churches and organizations the local congregation is self-determining, but as to our Saviour, His will is final. (Mat-thew 23:10; 2 Cor. 8:19, 23).

We subscribe to the concept that civil authorities are ordained of God and must be obeyed, yet we deny the juris-diction of the state over conscience in matters of faith. We believe that Christians should be exemplary citizens, but we espouse the idea of complete religious liberty for all. (Mat-thew 22:20,21; Romans 13:1-7; Acts 4:19; 2 Timothy 2:1-2).

We cherish the final preservation of the saints but believe that all true Christians will persevere. (Psalms 89:29, 36; Philippians 1:6).

We reject the idea of apostolic succession in the ministry but believe that genuine Baptist churches are reproductions in kind of the apostolic pattern. (Matthew 16:18).

W. R. WHITE
President, Baylor University
Waco, Texas

* * *

In the seminary was the first time I asked myself why I am a Baptist. I was sure as to immersion. I felt that our genius should follow Paul on the Lord's Supper—let each of you examine himself.

The competency of the individual to approach God for himself is a primary doctrine of Baptists. His response to the conviction of the Holy Spirit in conviction which led to repentance and confession of Christ was to me the basis of church membership. Many other decisions have to be made as a Christian. These too may rely on the response of his approach to God.

As God did the regenerating it must have been real and did not have to be done again. But the volition of the individual largely determined his growth as a Christian.

Three things mark Baptists and we rejoice in them. First we have a simple doctrine. It is a personal experience with Christ through the Holy Spirit. It is a real experience that is convincing to us. There is no creed handed down from any Baptist organization.

Second, we have a democratic church. Each member has the right to vote from the youngest to the oldest on all subjects. The church is a local autonomy. No other Baptist body can control the local church. Nor does the church feel it is bound by action of the conventions. We are bound together by a rope of sand. Yet we move in unison about as well as more highly organized denominations. The unity of Baptists is also voluntary but very real. The fellowship includes a wide difference of thinking and varied interpretations. To me one of the glories of Baptists is that there is room for the liberal and for the most conservative in preachers and lay people.

The third thing I would mention is our passion for reaching people. That is the normal emotion of a new convert. In recent years it seems that the desire to reach others has increased. Not just to reach the privileged but the underprivileged. The wealthy and the tenant farmer, his wife and children. We are perfectly willing for any group that feels a little alien from some other group to organize their own church. We will have fellowship with them that go out from us.

A simple doctrine, a democratic church and a passion to reach the world are to me the glory of Baptists. I love the diversity more than the regimentation. But I would insist that other denominations be as free to work out their destiny as we are.

> J. C. WILKINSON
> Pastor Emeritus, First Baptist Church
> Athens, Georgia
> Past President
> Georgia Baptist Convention

*   *   *

There are numerous reasons why I am happy in the Baptist fellowship. The brief limits of this article admit the discussion of only one. That is, our conception of man. We believe that man is the direct creation of God, that he was made in God's image, with the capacity to think, to choose, and to act as a sovereign being. As such he must be free. Freedom is just as indispensable to the normal development of man as water is to the life of fish. In freedom man moves, grows, develops the potentialities with which God has endowed him. The Pharaohs, Caesars, and other dictators, ancient and modern, have dared to enter the throneroom of man's sovereignty and dictate not only how he should act but what he should think, and even whether or not he should worship. God Himself will not do that. He will surround a man with providences, will influence man through mother love and fatherly example, through the preaching of the Word, the wooing of the Spirit, the warning of dangers, and the allurements of righteousness, but He will not coerce man. God respects the sovereignty of man and, therefore, man can say "no" to God as freely as he can say "yes." With man's sovereignty and freedom comes his responsibility.

Such a conception of man is the basic reason for many of our fundamental Baptist doctrines, such as the soul's competency before God. This admits of no intermediary, such as priests or prelate. In fact, it excludes such, because "Every one of us shall give account of himself to God." (Rom. 12:14). Such a concept, also, explains in part the Baptist position on baptism. We hold it to be the personal act of a believer. Therefore, infant baptism is impossible. Such a concept of man explains our form of church government. Inasmuch as the individual is sovereign, he is called upon to think for himself and to vote his convictions. A democracy is not just a form of government; it is a spiritual necessity. In a democracy the individual must think, analyze, conclude, express his will. In so doing, opportunity is given for growth. The assumption and discharge of responsibility is necessary to the development of the individual. A dictatorship, whether by an individual or a group, is a much more convenient, and sometimes a much more effective form of government from the standpoint of mechanical efficiency. But it removes the necessity of struggle by the individualists among the masses and, therefore, robs them of the very elements essential to the development of mental and spiritual capacities and powers. Hitler produced a better war machine than America, but he did not produce better soldiers.

This same conception of man is responsible for the Baptist insistence upon religious liberty for all men—including those who would oppose or even destroy them. Liberty of conscience, freedom in matters of religion are among the basic and inalienable rights of the human race. The source of such rights does not issue from a benevolent dictator or any other kind of man-made government. Were such true, those who granted these rights could withdraw them. We hold with the founding fathers of our great republic that man is endowed by his Creator with these rights.

In the holding of such concepts there is deep fellowship and from them come ample motivations for service to God and man.

J. Howard Williams
President
Southwestern Baptist Theological
Seminary
Fort Worth, Texas

Date Due

MY 12 '60			
MY 27 '60			
JA 24 '63			

Demco 293-5